Teaching Languages with Screen Media

Advances in Digital Language Learning and Teaching

Series Editors: Michael Thomas, Liverpool John Moores University, UK; Mark Peterson, Kyoto University, Japan; Mark Warschauer, University of California – Irvine, USA

Today's language educators need support to understand how their learners are changing and the ways technology can be used to aid their teaching and learning strategies. The movement toward different modes of language learning – from presence-based to autonomous as well as blended and fully online modes – requires different skill sets such as e-moderation and new ways of designing and developing language learning tasks in the digital age. Theoretical studies that include practical case studies and high quality empirical studies incorporating critical perspectives are necessary to move the field further. This series is committed to providing such an outlet for high quality work on digital language learning and teaching. Volumes in the series focus on a number of areas including but not limited to:

- task-based learning and teaching approaches utilizing technology
- language-learner creativity
- e-moderation and teaching languages online
- blended language learning
- designing courses for online and distance language learning
- mobile-assisted language learning
- autonomous language learning, both in and outside of formal educational contexts
- the use of web 2.0/social media technologies
- immersive and virtual language-learning environments
- digital game-based language learning
- language educator professional development with digital technologies
- teaching language skills with technologies

Enquiries about the series can be made by contacting the series editors: Michael Thomas (m.thomas@ljmu.ac.uk), Mark Peterson (tufsmp@yahoo.com) and Mark Warschauer (markw@uci.edu).

Also available in the series:

Autonomous Language Learning with Technology: Beyond The Classroom, Chun Lai

Autonomy and Foreign Language Learning in a Virtual Learning Environment, Miranda Hamilton

Digital Games and Language Learning: Theory, Development and Implementation, edited by Mark Peterson, Kasumi Yamazaki and Michael Thomas

Language Teacher Education and Technology: Approaches and Practices, edited by Jeong-Bae Son and Scott Windeatt

Online Teaching and Learning: Sociocultural Perspectives, edited by Carla Meskill

Task-Based Language Learning in a Real-World Digital Environment: The European Digital Kitchen, edited by Paul Seedhouse

Teacher Education in Computer-Assisted Language Learning: A Sociocultural and Linguistic Perspective, Euline Cutrim Schmid

Teaching Languages with Technology: Communicative Approaches to Interactive Whiteboard Use, edited by Euline Cutrim Schmid and Shona Whyte

Technology-Enhanced Language Teaching and Learning: Lessons from the Covid-19 Pandemic, edited by Karim Sadeghi, Michael Thomas and Farah Ghaderi

Video Enhanced Observation for Language Teaching: Reflection and Professional Development, edited by Paul Seedhouse

WorldCALL: Sustainability and Computer-Assisted Language Learning, edited by Ana María Gimeno Sanz, Mike Levy, Françoise Blin and David Barr

Teaching Languages with Screen Media

Pedagogical Reflections

Edited by
Carmen Herrero and Marta F. Suarez

BLOOMSBURY ACADEMIC
LONDON · NEW YORK · OXFORD · NEW DELHI · SYDNEY

BLOOMSBURY ACADEMIC
Bloomsbury Publishing Plc
50 Bedford Square, London, WC1B 3DP, UK
1385 Broadway, New York, NY 10018, USA
29 Earlsfort Terrace, Dublin 2, Ireland

BLOOMSBURY, BLOOMSBURY ACADEMIC and the Diana logo are trademarks of
Bloomsbury Publishing Plc

First published in Great Britain 2023
Paperback edition published 2025

Copyright © Carmen Herrero and Marta F. Suarez and Contributors, 2023

Carmen Herrero and Marta F. Suarez and Contributors have asserted their right under the
Copyright, Designs and Patents Act, 1988, to be identified as Authors of this work.

For legal purposes the Acknowledgements on p. xvi constitute an extension
of this copyright page.

Cover design by James Watson
Cover image © shutterstock.com

All rights reserved. No part of this publication may be reproduced or transmitted
in any form or by any means, electronic or mechanical, including photocopying,
recording, or any information storage or retrieval system, without prior
permission in writing from the publishers.

Bloomsbury Publishing Plc does not have any control over, or responsibility for,
any third-party websites referred to or in this book. All internet addresses given
in this book were correct at the time of going to press. The author and publisher
regret any inconvenience caused if addresses have changed or sites have ceased
to exist, but can accept no responsibility for any such changes.

A catalogue record for this book is available from the British Library.

A catalogue record for this book is available from the Library of Congress.

ISBN: HB: 978-1-3502-1619-8
PB: 978-1-3502-1623-5
ePDF: 978-1-3502-1620-4
eBook: 978-1-3502-1621-1

Series: Advances in Digital Language Learning and Teaching

Typeset by RefineCatch Limited, Bungay, Suffolk

To find out more about our authors and books visit www.bloomsbury.com
and sign up for our newsletters.

Contents

List of Figures ix
List of Tables x
List of Contributors xi
Acknowledgements xvi

1 Screen Cultures and Language Education: Current and Future Trends in Teaching, Learning and Research *Carmen Herrero and Marta F. Suarez* 1

Part One: Entertainment Media: Informed Research and Practice

2 Screen Media in Language Education: Towards a Student-Centred Approach *Carmen Herrero, Marta F. Suarez and Alicia Sánchez-Requena* 17

3 Integrating Screen Media into the Language Curriculum *Carmen Herrero* 47

4 Bridging the Gaps Left by Boredom and Sociocultural Misperceptions: Does Foreign-Film Pedagogy Hold the Answer? *Mark Goodwin* 69

5 Teaching Languages to Generation Z Students: The Impact of the Use of Audiovisual Materials in the Spanish Classroom *Nazaret Pérez Nieto and Ares Llop Naya* 89

6 Language Education at the BBC: Past, Present and Future *Steven Barclay* 115

Part Two: Interactive Screen Media: Informed Research and Practice

7 Designing an International Tourism Fair To Improve Students' Learning with Collaborative Work *Azahara Veroz González and Soledad Díaz Alarcón* 139

8 Translating Film Reviews as a Means of Improving Students'
   Interlinguistic and Plurilingual Abilities *Mazal Oaknín*   159

9 Benefits and Drawbacks of Using Social Networking Sites in
   Higher Education: The Case of Facebook as a Transmedia
   English-Language Teaching Tool *Jelena Bobkina and
   Elena Domínguez Romero*   179

10 The Kinaesthetics of Gamification: Exploring the Theory
   behind Exergaming as a Potential Aid to Language Learning
   Chris McGuirk   199

11 Video-Based Approaches to Foreign-Language Pedagogy:
   Two Case Studies on Techno-CLIL in the Secondary School
   Classroom in Italy and the Netherlands *Michael Thomas
   and Valentina Morgana*   223

12 Participatory Video in Practice: Filming with Women from
   the Sudanese Community in Bradford *Simona Manni*   247

Glossary   265
Index   269

Figures

2.1	Functions of screen media in L2.	24
3.1	The intersection of screen media and language learning.	57
3.2	Film Education Framework.	58
5.1	Awareness of the usage of audiovisual materials in the Spanish class.	103
5.2	Types of exercises preferred by students.	105
5.3	Types of audiovisual materials preferred by students.	106
10.1	MI theory. Visual representation.	203
10.2	VAK learning styles model.	204
11.1	Space diagonal instructions in 3D world.	238
11.2	Space diagonal formula.	238
11.3	Appendix. Worksheet for teaching Pythagoras in 3D.	246

Tables

2.1	Stages for activities based on screen media.	32
2.2	Template to assess audiovisual materials for L2 teaching and learning.	36
7.1	Differences between collaborative and cooperative work.	143
7.2	Syllabus for this unit, from 2016 to 2017.	146
7.3	Syllabus for this unit, from 2018 to 2019.	148
8.1	Guide to pre-translation textual analysis based on Carreres, Noriega-Sánchez and Calduch (2018)'s model.	167
8.2	Application of the guide to pre-translation textual analysis based on Carreres, Noriega-Sánchez and Calduch (2018)'s model.	169
9.1	Overall results: students' attitude towards the use of Facebook as a teaching tool.	185
9.2	Uses of Facebook as a learning and teaching tool.	185
9.3	Students' attitude towards the usefulness of Facebook as a learning and teaching tool.	186
9.4	The usefulness of Facebook as a learning and teaching tool.	187
9.5	Drawbacks of Facebook as a learning and teaching tool.	188
9.6	Students' views on Facebook use in future versions of the English for Professional and Academic Communication (EPAC) course.	189
10.1	The DiAL-e Framework.	210
11.1	List of the twenty-seven subject-specific words selected from the science videos.	229
11.2	Students' scores in the vocabulary pre- and post-test.	230
11.3	Students' responses to statements on machinima.	240

Contributors

Steven Barclay is a Social Researcher and Historian. His expertise is in media, education and journalism. He has recently completed a research project on local news and information systems in the UK, and is working for City University London on a project on the life and career of broadcaster Alistair Cooke. His PhD was in the history of educational broadcasting in the UK. ORCID: 0000-0001-6080-8456.

Soledad Díaz-Alarcón is Senior Lecturer at the University of Córdoba, Spain, where she teaches translation and interpreting. Her research areas include literary translation (French into Spanish), particularly French narrative and nineteenth-century detective novels, and translation didactics. She is a prolific author with over thirty publications. She has also participated in numerous conferences and international research stays. She is currently involved in numerous projects such as INMOCOR (I+D+i project) and PROADMIN (I+D+i FEDER project), both funded by the Junta de Andalucía. Soledad is currently Editor-in-chief of the translation journal *Hikma: Revista de Traducción* and the *Nuevos Horizontes Electrónicos* series by UCO Press. ORCID: 0000-0002-8733-6396.

Jelena Bobkina is Senior Lecturer in the Department of Linguistics Applied to Science and Technology at the Technical University of Madrid (UPM), Spain, where she teaches English for specific purposes. Her main publication and research interests are in computer-assisted language learning, discourse analysis in digital media environments, and EFL/ESL teaching methodology. She belongs to the ENTELEARN (English, Technologies and Learning) Research Group and is an active member of numerous research projects on innovative teaching. She has published extensively in international refereed journals. ORCID: 0000-0003-0432-9957.

Elena Domínguez Romero is Associate Professor of English Language and Linguistics at the Complutense University of Madrid, Spain, where she coordinates the Master's programme in Teacher Training for English, German, French and Italian. Her recent research interests include evidentiality and positioning in media discourse as well as applied linguistics and innovation for research on teaching. Her publications comprise over seventy papers in international refereed journals, co-edited volumes and book chapters with Peter Lang, De Gruyter, Palgrave, Routledge, IGI Global, Multilingual Matters, Bloomsbury, Springer and McGraw Hill.

Mark Goodwin is Head of MFL at Merchant Taylors' Boys' School, Crosby, UK. An experienced modern foreign languages teacher with a particular interest in foreign film pedagogy, Mark has previously worked as Head of Spanish/MFL/Languages at three other schools spanning the independent and state sectors. Mark's PhD in Spanish Studies (University of Manchester, UK) followed an MA in Education (Edge Hill University, UK). During his PhD studies, Mark presented academic papers at several international conferences and his article 'An Analysis of the Success of the Cultural Topic at A level' was published in *Using Film and Media in the Language Classroom* (Multilingual Matters, 2019). Mark has been a committee member of the Independent Schools' Modern Languages Association.

Carmen Herrero is Principal Lecturer of Spanish Studies at Manchester Metropolitan University, UK. She leads the research group Film, Languages and Media Education (FLAME) and founded the Film in Language Teaching Association (FILTA) with Isabelle Vanderschelden. Her research focuses on film and screen studies, and the pedagogical applications of film and audiovisual media for language learning and teaching. She has published numerous articles on Spanish and Latin American cinema, and the use of movies, media and transmedia in language teaching and learning. She co-edited the volume *Using Film and Media in the Language Classroom* (Multilingual Matters, 2019). ORCID: 0000-0002-1392-4224.

Ares Llop Naya is the Batista i Roca Fellow at Fitzwilliam College and Associate Lecturer in the Spanish and Portuguese Department at the University of Cambridge, UK. She holds a PhD in Linguistics from the Universitat Autònoma de Barcelona, Spain, and two Masters in Teaching Spanish and Catalan L1/L2. She also worked in the School of Modern Languages at Cardiff University, UK and in the Faculty of Education at the University of Barcelona, Spain. Her research focuses on the relationship between theoretical linguistics, SLA research and MFL pedagogy. ORCID: 0000-0003-4365-4947.

Simona Manni is a filmmaker and has completed a PhD at the Digital Creativity Labs at the University of York, UK. After studying film theory in Italy and documentary production in the UK, Simona Manni started working as a freelance filmmaker in York in 2012. She has produced educational, marketing and event videos for local and national clients. Since 2015, she has specialized in participatory filmmaking in community settings, with a focus on promoting constructive and authentic communication between groups. Through this approach she has worked with asylum seekers, people recovering from mental health problems, homeless young people, women using support services, and care home residents living with dementia. Her research focuses on developing interactive films in communities to discuss and explore issues related to mental health.

Chris McGuirk is Lecturer in TESOL at the University of Central Lancashire, UK. He has been working in the field of TESOL for over twenty years, with a career that has seen him involved in a variety of areas, including EAP, materials development, bespoke training, functional skills and ESOL management. He is currently pursuing a PhD in Applied Linguistics with a focus on digital game-based language learning. Other research interests of his include language learning technology, third spaces and new media.

Valentina Morgana is Associate Professor of English Linguistics in the Faculty of Language Sciences and Foreign Literature at the Università Cattolica del Sacro Cuore in Milan, Italy. She holds a Doctorate in Education from the Department of Languages at the Open University, UK. Her research interests include applied linguistics (MALL and TBLT) and corpus linguistics. Her recent publications focus on mobile English language learning and technology-mediated task-based language teaching. She is co-editor of *Mobile Assisted Language Learning Across Educational Contexts* (Routledge, 2021). ORCID: 0000-0001-6086-3228.

Mazal Oaknín is Associate Professor (Teaching Focused) at UCL's Department of Spanish, Portuguese and Latin American Studies, UK, where she is also a Spanish Language Coordinator. Her research focuses on gender and identity in Spanish contemporary literature and teaching Spanish as a foreign language. Mazal is a Fellow of the Higher Education Academy and Co-Director of the e-Expert Seminar Series in Translation and Modern Language Education, a collaboration between UCL and the University of Córdoba, Spain. She is co-editor of *Literatura política y política literaria en España: Del Desastre del 98 a Felipe VI* (Peter Lang, 2015) and her work has appeared in journals such as *Espéculo*, *Fahrenheit 452*, *Alba Magazine*, *Transletters*, *Hikma* and *Argus*. Her monograph *Writing, Feminism and the Media in Spain* appeared in 2019 (Peter Lang). ORCID: 0000-0002-2816-5638.

Nazaret Pérez-Nieto is Lecturer in Spanish at the School of Modern Languages in Cardiff University, UK, where she teaches Spanish language and translation modules at undergraduate and postgraduate level. A sworn translator (English–Spanish) and Fellow of the Higher Education Academy, she currently holds the roles of Assessment and Feedback Lead, Programme Director of Spanish and Portuguese for the 'Languages for All' Programme, and Language Coordinator for Spanish Language modules. ORCID: 0000-0002-0650-3181.

Alicia Sánchez-Requena is Senior Lecturer in Spanish at Sheffield Hallam University, UK, and creator of the Spanish e-learning website HolaCandela. com. She completed her PhD in 2017 at Manchester Metropolitan University, UK. Her research is in the field of audiovisual translation in Foreign Language Education, and most of her research work has been in the modalities of dubbing and accessibility. She also worked as Visiting Lecturer at the University of Chester, UK, and Language Tutor at Manchester Metropolitan University, UK. Previously, she worked as a Spanish teacher at the Royal Grammar School, Guildford, UK. She read translation and interpreting at the University of Granada, Spain, and completed an MA degree in Applied Linguistics (Teaching Spanish as a Foreign Language) at the University Antonio de Nebrija in Madrid, Spain. ORCID: 0000-0003-0961-700X.

Marta F. Suarez is Lecturer in Latin American and Spanish Cultural Studies at Manchester Metropolitan University, UK. She holds a PhD in Screen Studies (from Liverpool John Moores University, UK). She has lectured on film theory, race on screen, screenwriting and genre. Her PhD thesis explores the portrayal of Latin American and African immigration in contemporary Spanish film, where she discusses issues of globalization, race and national identity in the context of the 2008–12 financial crisis. She has published on this topic in the *Routledge Companion of European Cinema* (Routledge, 2021) and in the edited collection *Migrants' Perspectives, Migrants in Perspective* (Edinburgh University Press, 2021). Her research interests include transmedia storytelling, transnational screens, and the intersections between cross-media adaptations, streaming platforms, computer games and expansive worlds. She is editor for *Open Screens*. ORCID: 0000-0001-7205-0339.

Michael Thomas is Professor of Education and Social Justice and Chair of the Centre for Educational Research (CERES) at Liverpool John Moores University, UK. He is the founder of four book series including *Palgrave Studies on Global Policy and Critical Futures in Education*. He is the author of three research monographs and over twenty edited volumes, mostly in the field of digital education. He has worked at universities in Germany, the UK and Japan, and is currently coordinating research projects on teacher education and gender equality in line with UN Sustainable Development Goals in Botswana, Ghana, Nigeria and South Africa. His research interests are in social justice, inequality, access to education and digital learning. ORCID: 0000-0001-6451-4439.

María Azahara Veroz-González holds a PhD in language and cultures (2014), specializing in translation, at the University of Córdoba, Spain. She is currently Lecturer in French at the University of Córdoba, Spain. She is also a lecturer on the Online Master's Degree in English Studies (OMIES) at the University of Jaén, Spain. Her research interests focus on new technologies in translation, specialized translation, and foreign language teaching. She coordinates UCOTerm, a website funded by the University of Córdoba dedicated to resources for scientific and technical translation. She is also involved in INMOCOR (I+D+i project, Junta de Andalucia), NEUROTRAD (I+D+i project, University of Malaga) and PROADMIN (I+D+i FEDER project, Junta de Andalucía). She is co-director of the annual E-Expert Seminar: Translation and Language Teaching held with UCL. She is a member of the research group Oriens HUM-940 (University of Córdoba) and TRADIT (UNED), and co-editor of the journal *Hikma: Translation Studies*. ORCID: 0000-0001-9544-4090.

Acknowledgements

We would first like to thank Isabelle Vanderschelden, who co-organized the conference, 'New Approaches to Transmedia and Language Pedagogy', which took place in July 2019 in Manchester (UK) with the support of the Open World Research Initiative, 'Cross-language Dynamics: Reshaping Community'. The inspiration for this book was drawn from this event, as seven of the chapters in this volume were presented as papers at that conference. This event was part of the *Teacher Training* and *Transmedia in Education* projects, and we are very grateful to the other members of the team that led and contributed to the workshops: Daniel Escandell Montiel and Sophie Guingouain. We would also like to thank the many language teachers that participated in the INSETs, and provided comments, feedback and suggestions. Needless to say, this volume would not have been possible without the contribution of the authors of the chapters.

We would like to thank the editorial staff at Bloomsbury for their support and to the anonymous reviewers of the volume who provided insightful comments that have been extremely helpful.

Beyond this, several people have been instrumental as the book developed. We would like to thank Manuela Escobar, Joaquín Fernández Barreiro, Rebecca Wynne-Walsh, Laura Ripper, James Wilkinson and, in particular, Ana Wilkinson, who read all the drafts and offered great critical comments and editing suggestions. The last mention should go to our families for their continuous and enthusiastic support. This book is dedicated to them.

Carmen Herrero and Marta F. Suarez
Manchester, UK

1

Screen Cultures and Language Education: Current and Future Trends in Teaching, Learning and Research

Carmen Herrero and Marta F. Suarez

Introduction

The evolution, uses and concepts associated with the screen are part of an ongoing debate among scholars from diverse disciplines (Monteiro 2017; Buckley, Campe and Casetti 2019). What is undeniable is the central role of screens in communications and for the understanding of the world nowadays. In the current communication age, visual culture reaches all aspects of our daily experiences (Apkon 2013). After all, as Monteiro (2017: 1) notes, 'contemporary culture is a screen culture [...] rooted in images, information, data or networks'. For most people, their everyday activities are characterized by their interaction with and dependence on small and large screens (mobile phones, tablets, television, computer screens, billboards, etc.). Indeed, screens are not only devices for entertainment activities, but have become indispensable equipment for work and education. They are powerful tools for communication exchanges with colleagues, friends and family, and facilitate connections to local and global networks. Thus, screen dependency and changes in visual practices have meant a 'radical shift in visual culture' due to three factors: the exponential growth in the shapes, sizes, technical specifications and uses of screens; the possibility of having layers of images or windows on a screen, which 'produces a new relationship between image, frame(s) and screen'; and the way in which mobile and touch screens have changed interactions with the screen (Monteiro 2017: 4–5). The adaptability, ubiquity and mobile nature of screen-based devices within the 'convergence culture' (Jenkins 2006) pose new challenges in defining the screen experience (Verhoeff 2012). Furthermore, the current explosion of screens is linked to new media which, as Chateauand and Moure (2016: 6) argue, 'expand the screen's function beyond the optical' (i.e. display or projection), traditionally associated with cinema and television.

Likewise, with the new technologies and broadband internet facilities, video games audiences are evolving. As Engelstätter and Ward (2022) note, video games have become 'more mainstream' due to the facilities for digital game distribution to mobile devices and the increasing importance of 'social video' in video game streaming sites (Twitch, YouTube Gaming, or Facebook Gaming). Moreover, it is the biggest entertainment industry in the world, far larger than cinema and music combined. It is a growing and profitable business focused on providing leisure and all kinds of experiences to its users and participants, from sports simulators to immersive augmented reality games. Data from 2022 shows that gaming 'is among the biggest entertainment platforms', as 79 per cent of the world's online population now engages with games (Newzoo 2020).

In this era of digital communications and given the range of media texts, genres and formats, the use of screens in the current streaming video ecology opens new avenues for second and modern foreign language (L2) education. Increasingly, more language teachers are aware of the central role of visual culture and how it is intrinsically linked to technological and cultural changes. Thus, the search for texts and activities that connect with students' real-life experiences and offer greater authenticity gives more prominence to the screen. The range of screen products used today in L2 education has also expanded considerably as learners do not only see screen media consumption as a leisure activity but as a tool for learning and acquiring and developing new skills. The new features of the media landscape provide students with ample opportunities to develop a wide range of competences (visual/film/media literacy, multimodal communication, critical thinking and digital skills, among others), as current technologies allow users of screen media to be consumers and producers (prosumers). With the proliferation of social online video services, there is an increasing number of content creators who post and upload their own content to social video platforms (YouTube, Instagram, Facebook and TikTok) (Kaye et al. 2022). Similarly, video games are engaging media that combine the audiovisual experience with interaction, as the player takes a central role in the development of the story and/or gameplay. As this is a medium that is relevant to many, it opens a window of opportunity to connect with more learners and enhance their motivation for L2 learning, particularly as the younger learners are more likely to engage with games. The application of digital games and gamification in L2 learning are areas in expansion and potentially of great pedagogical value

(Peterson 2013; Reinhardt 2017, 2019; Peterson, Yamazaki and Thomas 2021). In this context, this volume attempts to address some of the opportunities and challenges related to the integration of screen products in L2 education. In this book, we have also used screen media as a wide-ranging term to refer to media produced for the screen and consumed through the screen.

As a broad research field, screen studies comprise different domains: cultural studies, film and television studies, media studies, and video games studies. In this context, the scholarship on screen media and language education is an emerging area that brings together second language acquisition (SLA) and computer-assisted language learning (CALL) studies, new literacy studies and digital education, applied linguistics and audiovisual translation studies among others. The editors of this book have been involved in research and praxis related to the use and applications of film for language teaching and learning, UX (user experience) research for the development of TESOL and MFL teacher training, and the design of targeted resources (FILTA 2010; Herrero 2019a; Herrero and Vanderschelden 2019). Since 2013, the research group Film, Languages and Media in Education (FLAME) at Manchester Metropolitan University has been dedicated to the development of research and knowledge-exchange activities exploring innovative and effective pedagogical approaches to L2 learning and teaching with film and other screen media. This book is partially based on the contributions to the international conference, 'New Approaches to Transmedia and Language Pedagogy', organized by FLAME with the support of the Open World Research Initiative (OWRI), 'Cross-language Dynamics: Reshaping Community', in 2019. This interdisciplinary conference focused on research related to film, video games and visual arts in language education, and the applications of transmedia education to L2 across different levels. All of these are rapidly growing topics as more language educators are making use of screen media and transmedia realia which are closer to the experiences that students are familiar with.

In this context, this volume provides readers with theory-led developments and research-based practical applications related to the use of screen media for improving and enhancing the learning processes in a variety of L2 levels and educational environments. The chapters presented in this book offer concrete examples of how screen media – including film, television, social media, advertising, video games, mobile media, music videos and digital media – are embedded in L2 teaching practices in different countries. Furthermore, as the contributions to this volume reveal, learner engagement extends far beyond the formal space of the classroom to include the informal learning that takes place in digital-based spaces with exposure to the target language in entertainment activities (e.g. viewing for pleasure, creating videos, playing video games on streaming services, etc.). The findings presented in this volume also give practical suggestions and open up new avenues for pedagogical innovation and research that have implications for teachers, schools, language educators, policymakers, and educational material writers and publishers.

Overview of the book

The first part of the book focuses on entertainment media, practice-informed research, and examples of practice in L2 teaching and learning. Chapter 2, 'Screen media in language education: Towards a student-centred approach', explores how screen media can be embedded in L2 teaching. Herrero, Suarez and Sánchez-Requena's chapter examines the increasing consumption of screen culture (film, television, social media, mobile apps and video games) and proposes a framework for a far-reaching integration of visual media into L2 learning and teaching, beyond being a linguistic and cultural resource. Due to the power of user-generated content on social media channels, this section offers valuable guidelines for the selection and integration of screen media materials into L2 teaching. It also provides some examples of screen media projects aimed at encouraging L2 learners to be active producers of content. Chapter 3, 'Integrating screen media into the language curriculum', is devoted more specifically to teacher training issues and the development of resources based on short films and video games. Carmen Herrero's contribution presents findings from the *Teacher Training* project, *Film, Languages and Pedagogy Training*, and the *Transmedia in Education* project (2016–21). The projects investigated the ways in which films can be integrated into L2 curriculum design, and respond to the practical challenges and gaps in training and resources identified by L2 teachers and trainees during a series of research-in-action interventions. Chapter 4, 'Bridging the gaps left by boredom and sociocultural misperceptions: Does foreign film pedagogy hold the answer?', focuses more specifically on how using Spanish film in the classroom can enrich students' experience and knowledge of the Spanish language and Spain in the context of the reformed A-Level syllabus, part of the English national curriculum. Given the falling numbers of L2 students and the uncertainty of the current L2 provision in English schools, Mark Goodwin calls for enhancing learners' motivation and addressing a lack of intercultural appreciation through better integration and exploitation of films in the language curriculum. Chapter 5, 'Teaching languages to Generation Z students: The impact of the use of audiovisual materials in the Spanish classroom', shows how the increase in audiovisual resources in L2 (TV series, films and music videos) allows teachers to access a wider range of engaging and dynamic materials. In the context of UK higher education, Nazaret Pérez Nieto and Ares Llop Naya evaluate students' perceptions of activities based on audiovisual materials and conclude that, when used effectively, they can increase students' motivation. Finally, Steven Barclay's chapter, 'Language education at the BBC: Past, present and future', examines the history of the BBC's language education broadcasting using original archival research and oral interviews. For decades, the BBC has innovated in pedagogy, taking new curriculum development opportunities as they appeared, and used an effective feedback mechanism to ensure popularity in schools. Given the renewed importance of the BBC educational provision during the COVID-19 pandemic, the author argues that the same structural, social and political factors that influenced the course of educational broadcasting will continue to influence audiovisual and transmedia education in the present and future.

The second part takes as its starting point the participatory nature of popular culture and the shifts that are taking place in contemporary media culture. This section focuses on interactive screen media and how language pedagogy should respond and realign to new learning experiences and provide further evidence of the value of transmedia practices in which students become prosumers (consumers and producers) of media content. The chapters in this volume illustrate how screen media can be exploited to support L2 teaching and learning, by drawing on a wide range of theories and approaches (SLA, CALL and audiovisual translation studies, new media studies, and film and video games studies). The first two chapters consider some of the benefits of translation applied to L2 teaching and learning: improving learners' linguistic and plurilingual abilities; enhancing motivation; fostering professional skills, such as collaborative and cooperative learning skills; and contributing to the development of mediation competence. Chapter 7, 'Designing an international tourism fair to improve students' learning with collaborative work', reports on a project in which undergraduate students at the University of Córdoba (Spain) produced audiovisual material on a French-speaking region as part of a module on French culture and civilization. M. Azahara Veroz González and Soledad Díaz Alarcón's contribution showcases the value of applying collaborative learning practice and the translation strategies and techniques to enhance students' engagement. Chapter 8, 'Translating film reviews as a means of improving students' interlinguistic and plurilingual abilities', explores the potential of film reviews for second language acquisition. In this chapter, Mazal Oaknín presents a case study based on the use of film reviews in the translation classroom for multilingual learners of Spanish in higher education. This chapter offers practical guidelines on how teachers might choose film reviews that are best suited for this purpose. Chapter 9, 'Benefits and drawbacks of using social networking sites in higher education: The case of Facebook as a transmedia English language teaching tool', discusses how to reduce the gap between traditional teaching practices and the sociotechnical conditions of today's communication. Jelena Bobkina and Elena Domínguez Romero present a classroom-based study conducted with a group of undergraduate engineering students from the Universidad Politécnica de Madrid in Spain. The study examines the benefits of social networking sites as transmedia language-teaching tools to enhance collaboration, reflection and autonomous learning. In chapter 10, 'The kinaesthetics of gamification: Exploring the theory behind exergaming as a potential aid to language learning', Chris McGuirk concentrates on the possible benefits of exergaming as a form of serious gaming to enhance language learning. More specifically, it looks at how kinaesthetic learning through exergames may benefit the language-learning process by helping to create an appropriate learning environment and mindset. Chapter 11, 'Video-based approaches to foreign language pedagogy: Two case studies on techno-CLIL in the secondary school classroom in Italy and the Netherlands', focuses on the dynamics of oral interaction and video-tasks. Michael Thomas and Valentina Morgana's contribution examines findings from two case studies on the use of video and Content and Language Integrated Learning (CLIL), an approach aimed at teaching learners about a particular topic in the target language. The first case study investigates the ways in which a CLIL approach was used to support multimodal types of input (captioned videos) to improve the acquisition of English subject-specific vocabulary with Italian learners of English in the secondary classroom. The second case study examines the use of machinima within a 3D immersive world, alongside a CLIL approach in the secondary mathematics classroom in the Netherlands. The final chapter, 'Participatory video in practice: Filming with women from the Sudanese community in Bradford', describes the practice of participatory filmmaking, an approach through which a professional filmmaker steps into a community to pass on media skills to its members. The aim of participatory filmmaking is to encourage people to reflect on issues that affect them, and to represent themselves and their community by taking control of the audiovisual language. To illustrate some of the dynamics of participatory filmmaking, Simona Manni presents a case study of her own practice working with the Sudanese community in Bradford. The project provides a model for involving migrants and refugees in participatory filmmaking where L2 learning is informal and implicit, but highly relevant.

Current and future trends: Screen culture in teaching, learning and research

The shift towards digital connectivity and reliance on social media and technology for work and personal life was already taking place before COVID-19, but the pandemic has accelerated the process and contributed to the expansion of visual and screen media communication. A recent research report from the UK media regulator Ofcom (2020) evidences the impact of this trend due to lockdown restrictions. The temporary closure of businesses, schools and higher education institutions in 2020 meant a rise in screen time and its uses for leisure and educational activities, with smartphones being the most used device.[1] This shift has given prominence to educational videos and has also impacted the increase of informal online learning, with the language learning app Duolingo being the most popular in the UK (Ofcom 2020).

The rise of online learning due to the disruption brought by the COVID-19 pandemic has also changed education dramatically, as online services had a crucial role in education during the lockdowns (See Kalantzis and Cope 2020). Up until the COVID-19 crisis hit, screen devices were mainly only essential for online courses. However, during 2020, even the most reluctant teachers had to adapt to teaching with screens. The scale of their use for educational purposes is evident in the adaptation of platforms such as Google Classroom or Microsoft Teams. The restrictions on face-to-face schooling during the pandemic have provided more evidence of how many language teachers are still struggling to understand the potential of new media when taking their teaching fully online. In fact, one could argue that, in today's rapidly changing media landscape, it is critical to understand media-use patterns and to examine the challenges and teacher-training needs. This situation has stretched the limits of education systems around the world and has also made the use of all sorts of educational technologies a priority to provide remote learning opportunities for students while schools and universities were forced to close. Examples of the solutions put forward to help learners to study remotely are broadcasting video lessons through television and radio, websites and portals, combined with social media

(Facebook and YouTube), and the making of videos and audio lessons through the medium of mobile phones (see Barclay's chapter in this volume).[2] Maybe now more than ever, teaching and learning experiences rely on the exchange and visualization of information on screen, and language education is not an exception. No doubt this will be the beginning of a new era in the language education field, the outcomes of which will soon be visible.

Incorporating screen media at the heart of L2 curricula and syllabi requires one to bear in mind the restless fluidity of technological advances and their impact on media. When discussing current and future trends of screen cultures in L2, it might be worth briefly considering the delineations of the field covered here. A useful starting point to understand this 'new technoculture' is the taxonomy of 'new media' proposed by Lister et al. (2009: 12–13), which includes the following elements: 'new textual experiences' (genres, textual forms and patterns of media consumption); 'new ways of representing the world' (immersive virtual environment, screen-based interactive multimedia, etc.); 'new relationships between subjects (users and consumers) and media technologies'; new experiences of the relationships between embodiment, identity and community 'that alter our personal and social experiences'; 'new conceptions of biological body's relationship to technological media' that blurred the distinction between real and virtual; and 'new patterns of organisation and production' due to the repositioning and amalgamations in the media industry and the impact on access and ownership. This taxonomy will provide a guide for identifying some of the current and future developments in relation to L2 education and screen media. However, in many respects, the distinction between digital and non-digital media relies not so much on the technological changes but on the new social practices in which they are anchored. Thus, many researchers argue that it is crucial to reuse and transfer categories and conventions from pre-existing frameworks and practices (Bateman 2021: 6).

The 'new textual experiences' provide opportunities to engage with a wider range of screen genres and textual forms. Traditional genres are easy to access (music videos, commercials, sketches, sitcoms and educational videos, for example), but there is also a growing taxonomy of Web 2.0 audiovisual subgenres. Among the most popular types of YouTube videos, there are numerous examples that can inspire L2 learners and provide templates for video creation: video blogs (vlogs), video tutorials, video podcasts, ask me anything (AMA) videos, whiteboard videos, listicle videos (lists with the 'best of' or the 'top list of'), product reviews, challenge videos, unboxing videos, behind the scenes videos, explainer videos, product demo videos, video testimonials, reaction videos, webinar teasers, community-based videos, Q&A videos, product-launch videos, etc. These subgenres are characterized by a short and effective format that can gain the audience's attention and provide a great variety of content and styles. Their diversity offers an extensive catalogue of opportunities for activities and tasks, as well as models for assignments, for all proficiency levels (see Pérez Prieto and Llop Naya's chapter in this volume).

Due to 'new relationships between subjects (users and consumers) and media technologies' (Lister et al. 2009: 12), it is equally important to think about the patterns of media consumption, which focus on a more personalized, interactive and immersive entertainment experience. The shift towards audiences as consumers of media is more than a simple metaphor. As transmedia expert Robert Pratten (Herrero 2019c: online) suggests, it could be useful to consider the connections between transmedia and education 'by building a learning environment around the learner'. What that means 'is trying to fit in with their existing behaviours [...] not just the way they like to learn but [considering] what they are doing at certain times of the day, what devices they used' and 'how did they like to spend their free time'. This consideration of the behaviour or profile of the learner makes the 'participatory' experience an exemplary model for personalized learning. As Pratten notes, for the learning experience to be 'relevant' to the individual, it should be 'contextual' and with a 'goal' in order to enhance the learner's engagement and journey into 'problem-solving' (see Bobkina and Domínguez Romero's and Veroz and Díaz Alarcón's chapters, as well as Herrero's, Manni's, and Herrero, Suarez and Sánchez-Requena's, in this volume).

The preference of younger generations (Gen Z and Millennial) for social and interactive media is one of the greatest challenges that teachers may face. As noted by Michael Thomas and Valentina Morgan in this volume, immersive virtual environments and screen-based interactive multimedia are part of advances in L2 education which provide learners with real-life experiences, similar to activities outside the classroom. In many ways gamification (applying game principles in non-game contexts) is a good strategy to stimulate an affective involvement towards the second language with overall positive effects on individuals (Hamari, Koivisto and Sarsa 2014). Similarly, games and competitive e-sports are ideal tools to engage learners' attention (see Chris McGuirk's chapter in this volume).

The gaming experience, video gaming (Pokémon, Minecraft and many other games based on brands and franchises) and live-in game events are growing in popularity and 'reinforcing the steady blurring between the real and virtual' (Westcott et al. 2022). Stemming from this shift, AR/VR hardware and gaming in 3D virtual worlds represent an opportunity to further enhance learners' engagement. For example, they can provide alternatives to real experiences, such as the 'period of residence abroad', and make this type of experiences more inclusive to learners who, for whatever reason, are not able to visit the country/ies of the language they are studying – particularly when, after two years of physical distance due to the pandemic, students have become more used to digitalized and virtualized experiences. Of course, all these activities generate other ethical, financial and practical questions that the language instructor should take into consideration when implementing, related to privacy issues, monetization, appropriate training (digital skills) and curriculum constraints.

Many educators have called for including a plurilingual perspective and the incorporation of translanguaging into L2 learning and teaching as part of a broader view of literacies that are shaping language education pedagogy (see Oaknín's and Veroz González and Díaz Alarcón's chapters in this volume). Contemporary visual and media culture is fundamentally transnational and *glocal* as the entertainment industry tries to adapt to global markets. Streaming video on-demand (SVOD) services have grown and attracted subscribers from around the globe using personalized data to offer a menu of local, national and international media products. Because of the new viewing habits, there is a new sense of community that builds strong social transnational connections among the fandoms. For instance, Netflix products such as *Money Heist* (Antena 3 and Netflix 2017–21), *Sense 8* (Netflix 2016–18), *Squid Game* (Netflix 2021) and *Stranger Things* (Netflix 2016–22) or the anime *One Piece* (Toei Animation 1999–present) gain the favour of millions of fans across the globe and, in many ways, offer a rich transcultural and multilingual experience of great value in L2 learning and teaching.

The consumption of user-generated video content is now more popular than the consumption of television or video streaming services, according to a recently published report on 'Digital media trends' (Westcott et al. 2022). In essence, the 'new patterns of organisation and production' (Lister et al. 2009: 13) offer attractive possibilities for integration of content creation as a way of socializing and boosting self-expression in L2, particularly within the younger generations. One of the current trends is transmedia storytelling, which implies telling a single story or story experience across multiple platforms and formats, each expanding the content of the others. Digital storytelling without dialogues (e.g. short films without verbal communication, or video games that rely entirely on visual and non-verbal clues) is particularly suitable for supporting the development of transmedia literacy, which implies the ability to recognize, understand and interact with complex, multimodal narratives (Rutledge 2019). It provides an ideal framework for working with all languages at all levels as it fosters the development of a wide range of skills (intercultural awareness, critical thinking and creativity, digital skills and language skills) (see Herrero's chapter in this volume). Furthermore, transmedia communication strategies can facilitate a synergy between L2 classes and content subjects (Herrero 2021).

In short, the core characteristics of 'new media' ('digital, interactive, hypertextual, virtual, networked and simulated') imply a radical cultural change in media ecology in terms of production, distribution and use (Lister et al. 2009: 11–13). There is no doubt that its impact in the L2 classroom will keep growing during the next decade. Overall, the current and future patterns of screen media consumption and trends in education entail not only media consumption, but the production of different artefacts that actively engage learners in participatory practices and prepare them to be critical prosumers and responsible citizens. Students can make the most of multimodal practices in face-to face and in virtual and mobile practice. Consequently, the role of the L2 teacher as curator of media is vital, as in the selection process language instructors should consider screen media multimodal patterns and social and gender representations (Herrero 2019b; Contreras Llave 2022). More than ever, as the media and entertainment landscape changes, pre-service and in-service L2 training needs to respond to the expansion of social media and evolving preferences of younger generations, skills and knowledge to connect, gather information and offer relevant and engaging teaching materials and projects in which learners are 'prosumers' and active designers of meaning. Ultimately, to fully exploit screen media for L2 learning requires a more systematic approach to gamified and screen media-pedagogical practices, based on both teacher-informed designed resources and student-centred learning.

Notes

1   The increase in screen use was significant during the COVID-19 pandemic in 2020: 'an average of 3 hours 37 minutes a day on smartphones, tablets, and computers (nine minutes more than in 2019) as well as an average of 1 hour 21 minutes a day watching online services such as Netflix and BBC iPlayer on television sets (24 minutes more than in 2019)' (Ofcom: 2021: 3). As for the use of mobile phones, 'UK internet users spent nearly four times as much time on smartphones (an average of 2 hours 19 minutes a day) than they did on computers (37 minutes)' (Ofcom, 2021: 3).

2   See, for example, the reports collected by UNESCO on educational responses to the COVID-19 crisis across the world: https://en.unesco.org/covid19/educationresponse/nationalresponses.

References

Apkon, S. (2013), *The Age of the Image: Redefining Literacy in a World of Screens*, New York: Farrar, Straus and Giroux.

Bateman, J. (2021), 'What Are Digital Media?', *Discourse, Context & Media*, 41 (100502). Available online: https://doi.org/10.1016/j.dcm.2021.100502.

Buckley, C., R. Campe and F. Casetti, eds (2019), *Screen Genealogies: From Optical Device to Environmental Medium*, Amsterdam: Amsterdam University Press.

Chateauand, D., and J. Moure, eds (2016), *Screens. From Materiality to Spectatorship: A Historical and Theoretical Reassessment*, Amsterdam: Amsterdam University Press.

Contreras Llave, N. (2022), 'Cine y perspectiva de género como herramienta de transformación social en la didáctica de español como lengua extranjera', PhD thesis, Faculty of Education: Universidad de Alicante.

Engelstätter, B., and M. R. Ward (2022), 'Video Games Become More Mainstream', *Entertainment Computing* 42: 100494.

Film in Language Teaching Association (2010), *Film in Language Teaching Association* (FILTA). Available online: http://www.filta.org.uk.

Film, Languages and Media in Education (2013), *Film, Languages and Media in Education* (FLAME). Available online: https://www.mmu.ac.uk/languages/flame/.

Hamari, J., J. Koivisto and H. Sarsa (2014), 'Does Gamification Work? A Literature Review of Empirical Studies on Gamification', in R. Sprague (ed.), *Proceedings of the 47th Hawaii International Conference on System Sciences*, 3025–34, Los Alamitos, CA: IEEE Computer Society.

Herrero, C. (2019a), 'Conclusion: Present and Future directions for Video, Film and Audiovisual Media in Language Teaching', in C. Herrero and I. Vanderschelden (eds), *Using Film and Media in the Language Classroom: Reflections on Research-led Teaching*, 188–97, Bristol: Multilingual Matters.

Herrero, C. (2019b), 'Medios audiovisuales', in J. Muñoz-Basols, E. Gironzetti and M. Lacorte (eds), *The Routledge Handbook of Spanish Language Teaching: Metodologías, contextos y recursos para la enseñanza del español L2*, 565–82, London and New York: Routledge.

Herrero, C. (2019c), 'Transmedia in Education: An Interview with Robert Pratten', *MMUTube* [video]. Available online: https://mmutube.mmu.ac.uk/media/Transmedia+and+Education-+Interview+with+Robert+Pratten.+Interview+by+Carmen+Herrero/1_e7wkfs5b.

Herrero, C. (2021), 'La educación transmedia como estrategia innovadora para integrar lengua y cultura en la enseñanza de ELE', *Doblele. Revista de lengua y literatura*, 7: 50–66.

Herrero, C., and I. Vanderschelden, eds (2019), *Using Film and Media in the Language Classroom: Reflections on Research-led Teaching*, Bristol: Multilingual Matters.

Jenkins, H. (2006), *Convergence Culture: Where Old and New Media Collide*, New York: New York University Press.

Kalantzis, M., and B. Cope (2020), 'After The COVID-19 Crisis: Why Higher Education May (and Perhaps Should) Never Be the Same', *ACCESS: Contemporary Issues in Education* 40 (1): 51–5.

Kaye, D., B. Valdovinos, J. Zeng and P. Wikstrom (2022), *TikTok: Creativity and Culture in Short Video*, Cambridge: Polity Press.

Lister, M., J. Dovey, S. Giddings, I. Grant and K. Kelly, eds (2009), *New Media. A Critical Introduction*, 2nd ed., London and New York: Routledge.

Monteiro, S., ed. (2017), *The Screen Media Reader. Culture, Theory, Practice*, New York and London: Bloomsbury.

Newzoo (2022), 'How Consumers are Engaging with Games in 2022', *Newzoo Consumer Insights Report*. Available online: https://newzoo.com/insights/trend-reports/how-consumers-are-engaging-with-games-in-2022.

Ofcom (2021), *Online Nation. 2021 Report*. 9 June. Available online: https://www.ofcom.org.uk/__data/assets/pdf_file/0013/220414/online-nation-2021-report.pdf.

Peterson, M. (2013), *Computer Games and Language Learning*, New York: Palgrave Macmillan

Peterson, M., K. Yamazaki and M. Thomas, eds (2021), *Digital Games and Language Learning: Theory, Development and Implementation*, London and New York: Bloomsbury Publishing.

Reinhardt, J. (2017), 'Digital Gaming in L2 Teaching and Learning', in C. A. Chapelle and S. Sauro (eds), *The Handbook of Technology and Second Language Teaching and Learning*, 202–16, Hoboken, NJ: John Wiley & Sons.

Reinhardt, J. (2019), *Gameful Second and Foreign Language Teaching and Learning: Theory, Research, and Practice*, Basingstoke: Palgrave Macmillan.

Rutledge, P. (2019), 'Transmedia Psychology: Creating Compelling and Immersive Experiences', in M. Freeman and R. R. Gambarato (eds), *The Routledge Companion to Transmedia Studies*, 350–63, New York: Routledge.

Verhoeff, N. (2012), *Mobile Screens: The Visual Regime of Navigation*, Amsterdam: Amsterdam University Press.

Westcot, K., J. Arbanas, C. Arkenberg and B. Auxier (2022), 'Digital Media Trends, 16th edition: Toward the Metaverse', *Deloitte Insights Magazine*. Available online: https://www2.deloitte.com/us/en/insights/industry/technology/digital-media-trends-consumption-habits-survey/summary.html#.

Part One

Entertainment Media: Informed Research and Practice

2

Screen Media in Language Education: Towards a Student-Centred Approach

Carmen Herrero, Marta F. Suarez and
Alicia Sánchez-Requena

Introduction

The term 'screen culture' is often used to refer to media that rely primarily on 'images more than language, a modern form of visual culture' (Butsch 2019: 2). It includes film, television and other digital media that have become a mainstay of our lives, such as social media, mobile apps or digital games. This upward trend is happening because the range of screen media continues to expand, and, at the same time, the phenomenon of media convergence increases 'the flow of content through multiple media platforms' (Jenkins 2006: 2). Thus, screen media has enormous potential for achieving a more active engagement with authentic cultural products mediated by technology in a highly visual, digital landscape.

By reflecting on today's 'media ecology' (Scolari 2012), this chapter analyses the possibilities and challenges offered by screen media in the field of second/foreign language (L2) education. It proposes a broader framework for the integration of visual media as a linguistic and transcultural resource in L2 learning and teaching. It does so by addressing the following questions:

1. How can screen media complement current pedagogical approaches and more traditional methodologies?
2. How do language learners (from children to adults) use screen media as consumers and producers?
3. Which skills are they using or acquiring when interacting with screen media in L2?
4. What are the challenges experienced by language learners and teachers when using a range of screen media, and how can these be addressed?

Adopting a multidisciplinary theoretical approach (applied linguistics, second language acquisition, audiovisual translation, screen studies and transmedia studies), this chapter seeks to provide some guidelines to facilitate a meaningful and efficient integration of screen media into L2 lesson plans and classroom tasks. The first part of this chapter provides an overview of the uses of audiovisual media pushed by the technological advances that have taken place since the late twentieth century. It draws particular attention to current opportunities for exploiting screen media in language education due to their accessibility through streaming platforms such as Amazon Prime Video, Netflix or YouTube. It also addresses the use of social media, mobile apps and digital games for language learning, reflecting on the opportunities that these media offer to educators and learners. This section proposes a flexible model for exploiting screen media as a learning tool across different language-learning contexts and levels. The aim is to guide teachers who wish to incorporate screen media as a more pertinent component of curriculum content. It offers a template for selecting screen media products for L2 teaching and learning, considering objectives and issues such as themes and content, genres and linguistic characteristics (vocabulary, speed, accents, etc.), among others. The second part of this chapter, recognizing that activities involving screen media should be interactive, engaging, productive and relevant, examines some real examples of L2 projects, including audiovisual translation tasks and video-making.

From audiovisual media to screen cultures

Before considering the applications and practicalities of working with screen media in the language classroom, this section reviews how they have been used to date. Screen media products have been apt resources for L2 teaching since films were screened or distributed worldwide in their original version. Their usage has been intrinsically linked to the development of new technologies. Since the 1970s, videocassette recorders and video cameras have provided exposure to authentic materials (news, adverts, documentaries, etc.). The development of satellite television and interactive video opened new possibilities; and, since the 1980s, with the wider distribution of Video Home System (or VHS), screen media products were adopted progressively for language instruction to expose students to popular culture. In the case of films, the mass production of DVDs and the successor to this format, the Blu-ray Disc, accelerated this trend. They facilitated language in action by fostering meaningful classroom activities working with a range of special features: different language versions, options for subtitles, direct scene access, and the bonus materials included in some of the DVDs (teasers, trailers, 'making-of' documentaries, music videos from the soundtrack, commentaries from and interviews with the director, actors, producers or the film crew, etc.).

Although in the early or first half of the 1990s professional video and television materials were purposely produced for L2 teaching and learning, these film and video programmes were mainly used in activities that did not promote a creative approach or as 'a bit of time-filling end-of-term entertainment' (Voller and Widdows 1993: 342). In general, rather than efficiently integrating these authentic resources into the language curriculum, videos were associated with entertainment activities. Progressively, films, videos and TV series were seen as useful tools in a communicative approach. In this context, language teachers were encouraged to plan video-based lessons to facilitate more effective learning. For example, visual content was exploited as a stimulus for follow-up writing exercises, discussion activities, or to present language in a specific situation leading to other tasks. Over the last thirty years, the increasing popularity of video in L2 classrooms has led to the creation of new publications that include activities, techniques and 'recipes' to make the most of 'authentic' audiovisual materials (Canning-Wilson 2000; Stemplensky and Tomalin 2001; Sherman 2003).

As video cameras became increasingly available, language instructors began to experiment with video recording for language instruction and assessment (Lonergan 1984). In a similar vein, language educational experts started to put forward compelling reasons for using films and involving students in video creation to mobilize a stronger affective and creative engagement with the language tasks (Bahloul and Graham 2012; Keddie 2014; Goldstein and Driver 2015; Anderson and Macleroy 2016).

During the last decade, one can see how the dynamics of contemporary media and visual culture have radically transformed the entertainment landscape. The growing popularity of streaming services, which are tailored to personal viewing habits, has opened new avenues for incorporating more visual content into L2 instruction. In many ways, YouTube was a pioneer in this educational trend and the possibilities that it offers as a teaching resource are still relevant today. Burke, Snyder and Rager (2009) have rightly identified some of the advantages of using YouTube as an instructional tool: it offers a plethora of authentic video materials that increase motivation; it provides visual demonstrations and examples on topics that are part of classroom content; and it facilitates discussion during the lessons, enhancing critical thinking. Hence, language scholars have emphasized the various opportunities that YouTube presents for language learning and teaching (Brook 2011). YouTube can enhance learners' listening skills, increase their exposure to regional varieties, improve pronunciation skills and vocabulary acquisition (Watkins and Wilkins 2011; Kabooha and Elyas 2018), as well as encourage authentic writing (Mayora 2009). It provides a wealth of examples of multimodal texts and genres, as well as opportunities for cultural and intercultural learning due to the social nature of some of its content and affordances (Benson 2015; Seeger 2019). Ultimately, YouTube is a platform that can provide many opportunities for video-making and can facilitate a great range of other tasks and activities, such as audiovisual translation exercises. Furthermore, as a 'language learning site', YouTube is an ideal platform for online self-regulated language learning (Wang and Chen 2020).

Streaming video offers plenty of possibilities for a personalized and meaningful experience that engages learners actively with participatory culture (Herrero and Vanderschelden 2019). The 'streaming video ecology' provides a relatively more diverse menu of programmes and a multilayered experience of audiovisual products from and across the world. Netflix is the new leader in this experience, although other platforms are steadily increasing membership and audiences. The popularity and diversity of TV series are now characteristics of a thriving media ecosystem, a phenomenon accelerated by the COVID-19 outbreak and subsequent lockdowns that took place across the world. The streaming video ecology has facilitated new viewing styles. Quite often, all episodes are available for binge-watching and can be viewed at any time, in any place, on any device with streaming capabilities. As noted by Herrero (2019b: 192), the impact of these 'trends on the learning practices of the millennial and post-millennial learners are starting to be visible'. For example, the accessibility and popularity of some series have had a direct impact on the increasing popularity of some languages (as is the case for Korean in the UK). However, as noted by Wang and Cheng (2020) in relation to YouTube, students tend to take a passive approach and attitude. Thus, to make the most of the technological advances offered by these platforms, it is important to encourage students to reflect critically on their online learning and prepare lesson plans.

Video content is the most popular content on social media platforms (TikTok, Facebook, Instagram, Twitter, LinkedIn, among others). Expectedly, similar concerns and successes have been described by scholars about the use of social media in the L2 classroom. For Reinhardt (2019: 31), research into the use of social media for language learning has demonstrated that 'used informally, [it] can afford the development of intercultural, sociopragmatic, and audience awareness, language learner and user identities, and particular literacies'. The potential for the use of social media in the L2 classroom has been widely studied, with a plethora of scholarship pointing out the benefits of integrating it into the language classroom (Alm 2015; Wong, Sing-Chai and Poh-Aw 2017; Reinhardt 2019; Barrot 2021). However, some authors also highlight the limitations of using these resources in the classroom without careful consideration. For example, Reinhardt (2018: 23) indicates that students dislike using social media when there is 'pressure to be grammatically perfect or show more content expertise than they feel they have'. In a later study (Reinhardt 2019), the author also reminds educators that most of these platforms are commercial enterprises, and some scrutiny is recommended before using them with an educational aim. The need to ensure that the use of social media in the classroom is meaningful and relevant is also emphasized by Lantz-Andersson (2018), who suggests that these tasks should be mediated by the educator. Alm (2015) notes that the attitude of learners towards these platforms and networks impacts their engagement, as some prefer not to use social media, some feel overexposed when using L2 in situations that are visible to their private networks, and some do not know anyone with whom to practise the L2 in a meaningful and authentic way. In some of these cases, the educator might be able to offer alternatives, such as creating hidden private groups, setting activities to interact with a certain page or person, suggesting accounts to follow, and sharing a class account for general use during class time, etc. Similarly, Ko (2019), as Reinhardt (2018) above, also discusses challenges derived from learners' confidence in using the target language in these spaces, particularly in regard to how their language accuracy might compare to other learners. To this, Ko (2019) also adds constraints related to the use of personal devices (such as battery life or distractions). Despite the limitations, Reinhardt (2018) asserts that research has evidenced the potential of social media to enhance language learning and foster collaboration, develop linguistic and cultural competences, and provide opportunities for learning autonomy.

While much has been written on the use of film and television for learning, the use of digital games has been less widely explored as a whole. Reinhardt and Sykes (2014) developed a framework for categorizing and analysing L2 teaching and learning research and practice, where the authors distinguish between 'game-enhanced, game-based, or game-informed' materials and projects. Game-enhanced practice refers to the use of 'off the shelf' games, those which were designed for entertainment and have no educational aims in their design, even though they might be used for this purpose. Here one might find activities with traditional games played in the target language, such as playing Ludo when learning to count in the L2, integrating games from TV shows, the use of computer games where the language is set to the target language, or even using versions of Wordle in the L2. The second category, which is game-based, refers to the use of educational games where aspects of learning have been considered by design. Here one might find spelling games, educational learning apps, vocabulary games, etc. Finally, the third category (game-informed) explores practices and research that apply game principles to contexts not originally intended to have any gaming feature. This is the category where gamification processes take place, for example.

The studies exploring the value of integrating digital games (such as mobile games, computer games or console games) indicate that games enhance learning but that they might be challenging to implement within the curriculum. Kawaguchi and Watkins (2015) found that the cost and the teacher's digital literacy were barriers for successfully implementing games into the classroom, while Yudintseva (2015) also indicated that some learners might still prefer traditional learning through repetition and textbooks. Many projects approach learning activities through play to supplement very specific areas of the curriculum, such as learning thematic vocabulary, or as an activity that can complement learning outside the classroom. Brevik (2019) found that learners who were engaged with gaming in the L2 progressed quickly and further than learners who practised the L2 in social media or general internet surfing. The author also notes in this study that those who played games were also more likely to engage in other activities connected to these games, particularly reading novels that expanded the storytelling. Beyond this, gamers might also read walkthroughs, interact with other users to answer questions about the game, and watch videos to help them complete a particular level or puzzle, etc. Reinders (2012), Chen and Yang (2013), Chik (2014), Janebi Enayat and Haghighatpasand (2019), Calvo-Ferrer and Belda-Medina (2021) and Li (2022) all explore the impact of playing digital games outside the classroom as a way to improve language skills, with their research findings showing improvements in areas such as listening, reading, writing, vocabulary and motivation.

Overlapping sometimes with digital games, learning apps have also shown great potential for complementing learning. However, studies have shown that they work best when their use is mediated by a tutor and learners' digital literacy is addressed (Finardi, Leao and Amorim 2016; Reinhardt 2018). Heil et al.

(2016) conclude that while commercial learning apps might enhance vocabulary, they often work with it as isolated units and do not help with contextualization, a point also made by Nami (2020). Loewen et al. (2019) also review commercial apps and report favourable learning outcomes, although they note obstacles, such as frustration with the materials or differences in learners' motivation. Barriers related to the digital literacy of the learners are also discussed by Puebla et al. (2022). Overall, however, the use of apps to support learning in or outside the classroom offers great potential to target specific areas or as autonomous learning.

Using screen media: functions, practical guidelines

Considering the variety of screen media, this section aims to offer a framework for exploiting media artefacts across different language-learning contexts and levels. The first objective is to offer criteria for selecting among and working with screen media products; the second objective is to present some existing resources and practical examples that can guide or serve as a model for language teachers who wish to introduce screen media as a central component of curriculum content. Given the versatility of its applications, it is important to start not so much with the advantages (or lack of them) but concentrate on the roles or functions of screen media in L2 teaching and learning. Herrero (2019a: 572) has presented a taxonomy based on the relationship between audiovisual media and the L2 classroom organized into five functions (see Figure 2.1). These categories will guide the discussion on the strategies for using screen media in L2 teaching. It should be noted that the division between the functions is not absolute, since certain proposals can relate to more than one of the functions.

For the first function, the development of communicative language competence, we can take as a reference the *Common European Framework of Reference for Languages: Learning, Teaching and Assessment* (Council of Europe 2001). This curriculum map proposes an action-oriented approach to language learning. Its methodology draws on the communicative language competences (grammatical, semantic, phonological, orthographic, sociolinguistic, pragmatic, discourse, functional, plurilingual and pluricultural competence). These competences are developed 'in language activities involving language processes to produce and/or receive texts in relation to themes in specific domains, activating those strategies which seem most appropriate for carrying out the

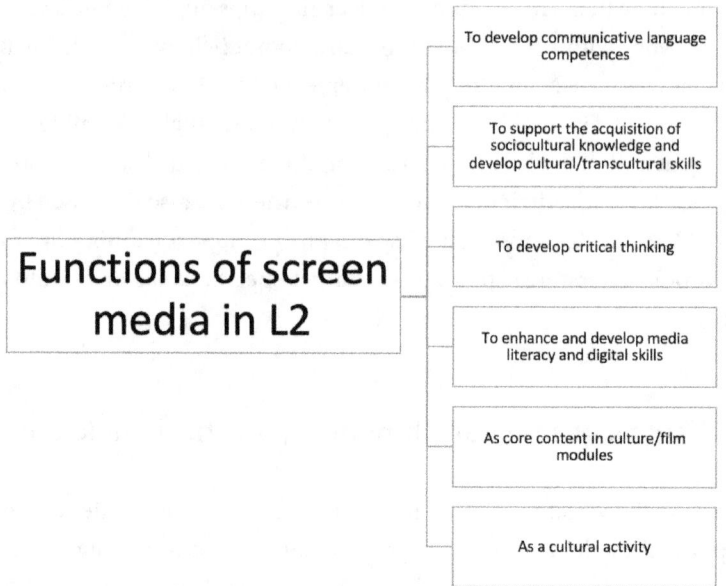

Figure 2.1 Functions of screen media in L2. Source: adapted and translated from Herrero 2019a: 572.

tasks to be accomplished' (Council of Europe 2001: 9). Logically, one of the ways of learning a language is the direct exposure to authentic use of language in L2 by consuming screen media products (see also Council of Europe 2018). Different studies advocate for the value of audiovisual content being a source of diverse linguistic variation. First, they offer examples of grammar in action (Canning-Wilson 2000), and different types of accents and language variations. Videos, digital games, social media apps, films and TV series and programmes can provide a rich exposure to vocabulary and, some argue, can facilitate incidental lexical acquisition. Webb and Rodgers's studies (2009a; 2009b) found that the knowledge of 3,000 word families (plus proper names and other marginal words) facilitated the understanding of 95 per cent of British or American films. Their analysis of vocabulary in television programmes found that between 2,000 and 4,000 words reach a 95-per-cent coverage. In addition, these authors noted that rare vocabulary was less present and that there was greater lexical variation between episodes. There are some practical recommendations that can be extrapolated from this research. For example, regular work with screen media helps to increase incidental vocabulary acquisition; and pre-viewing activities and a segment (or clip) approach can reduce the vocabulary demands of audiovisual input.

As a source of conversational language, videos involving extensive use of frequent words can improve vocabulary acquisition (Quaglio 2009; Jones and Horak 2014; Kabooha and Elyas 2018). To provide a valuable and effective learning experience, Frumuselu's (2019) study supports the use of television series and sitcoms with intralingual and interlingual subtitles for long- and short-term retention of colloquial expressions. Furthermore, it is generally accepted that the association of words with visual images can support the acquisitor of new vocabulary. Other recent studies have investigated the impact of intralingual and interlingual subtitles to enhance language acquisition (Vanderplank 2016) and how watching captioned videos with visual prompts boosts vocabulary learning (Cokely and Muñoz 2019). Similarly, studies led by Reinhardt (2018, 2019) provide evidence for learners' development of intercultural and linguistic skills through the use of digital games, social media platforms and mobile apps.

Many argue that screen media are ideal tools to enhance listening comprehension and pronunciation skills (Oddone 2011; Chang and Chang 2014; Metruk 2018). In the last two decades, the applications of audiovisual translation to L2 learning and teaching have produced a significant number of studies that support the use of subtitles for the development of lexical acquisition, as mentioned above, as well as aural comprehension (Talaván 2019, 2020; Incalcaterra McLoughlin, Lertola and Talaván 2020). A recent study using eye-tracking has investigated the benefits of captioned video to enhance the acquisition of pronunciation skills with Spanish learners of English as L2 (Mora and Cerviño-Povedano 2019). Similarly, dubbing improves pronunciation, intonation and fluency (Sánchez-Requena 2016, 2017). The use of audio description fosters oral fluency, autonomous learning and enhances learners' motivation (Herrero and Escobar 2020; Herrero et al. 2020; Navarrete 2020).

As authentic materials, films and television series contain a variety of languages in use and registers (formal, informal, regional and social variations). They are particularly useful for learning pragmatic language features and increasing language awareness of different varieties (Rose 2001; Martínez-Flor 2007; Boku 2008; Bruti 2015, 2020). Film, television series or even clips exposed students to non-verbal elements that provide context to better understand the meaning of the message, features also present in many digital games and visual storytelling. This becomes particularly important for foreign language teaching in specialized domains (law, politics, economics, tourism, medicine, etc.) 'where domain-specific discursive, pragmatic, and cultural features can create significant obstacles for language learners' (Bonsignori 2018: 58).

The second function identifies the exposure and meaningful use of screen media as a source of cultural knowledge that can assist students on their journey as cultural mediators. In their different formats and genres, from adverts to soap operas, video games and films, viewing screen media artefacts has been equally beneficial to the development of language learners' intercultural competence (Pegrum 2008; Yang and Fleming 2013; Benson 2015; Reinhardt 2019; Tomlinson 2019; Zhang 2019). Given the communicative needs of today's globalized world, the concept of transcultural competence can be seen as more appropriate to account for the multilingual and multicultural environments (Pennycook 2006; Kramsch 2014). Blell and Doff (2014: 83) propose the need to develop transcultural communication that aims at 'the successful understanding of people in dynamized inter- and trans-cultural processes, either in face-to-face or text-conducted (e.g. literature, film, music) encounters'. Screen media can support the integration of critical perspectives for social action in the L2 classroom by giving visibility to the representation of multiple identities (religion, class and race). A critical feminist paradigm, in conjunction with activities aimed at developing visual and multimodal literacies, can support the decoding of gender stereotypes or inequalities in audiovisual materials and teaching resources based on screen media (Contreras Llave 2022). Films and TV series that include multilingual perspectives, cross-border encounters and the effects of globalization are particularly useful for embedding a transcultural and transnational approach in the L2 classroom. Transnational and multilingual films and television series have a great didactic potential as they illustrate the complexity, diversity and plurality of the notions of culture, identity and belonging, triggering a reflection on cultural diversity and opening up fruitful discussions on the representation of multilingual life (Herrero 2022a; Vanderschelden 2022).

The third function focuses on using screen media to develop media literacy. The technological advances and tools facilitate the involvement of language learners as *prosumers*: consumers and producers of content (user-generated content), including the capacity for creating, remixing and sharing media. Applied to teaching and learning, it means supporting learners in the development of the knowledge and skills required to become visually literate and competent producers of media. It involves guiding students in the meaning-making processes that enable them to become more active readers of screen media artefacts as multimodal texts. As for language learning, it implies the ability to decode and critically interpret multimodal texts, understanding the contexts and intercultural/transcultural discourses and codes, as well as fostering the ability to be active producers of media content.

The fourth function relates to undergraduate or postgraduate modules dedicated to the study of film, television or screen media per se. The approach for these units can follow a national or transnational perspective or a comparative model – for example, Cinema and Literature or Cinema and History.

The last function focuses on cultural activities with screen media. It can include practical filmmaking and television production training sessions, film clubs or film festivals (see, for example, the programme of activities offered by Into Film in the UK). The Beyond Babel Multilingual Film Festival in Manchester is an example of school outreach as a community engagement cultural programme, i.e. round table with filmmakers, debates and Q&A sessions, and didactic resources (Herrero 2020).

Using screen media: designing activities

The following section provides a guide to designing activities and learning projects for L2 teaching, the criteria to be considered in the process of selecting screen media, and the different ways of sequencing activities. Using visual resources requires careful selection, planning and delivery, attending to the learning aims and contents of the academic curriculum – for example, the function of the text, the type of activities and tasks, and the pedagogical approach adopted. Together with considering media devices, products and software, the preparation of assessment and rubrics plays a key role in screen media projects. Thaler (2014: 22) suggests the following criteria: auditory features, visual features, relation between sound and image, relevance, and methodology. The model presented in this chapter adopts Herrero's (2019a) criteria, which include linguistic criteria, potential for interdisciplinary projects and the development of media and digital competences, among others (see template included in the Appendix). The first criterion requires the assessment of those factors that can facilitate or hinder linguistic comprehension. Among the factors to take into consideration are the length of the visual text, the number of characters, and the quality and complexity of the language (dialect, use of specialized vocabulary, speed, etc.). Overall, it is important to weigh up these elements attending to the relevance, pedagogical suitability and exploitability for the proficiency level of the learners. It is worth noting that the increasing use of videos with no dialogues provides a good alternative and can generate a broad range of tasks for all proficiency levels (A1–C2). Another criterion is the type of competences that are going to be developed: functional communicative competences; pragmatic and sociolinguistic competences; cultural, intercultural/transcultural competences; and/or digital and media competences, including visual and multimodal competences. As discussed in the previous section, a wider range of competences and skills should be fostered and assessed in the language curriculum. Therefore, one of the imperatives when selecting screen media is considering how they can be used to promote the so-called 'twenty-first-century skills' (critical thinking, problem solving, creativity, teamwork and digital literacy) and support self-regulated language learning and language awareness.

A critical issue when selecting an audiovisual text is the thematic content. For example, one should consider whether the themes are appropriate for the age and culture/s of the students and their potential interest in the narrative and the characters. In the case of films or television series, a careful weighing of the complexity of the narrative structure and its main components (causality, time and space) is essential. In the case of digital games, the digital literacy of the learners and the age classification of the game should be considered. If the story is presented in a complex manner (i.e. flashbacks or parallel actions), it can negatively affect learners' engagement and ability to grasp the story development; while a linear story with fewer subplots is easier to follow. Style, aesthetic qualities and cinematographic techniques are particularly important as they affect the cognitive and affective processes as well as how the audience/learners experience the viewing. Moreover, the selection should also bear in mind both traditional genres as well as the new genres and patterns of media consumption: animations, machinima, fandom, lip-dub, presentations (TED), remix and mashup, sketches, video-tutorials and 'how to…', screencast, webseries, vlogs, video games, interactive comics, etc. Similarly, the gameplay and genre of a digital game might also encourage or discourage participation and engagement, so canvassing the preferences of learners could be important.

Digital media and online platforms are changing the way media messages are constructed and shared through mobile screens (tablets and mobile phones). Therefore, the integration of digital video in L2 activities and projects requires us to consider practical questions: What kind of devices do learners have? What is the purpose of bringing them into the L2 classroom? Are they required to bring a device with internet capabilities? Who is covering the costs related to connection, access or subscription? It is also important to pay attention to what learners do with screens in their free time and what technologies they use, as well as the potential for distractions in the classroom when using their own devices.

When dealing with screen media, copyright restrictions must also be taken into consideration. The World Intellectual Property Organization accepts the free use of works for teaching purposes if it is compatible with 'fair practice, but quite often there are grey areas and not all screen media has the same type of copyright. In the UK, the Copyright Law (UK Copyright Service 2022) approves the use of stills in learning materials to a certain degree for research and educational purposes. However, these need to be used as examples within the text and clearly referenced within it; they cannot be used solely for decorative purposes; they must have an evident educational aim and be integrated within an argument or lead to one; the total used cannot be more than ten per cent of the original work; and the resource must be free to access. However, marketing materials are not included in this allowance and the use of promotional posters or DVD covers has different policies. The screening of screen media can also be complex depending on the material and the way in which it is shown. For example, many films and TV series can be screened in-class as long as they serve an educational purpose and there is a task attached to them, but not as entertainment or void of a learning objective. They can be shown in a classroom but not if the lesson is being recorded and made available later on. If the lesson is online, as was the case during most of 2020 and 2021 across many institutions due to COVID-19 regulations, the screening might fall under streaming laws for which there are more complex considerations and restrictions. Although the legislation is different in each country, it is commonly accepted that works with non-Creative Commons licence cannot be shared or employed for commercial use. Thus, if the resources are going to be published or used in handouts attached to paid courses, it might not be possible to include certain examples, stills or clips. In this regard, short films are usually more accessible, and it is more likely that the producers and filmmakers grant permission to use their media products for different purposes. This is particularly relevant if teachers intend to develop projects using screen material beyond their classes. Bearing this in mind, the next step is to consider how the media product will be used in the classroom. This could include the display of a video or its editing. For the latter, audiovisual translation techniques (subtitling, dubbing, audio description, etc.) are an excellent way of exploiting L2 material. Especially in the past two decades, there has been a growing wave of researchers interested in evidencing the benefits of students using audiovisual translation techniques actively in the language classroom. For example, *ClipFlair* (2011), an EU-funded platform, contains numerous activities within existing videos (organized by language, topic and level) to work with both voice and captions. Students can add their voice to the videos using techniques such as dubbing, audio description or narration. They can also add captions in the same language as the video or in a L2. There are a variety of aims including increasing students' speed, working on creative writing, improving listening comprehension, or learning and revising vocabulary (Sokoli and Zabalbeascoa Terran 2019).

Finding screen media material and resources to include in classes can be time-consuming. One solution is to identify reliable channels or playlists that are suitable in terms of content, such as the BBC's YouTube Channel, the TED talk series, and the Movieclips.com website (Magasic 2017). Another useful site for educators in the UK is Box of Broadcast, Learning on Screen's on-demand TV and radio service for education. This archive includes over 2.7 million broadcasts and most of the TV material comes with a transcript and metadata for search purposes. Many publishers of textbooks and language materials now have video channels on YouTube and the same can be said for many educators who regularly upload short videos and lessons to the site. *Europeana* is another platform that brings together cultural heritage collections including television archives and films from Europe. In the UK, the British Film Institute holds in the BFI National Archive one of the largest film and television collections in the world and it connects with partner archives across the UK.[1] Similar archives of moving images can be found in the USA.[2] Another recommendation is to find lists of videos, short films and films curated by language teachers. For example, Lumière (originally known as the Library of Foreign Language Film Clips and created by the Berkeley Language Center) is an online library that contains 20,603 clips drawn from 6,786 films in sixty-five languages (see Kaiser and Shibahara 2014). The Instituto Cervantes has a catalogue of Spanish-speaking voices (Catálogo de Voces Hispánicas), which functions as a database of short audiovisual examples of registers and accents across Latin American countries and Spanish regions.[3] Furthermore, the Film in Language Teaching Association's community site has an area dedicated to videos that comprise over two hundred collected videos recommended by language teachers (trailers, teasers, adverts, clips, short films, educational videos, etc.).

Most of the materials above are authentic materials created in the target language but used by educators of this language as L2. This is one of the two most common types of screen media products that can be included in the L2 classroom. First, those created for the industry but exploited by educators and students for learning purposes. This category comprises a broad range of screen media (films, short films, series, documentaries, trailers, adverts, interviews, video games, among others) that can be used as a whole or just as an extract. Secondly, there are screen media products created specifically for the language classroom, such as the videos created by publishers of textbooks, which are often included as part of a DVD or hosted on a Vimeo or YouTube channel. Another example is HolaCandela.com (Sánchez-Requena 2020), a website for learners of Spanish that includes a series of episodes created with a specific focus. The site provides activities in the same format as A-level exams in the UK, but they can also be used by any other learner. The series casts non-professional actors who employ adequate speed and vocabulary for the purpose of the project.

Using digital videos, film or television series per se does not necessarily contribute to language learning, and 'the learning outcomes depend largely on the way videos are used as part of the overall learning environment, e.g. how viewing or producing videos is integrated into other learning resources and tasks' (Karppinen 2005: 245). There are numerous types of activities based on videos, films and TV series, normally divided into three stages: pre-viewing, while-viewing and post-viewing activities (see Table 2.1). The pre-viewing activities are aimed at stimulating the interest of learners, helping learners formulate hypotheses about the topic or themes, and facilitating the comprehension of the video or film. Most of the activities are language-based exercises that introduce vocabulary and plot, the production team (director and cast) and the sociohistorical context. The while-viewing sequence is mainly aimed at exploiting the paralinguistic elements (gestures, body language, etc.), paying attention to cinematography (colour, composition, type of shots and angles, etc.), sound (dialogue, music, ambient sounds), and identifying key scenes. An example of an aural comprehension activity for this sequence is matching quotes from the film to the characters. The post-viewing tasks often involve a detailed analysis of the characters and themes, as well as the formal characteristics of the work. All these activities are ideal for introducing students 'to different types of popular culture and engaging them with critical questions about the relationship between information and power, through the critical analysis of socio-political issues and intercultural relationships' (Chan and Herrero 2010: 11). The production of oral and written responses to the films (discussion or debate, film reviews, etc.) can be combined with other extension

Table 2.1 Stages for activities based on screen media (based on Herrero 2019a)

	Textual and lexical competence	**Phonological and phonetic competence**	**Grammatical competence**
Pre-viewing	Undertake comprehension activities with different types of texts (synopsis, topic and cultural contextualization, filmmaker's biography, etc.) to become familiar with film and subject vocabulary.	Present and contextualize relevant elements for pronunciation and intonation.	Use grammatical structures to express probability or hypotheses about the text (topics, genres, etc.).
While viewing	Identify sentences within the dialogue and their importance in the context of the audiovisual text.	Recognize geographical characteristics present in the audiovisual text.	Provide context to use certain grammar structures (colloquial register, imperfect tense, conditional tense, etc.).
Post-viewing	Expand vocabulary by connective or descriptive activities applied to different semantic fields (physical and personality description of the characters, geographical spaces, topics and themes, etc.).	Dub the dialogue between two actors in a scene or create the audiodescription of a scene.	Practise grammatical structures that appear in the audiovisual text in a specific activity or as an integral part of one of the final creative tasks.
	Sociolinguistic and pragmatic competence	**Cultural and intercultural competence**	**Digital, multimodal and film competence**
Pre-viewing	Form hypotheses about types of linguistic registers (social class, ethnic or professional group).	Awake curiosity and introduce the audiovisual text and the models (temporal, geographical, cultural, etc.).	Analyse the poster and/or the trailer or teaser to become familiar with the key concepts of the multimodal composition.
While viewing	Recognize linguistic indicators for social relationships, courtesy rules and popular expressions (sayings, idioms, etc.)	Identify associated values with the target culture; compare socio-cultural models.	Analyse stylistic resources in key sequences or stills to infer how meaning is generated.

(continued)

Post-viewing	Increase the comprehension and production of pragmatic meaning from a critical analysis of the varied semiotic resources present in the audiovisual text.	Analyse cultural and intertextual models. Critically reflect on the values linked to the target culture and the learners' culture(s).	Design and create a visual product (poster, trailer, visual concept map, infographic, etc.). Write a film review video, blog, journal, etc.) individually or collaboratively.

activities, such as research projects on the themes, director, stars, etc., to develop cultural and transcultural competences, as well as digital skills. Examples of these types of sequences are available in the study guides organized by language level, topic and learning aims created by the Film in Language Teaching Association (FILTA) for Arabic, English, French, German, Italian, Mandarin, Spanish and Urdu.

Project-based learning based on screen media involves the extensive use of learners' linguistic resources in the target language as well as working collaboratively on tasks aimed at developing a wide range of competences: mediation, critical skills, teamwork, plurilingual and pluricultural competences. The focus of a task is not only on improving language skills, but creating a product (e.g. a blog, a video essay or a subtitling project). The outcome of this 'real' product must be evaluated using a descriptor and, therefore, it is essential to collect evidence of students' progress. Due to the multimodal nature of these projects, there are usually several components or learning skills that can be enhanced and rubrics are particularly useful for making students aware of their own progress (see Herrero, Sánchez-Requena and Escobar 2017 for a model of rubrics for an audiovisual translation project). Another excellent example of project work was carried out by Alonso-Pérez (2019) at Sheffield Hallam University with a group of second-year learners with B1–B2 Spanish. The subtitling project with short films culminated in a Spanish film festival, where students presented their work and competed for the best subtitled short film category.

The advent of digital communications has facilitated the convergence of traditional and new media allowing learners to be active producers of media content, also referred to as user-generated content. There are numerous resources aimed at language teaching for supporting students' filmmaking. For example, the *Connecta* Project (2021), run by the University of Roehampton and funded by Creative Multilingualism, has created a series of guides in English, French, German and Spanish that include information on how to script, shoot, edit and subtitle a film. *LessonStream* is a community of teachers and educators, founded by Jamie Keddie, that uses storytelling to teach English. User-generated content projects enhance learners' creativity. For instance, the Multilingual Digital Storytelling project, developed by researchers at Goldsmiths, University of London, brings together mainstream and complementary schools in the UK and in six other countries to create and share their creations. Another valuable example of user-generated content can be found in the 'Culturema' (2012), a project created by Celia Carracedo. It includes short films and other resources created by students learning Spanish language and culture at the Chinese University of Hong Kong (Carracedo 2017). The project, 'Open Educational Resources for Students by Students', carried out at Manchester Metropolitan University, demonstrates the educational possibilities of transmedia practices and open educational resources (Herrero 2022b). Outside of formal education, it is worth noting the short films projects developed by Jorge García Martín with his students in the Language School Séneca in Riga, Latvia.[4]

Educators of English as an L2 might find the site *Film English* particularly useful for the range of activities and resources available. For some practical projects and suggestions for activities using social media, see Antenos-Conforti (2009), Suarez (2014), Barroso (2020) or Lee (2022). Work on the use of games and quizzes in the classroom has also provided a wide range of suggestions for implementing them, such as Suarez (2011, 2013, 2014), Chen and Yang (2013), Janebi Enayat and Haghighatpasand (2019) or Calvo-Ferrer and Belda-Medina (2021).

Conclusions

This chapter has highlighted how certain pedagogical approaches have shown the need to bring educational practices in L2 teaching closer to twenty-first-century learners. This is of particular importance at a time when screens are an essential dimension of learners' interests and modes of communication. Despite the challenges of integrating screen media products into curricular objectives and classroom activities, the variety of multimodal texts and genres available through numerous platforms (YouTube, Vimeo, Netflix, etc.) makes it easier to meet pre-existing pedagogical objectives. Furthermore, learning with and through screens helps L2 learners to develop analytical reasoning and cross-cultural sensitivity in media contexts with which they are familiar. We have argued that it is necessary to provide as many audiovisual resources as possible to interpret and manage autonomous and collaborative learning through the realization of video projects. This type of project-based learning not only enables the use of tools, apps and software in real contexts, but also facilitates the development of other competences (problem solving, willingness to learn, collaboration, creativity, innovation, groupwork skills, etc.).

This chapter has presented research and evidence-based practices that demonstrate the benefits of using screen media and how it can be integrated into foreign language classes. First, traditional and new formats and genres enhance the connection between L2 teaching and popular culture. As 'authentic' texts mediated by technology, screen media has the potential to effectively engage learners and stimulate a positive emotional experience that is meaningful and enjoyable, and reduce or regulate other emotional aspects, such as anxiety and insecurity. In addition to increasing motivation, multimodal artefacts have the capacity to support learners in their appreciation, use and production of multimodal texts, and the development of a wide range of competences. The chapter has included criteria to consider a more systematic exploiting of screen media, including practical models of user-generated content creation, to enhance learners' autonomy and foster their motivation.

The growing number of research-led publications in this field are bringing together evidence of the successful application of techniques, models and practices for using screen media to enhance language learning. However, to continue to take advantage of the opportunities created by today's highly visual and digital research landscape and the variety of tools available, it is imperative that teachers train and collaborate with other teachers in professional language-learning environments. More than ever, teachers need to improve their knowledge, professional skills and teaching practices, and keep up to date as technology evolves and visual cultures continue to shape local and global interactions.

Appendix

Table 2.2 Template to assess audiovisual materials for L2 teaching and learning

LEARNERS	
Educational level Linguistic level Film, visual literacy level, etc.	
GENERAL INFORMATION	
Title of the audiovisual material	
Director(s)	
Cast	
Other information (producer, composer, etc.)	
Synopsis	
Age rating and specific classification considerations	
Duration	
Intellectual property	Copyright Creative Commons Copyleft
SUPPORT	
Format	DVD Digital
Subtitles	L1 L2
Audiodescription	L1 L2
Extras	Posters or images Making-of Trailer / Teaser Other
Quality	Sound Image

(continued)

LINGUISTIC CRITERIA	
Linguistic content	Language varieties
	Grammatical content
	Lexical content
	Functional content
Communicative content	
Cultural content	
Intercultural/transcultural content	

INTERDISCIPLINARY CRITERIA	
Themes and applications to interdisciplinary projects	

PRACTICAL APPLICATION CRITERIA FOR MEDIATIC AND AUDIOVISUAL COMPETENCE	
Ability to effectively use multimodal resources	Spatial design (architectonic, geographical meanings)
	Gestural design (gestures, body language, kinesics, etc.)
	Visual design (images and colours)
	Linguistic design (verbal and written script)
	Audio design (music, sound effects, etc.)
	Synaesthesia and semiotic orchestration
Ability to effectively develop learners' film /visual / media competence (comprehension and critical analysis, and ability to develop audiovisual creation activities)	Director (author)
	Format (feature film, medium-length film, short film)
	Topic(s)
	Genre(s)
	Historical context
	Narrative and point of view
	Characters
	Style and aesthetics
	(filming, camera angles, light and colours, soundtrack, space, costumes, make-up, performance)

CRITERIA FOR THE DEVELOPMENT OF DIGITAL COMPETENCIES	
Ability to develop digital competence	

Notes

1 The BFI National Archive comprises regional and national archives (see https://www2.bfi.org.uk/britain-on-film/regional-national-archives).
2 See, for example, the guide provided by the Columbia University Libraries: https://guides.library.columbia.edu/c.php?g=568074&p=3914591.
3 http://cvc.cervantes.es/lengua/voces_hispanicas/.
4 A webinar presenting these projects is available here: https://tinyurl.com/2m94d2st.

References

Alm, A. (2015), '"Facebook" for Informal Language Learning: Perspectives from Tertiary Language Students', *The EuroCALL Review*, 23 (2): 3–18.

Alonso-Pérez, R. (2019), 'Enhancing Student Motivation in Foreign Language Learning through Film Subtitling Projects', in C. Herrero and I. Vanderschelden (eds), *Using Film and Media in the Language Classroom: Reflections on Research-led Teaching*, 108–26, Bristol: Multilingual Matters.

Anderson, J., and V. Macleroy (2016), *Multilingual Digital Storytelling*, London: Routledge.

Antenos-Conforti, E. (2009), 'Microblogging on Twitter: Social Networking in Intermediate Italian Classes', in L. Lomicka and G. Lords (eds), *The Next Generation: Social Networking and Online Collaboration in Foreign Language Learning*, 59–90, San Marcos: Calico.

Bahloul, M., and C. Graham, eds (2012), *Lights! Camera! Action and the Brain: The Use of Film in Education*, Newcastle upon Tyne: Cambridge Scholars Publishing.

Barroso, L. G. (2020), 'Aprendiendo español al ritmo de Tik-Tok en el entorno virtual', *Actas del X Encuentro Práctico de Profesores de Español en Nueva Delhi*, 2020, Nueva Delhi: Instituto Cervantes. Available online: https://cvc.cervantes.es/ensenanza/biblioteca_ele/publicaciones_centros/PDF/delhi_2020/09_garcia-barroso.pdf.

Barrot, J. S. (2021), 'Social Media as a Language Learning Environment: A Systematic Review of the Literature (2008–2019)', *Computer Assisted Language Learning*, 1–29.

Benson, P. (2015), 'Commenting to Learn: Evidence of Language and Intercultural Learning in Comments on YouTube Videos', *Language Learning and Technology*, 19 (3): 88–105.

Blell, G., and S. Doff (2014), 'It Takes More than Two for This Tango: Moving beyond the Self/Other-Binary in Teaching about Culture in the Global EFL-Classroom', *Zeitschrift für Interkulturellen Fremdsprachenunterricht*, 19 (1): 78–96.

Boku, M. (2008), 'A Study of EFL Learners' Pragmatic Competence Using a Movie Scene', *The Association for Teaching English through Movies*, 13: 30–45.

Bonsignori, V. (2018), 'Using Films and TV Series for ESP Teaching: A Multimodal Perspective', in B. Crawford Camiciottoli and M. C. Campoy Cubillo (eds), *Multimodal Perspectives on English Language Teaching in Higher Education*, 77: 58–69.

Brevik, L. M. (2019), 'Gamers, Surfers, Social Media Users: Unpacking the Role of Interest in English', *Journal of Computer Assisted Learning*, 35 (5): 595–606.

Brook, J. (2011), 'The Affordances of YouTube for Language Learning and Teaching', *Hawaii Pacific University TESOL Working Paper Series* 9 (1,2): 37–56.

Bruti, S. (2015), 'Teaching Learners How to Use Pragmatic Routines Through Audiovisual Material', in B. Crawford-Camiciottoli and I. Fortanet-Gómez (eds), *Multimodal Analysis in Academic Settings: From Research to Teaching*, 213–36, London: Routledge.

Bruti, S. (2020), 'Teen Talk in TV Series as a Model of Linguistic Innovation and Emotional Language' in V. Werner and T. Tegge (eds), *Pop Culture in Language Education*, 33–49, London: Routledge.

Burke, S., S. Snyder and R. C. Rager (2009), 'An Assessment of Faculty Usage of YouTube as a Teaching Resource', *The Internet Journal of Allied Health Sciences and Practice*, 7 (1): 1–8.

Butsch, R. (2019), *Screen Culture: A Global History*, Cambridge: Polity Press.

Calvo-Ferrer, J. R., and J. Belda-Medina (2021), 'The Effect of Multiplayer Video Games on Incidental and Intentional L2 Vocabulary Learning: The Case of Among Us', *Multimodal Technologies and Interaction*, 5 (80): 1–16.

Canning-Wilson, C. (2000), 'Practical Aspects of Using Video in the Foreign Language Classroom', *The Internet TESL Journal*, 6 (11). Available online: http://iteslj.org/Articles/Canning-Video.2001 html.

Carracedo, C. (2017), 'Aprendizaje integrado de lengua y contenidos: Organización e intervención didáctica de un curso sobre cine en español en entornos universitarios de Hong Kong', PhD thesis, University Pablo de Olavide, Spain.

Chan, D., and C. Herrero (2010), *Using Film to Teach Languages*, Manchester: Cornerhouse. Available online: https://goo.gl/MhScf7.

Chang, C., and C. K. Chang (2014), 'Developing Students' Listening Metacognitive Strategies Using Online Videotext Self-Dictation-Generation Learning Activity', *The EUROCALL Review*, 22 (1): 3–19.

Chen, H. J. H., and T. Y. C. Yang (2013), 'The Impact of Adventure Video Games on Foreign Language Learning and the Perceptions of Learners', *Interactive Learning Environments*, 21 (2): 129–41.

Chik, A. (2014), 'Digital Gaming and Language Learning: Autonomy and Community', *Language Learning & Technology*, 18 (2): 85–100.

ClipFlair (2011), '*Foreign Language Learning through Interactive Revoicing and Captioning of Clips*'. Available online: http://clipflair.net.

Cokely, M., and C. Muñoz (2019), 'Captioned Video, Vocabulary and Visual Prompts: An Exploratory Study', in C. Herrero and I. Vanderschelden (eds), *Using Film and Media in the Language Classroom: Reflections on Research-led Teaching*, 61–75, Bristol: Multilingual Matters.

Connecta Project (2021), *Teaching Guides: Making Short Films*. Available online: https://www.creativeml.ox.ac.uk/teaching-guides-making-short-films/.

Contreras Llave, N. (2022), 'Cine y perspectiva de género como herramienta de transformación social en la didáctica de español como lengua extranjera', PhD thesis, Universidad de Alicante, Alicante, Spain.

Council of Europe (2001), *Common European Framework of Reference for Languages: Learning, Teaching, Assessment*, Cambridge: Cambridge University Press.

Council of Europe (2018), *Common European Framework of Reference for Languages: Learning, Teaching, Assessment. Companion Volume with New Descriptors*. Available online: http://rm.coe.int/cefr-companion-volume-with-new-descriptors-2018/1680787989.

Culturema (2012), *Culturema: sitio sobre cine y cultura*. Available online: http://www.culturema.com.

Europeana (nd), *Discover Inspiring European Cultural Heritage: Europeana*. Available online: https://www.europeana.eu/en.

Film English (nd), *Film English*. Available online: https://film-english.com/.

Film in Language Teaching Association (FILTA) (2010), 'The Film in Language Teaching Association'. Available online: http://www.filta.org.uk.

Finardi, K. R., R. G. Leao and G. B. Amorim (2016), 'Mobile Assisted Language Learning: Affordances and Limitations of Duolingo', *Education and Linguistics Research*, 2 (2): 48–65.

Frumuselu, A. D. C. (2019), '"A Friend in Need is a Film Indeed": Teaching Colloquial Expressions with Subtitled Television Series', in C. Herrero and I. Vanderschelden (eds), *Using Film and Media in the Language Classroom: Reflections on Research-led Teaching*, 92–107, Bristol: Multilingual Matters.

Goldstein, B., and P. Driver (2015), *Language Learning with Digital Video*, Cambridge: Cambridge University Press.

Heil, C. R., J. S. Wu, J. J. Lee and T. Schmidt (2016), 'A Review of Mobile Language Learning Applications: Trends, Challenges, and Opportunities', *The EuroCALL Review*, 24 (2): 32–50.

Herrero, C. (2019a), 'Medios audiovisuales', in J. Muñoz-Basols, E. Gironzetti and M. Lacorte (eds), *The Routledge Handbook of Spanish Language Teaching: Metodologías, contextos y recursos para la enseñanza del español L2*, 565–82, London and New York: Routledge.

Herrero, C. (2019b), 'Conclusion: Present and Future Directions for Video, Film and Audiovisual Media in Language Teaching', in C. Herrero and I. Vanderschelden (eds), *Using Film and Media in the Language Classroom: Reflections on Research-led Teaching*, 188–97, Bristol: Multilingual Matters.

Herrero, C. (2020), 'The Beyond Babel Multilingual Film Festival', *Journal of Film and Video*, 72 (1–2): 33–45.

Herrero, C. (2022a), 'Visual Explorations of a New Life: Language, Identity and Landscape in *El futuro perfecto* and *Ingen Ko På Isen*', in S. Brownlie and R. Abouddahab (eds), *Figures of the Migrant: The Roles of Literature and the Arts in Representing Migration*, 93–109, London and New York: Routledge.

Herrero, C. (2022b), 'La educación transmedia como estrategia innovadora para integrar lengua y cultura en la enseñanza de ELE', *Doblele. Revista de lengua y literatura*, 7: 50–66.

Herrero, C., and M. Escobar (2020), 'A Pedagogical Model for Integrating Film Education and Audio Description in Foreign Language Acquisition', in L. Incalcaterra McLoughlin, J. Lertola and N. Talaván (eds), *Audiovisual Translation in Applied Linguistics: Educational Perspectives*, 31–55, Amsterdam: John Benjamins.

Herrero, C., A. Sánchez-Requena and M. Escobar (2017), 'Una propuesta triple: Análisis fílmico, traducción audiovisual y enseñanza de lenguas extranjeras', *Building Bridges between Film Studies and Translation Studies, inTRAlinea*. Available online: http://www.intralinea.org/specials/article/una_propuesta_triple_analisis_filmico_traduccion_audiovisual_y_ensenanza.

Herrero, C., K. Valverde, T. Costal and A. Sánchez-Requena (2020), 'The Film and Creative Engagement Project: Audiovisual Accessibility and Telecollaboration', *Research in Education and Learning Innovation Archives*, 24: 89–104.

Herrero, C., and I. Vanderschelden, eds (2019), *Using Film and Media in the Language Classroom: Reflections on Research-led Teaching*, Bristol: Multilingual Matters.

Incalcaterra McLoughlin, L., J. Lertola and N. Talaván, eds (2020), *Audiovisual Translation in Applied Linguistics: Educational Perspectives*, 111, Amsterdam: John Benjamins.

Into Film (nd), *Into Film. Film in Education. Film Clubs*. Available online: https://www.intofilm.org.

Janebi Enayat, M., and M. Haghighatpasand (2019), 'Exploiting Adventure Video Games for Second Language Vocabulary Recall: A Mixed-Methods Study', *Innovation in Language Learning and Teaching*, 13 (1): 61–75.

Jenkins, H. (2006), *Convergence Culture. Where Old and New Media Collide*, New York and London: New York University Press.

Jones, C., and T. Horak (2014), 'Leave it Out! The Use of Soap Operas as Models of Spoken Discourse in the ELT Classroom', *The Journal of Language Learning and Teaching*, 4 (1): 1–14.

Kabooha, R., and T. Elyas (2018), 'The Effects of YouTube in Multimedia Instruction for Vocabulary Learning: Perceptions of EFL Students and Teachers', *English Language Teaching*, 11 (2): 72–81.

Kaiser, M., and C. Shibahara (2014), 'Film as Source Material in Advanced Foreign Language Classes', *L2 Journal*, 6: 1–13.

Karppinen, P. (2005), 'Meaningful Learning with Digital and Online Videos: Theoretical Perspectives', *AACE Review*, 13 (3): 233–50.

Kawaguchi, S., and J. Watkins (2015), 'Mobile Games for L2 learning: Student and Teacher Perspectives', *International Journal of Technologies in Learning*, 21 (2): 11–23.

Keddie, J. (2014), *Bringing Online Video into the Classroom*, Oxford: Oxford University Press.

Ko, M. H. (2019), 'Students' Reactions to Using Smartphones and Social Media for Vocabulary Feedback', *Computer Assisted Language Learning*, 32 (8): 920–44.

Kramsch, C. (2014), 'Language and Culture in Second Language Learning', in F. Sharifian (ed.), *The Routledge Handbook of Language and Culture*, 305–17, London: Routledge.

Lantz-Andersson, A. (2018), 'Language Play in a Second Language: Social Media as Contexts for Emerging Sociopragmatic Competence', *Education and Information Technologies*, 23 (2): 705–24.

Learning on Screen (n.d.), *Learning on Screen – Opening Up Access to Movie Image and Sound*. Available online: http://www.learningonscreen.com.

Lee, Y. J. (2022), 'Language Learning Affordances of Instagram and TikTok', *Innovation in Language Learning and Teaching*, IGI Global 1–16.

Lessonstream (nd), *Lessonstream.org*. Available online: http://lessonstream.org.

Li, J. (2022), 'A Systematic Review of Video Games for Second Language Acquisition', *Research Anthology on Developments in Gamification and Game-Based Learning*, 1345–71.

Loewen, S., D. Crowther, D. R. Isbell, K. M. Kim, J. Maloney, Z. F. Miller and H. Rawal (2019), 'Mobile-Assisted Language Learning: A Duolingo Case Study', *ReCALL*, 31 (3): 293–311.

Lonergan, J. (1984), *Video in Language Teaching*, Cambridge: Cambridge University Press.

Magasic, M. (2017), 'Learning Through Watching: Streaming Video in L2 English', *JALT CALL Journal*, 13 (3): 199–209.

Martínez-Flor, A. (2007), 'Analysing Request Modification Devices in Films: Implications for Pragmatic Learning in Instructed Foreign Language Contexts', in E. Soler and M. Safont Jordá (eds), *Intercultural Language Use and Language Learning*, 245–76, Dordrecht: Springer.

Mayora, C. A. (2009), 'Using *YouTube* to Encourage Authentic Writing in EFL Classrooms', *TESL Reporter*, 42 (1): 1–12.

Metruk, R. (2018), 'Extensive Listening Practice of EFL Learners with Authentic English Videos', *Teaching English with Technology*, 16 (4): 3–19.

Mora, J. C., and E. Cerviño-Povedano (2019), 'The Effects of Bimodal L2 Input on the Processing of Function Words by Spanish EFL learners: An Eye-tracking Study', in C. Herrero and I. Vanderschelden (eds), *Using Film and Media in the Language Classroom: Reflections on Research-led Teaching*, 76–91, Bristol: Multilingual Matters.

Multilingual Digital Storytelling (n.d.), *MDST Main Site. A Multilingual Digital Storytelling Project*. Available online: https://goldsmithsmdst.com/.

Nami, F. (2020), 'Educational Smartphone Apps for Language Learning in Higher Education: Students' Choices and Perceptions', *Australasian Journal of Educational Technology*, 36 (4): 82–95.

Navarrete, M. (2020), 'The Use of Audio Description in Foreign Language Education', in L. Incalterra McLoughlin, J. Lertola and N. Talaván (eds), *Audiovisual Translation in Applied Linguistics: Educational Perspectives*, 131–52, Amsterdam: John Benjamins.

Oddone, C. (2011), 'Using Videos from YouTube and Websites in the CLIL Classroom', *Studies About Languages*, 18: 105–10.

Pegrum, M. (2008), 'Film Culture and Identity: Critical Intercultural Literacies for the Language Classroom', *Language and International Communication*, 8 (2): 136–54.

Pennycook, A. (2006), *Global Englishes and Transcultural Flows*, London and New York: Routledge.

Puebla, C., T. Fievet, M. Tsopanidi and H. Clahsen (2022), 'Mobile-Assisted Language Learning in Older Adults: Chances and Challenges', *ReCALL*, 34 (2): 169–84.

Quaglio, P. (2009), *Television Dialogue: The Sitcom "Friends" vs Natural Conversation*, Amsterdam: John Benjamins.

Reinders, H., ed. (2012), *Digital Games in Language Learning and Teaching*, Basingstoke: Palgrave Macmillan.

Reinhardt, J. (2018), 'Social Media in the L2 classroom: Everyday Agency, Awareness, and Autonomy', in H. Castañeda-Peña, *Technology in ELT: Achievements and Challenges for ELT Development*, Bogotá: Universidad Distrital, 17–34.

Reinhardt, J. (2019), 'Social Media in Second and Foreign Language Teaching and Learning: Blogs, Wikis, and Social Networking', *Language Teaching*, 52 (1): 1–39.

Reinhardt, J., and J. Sykes (2014), 'Special Issue Commentary: Digital Game and Play Activity in L2 Teaching and Learning', *Language Learning & Technology*, 18 (2): 2–8.

Rose, K. R. (2001), 'Compliments and Compliment Responses in Film: Implications for Pragmatics Research and Language Teaching', *International Review of Applied Linguistics*, 39: 309–26.

Sánchez-Requena, A. (2016), 'Audiovisual Translation in Teaching Foreign Languages: Contributions of Revoicing to Improve Fluency and Pronunciation in Spontaneous Conversations', *Portalinguarum*, 26: 9–21.

Sánchez-Requena, A. (2017), 'Audiovisual Translation in Foreign Language Education: The Use of Intralingual Dubbing to Improve Speed, Intonation and Pronunciation in Spontaneous Speech', PhD thesis, Manchester Metropolitan University, UK.

Sánchez-Requena, A. (2020), '¡Vaya tela, Candela!', *TECLA. Revista de la Consejería de Educación en Reino Unido e Irlanda*, 10–14.

Scolari, C. (2012), 'Media Ecology: Exploring the Metaphor to Expand the Theory', *Communication Theory*, 22 (2): 204–25.

Seeger, I. (2019), 'Addressing "Super-Diversity" in the Language Classroom through Multilingual Films and Peer-generated YouTube Content', in C. Herrero and I. Vanderschelden (eds) *Using Film and Media in the Language Classroom: Reflections on Research-led Teaching*, 30–47, Bristol: Multilingual Matters.

Sherman, J. (2003), *Using Authentic Video in the Language Classroom*. Cambridge: Cambridge University Press.

Sokoli, S., and P. Zabalbeascoa Terran (2019), 'Audiovisual Activities and Multimodal Resources for Foreign Language Learning', in C. Herrero and I. Vanderschelden (eds), *Using Film and Media in the Language Classroom: Reflections on Research-led Teaching*, 170–87, Bristol: Multilingual Matters.

Stemplensky, S., and B. Tomalin (2001), *Film*. Oxford: Oxford University Press.

Suarez, M. F. (2011), 'El uso de la animación 3D como herramienta de aprendizaje de una segunda lengua', *Actas de las IV Jornadas Didácticas del Instituto Cervantes de Mánchester*, Instituto Cervantes Manchester. Available online: https://cvc.cervantes.es/ensenanza/biblioteca_ele/publicaciones_centros/PDF/manchester_2011/09_fernandez.pdf.

Suarez, M. F. (2013), 'Usando concursos televisivos como escenario de aprendizaje de una L2', *Actas de las V Jornadas Didácticas del Instituto Cervantes de Mánchester*, Instituto Cervantes Manchester. Available online: http://cvc.cervantes.es/ensenanza/biblioteca_ele/publicaciones_centros/PDF/manchester_2012/06_suarez.pdf.

Suarez, M. F. (2014), 'Actividades en entornos digitales: exposición a muestras reales de lengua', *Actas de las VI Jornadas Didácticas del Instituto Cervantes de Mánchester*, Instituto Cervantes Manchester. Available online: http://cvc.cervantes.es/ensenanza/biblioteca_ele/publicaciones_centros/PDF/manchester_2013-2014/03_suarez.pdf.

Talaván, N. (2019), 'Creative Audiovisual Translation Applied to Foreign Language Education: A Preliminary Approach', *Journal of Audiovisual Translation*, 2 (1): 53–74.

Talaván, N. (2020), 'The Didactic Value of AVT in Foreign Language Education', in L. Bogucki, and M. Deckert (eds), *The Palgrave Handbook of Audiovisual Translation and Media Accessibility*, 567–92, London: Palgrave Macmillan.

Thaler, E. (2014), *Teaching English with Film*. Paderborn: Schöningh.

Tomlinson, B. (2019), 'Developing Intercultural Awareness through Reflected Experience of Films and Other Visual Media', in C. Herrero and I. Vanderschelden (eds), *Using Film and Media in the Language Classroom: Reflections on Research-led Teaching*, 19–29, Bristol: Multilingual Matters.

UK Copyright Service (UKCS) (2019), *UK Copyright Law*. Available online: https://copyrightservice.co.uk/_f/8016/0700/6846/edupack.pdf.

Vanderplank, R. (2016), *Captioned Media in Foreign Language Learning and Teaching*, London: Palgrave MacMillan.

Vanderschelden, I. (2022), 'Screening Young Migrants and Cosmopolitan Mobility: Julie Bertuccelli's *La Cour de Babel*', in S. Brownlie and R. Abouddabah (eds), *Figures of the Migrant: The Roles of Literature and the Arts in Representing Migration*, 185–202, London and New York: Routledge.

Voller, P., and S. Widdows (1993), 'Feature Films as Text: A Framework for Classroom Use', *ELT Journal*, 47 (4): 342–53.

Wang, H., and C. W. Chen (2020), 'Learning English from YouTubers: English L2 Learners' Self-Regulated Language Learning on YouTube', *Innovation in Language Learning and Teaching*, 14 (4): 333–46.

Watkins, J., and M. Wilkins (2011), 'Using YouTube in the EFL Classroom', *Language Education in Asia*, 2 (1): 113–19.

Webb, S., and M. P. H. Rodgers (2009a), 'The Lexical Coverage of Movies', *Applied Linguistics*, 30 (3): 407–27.

Webb, S., and M. P. H. Rodgers (2009b), 'Vocabulary Demands of Television Programs', *Language Learning*, 59 (2): 335–66.

Wong, L. H., C. Sing-Chai and G. Poh-Aw (2017), 'Seamless Language Learning: Second Language Learning with Social Media', *Comunicar. Media Education Research Journal*, 25 (1): 9–20.

World Intellectual Property Organization (WIPO) (2022), *WIPO – World Intellectual Property Organization*. Available online: https://www.wipo.int.

Yang, L. H., and M. Fleming (2013), 'How Chinese College Students Make Sense of Foreign Films and TV Series: Implications for the Development of Intercultural Communicative Competence in ELT', *The Language Learning Journal*, 41 (3): 297–310.

Yudintseva, A. (2015), 'Synthesis of Research on Video Games for the Four Second Language Skills and Vocabulary Practice', *Open Journal of Social Sciences*, 3 (11): 81–98.

Zhang, L. (2019), 'The Affordances of TV Drama in Building L2 Chinese Learners' Intercultural Competence', PhD thesis, The University of Melbourne, Australia.

3

Integrating Screen Media into the Language Curriculum

Carmen Herrero

Introduction

One cannot dispute the value of visual communication for learners who are accustomed to creating and sharing images and videos with laptops and smartphones and who regularly use video as part of their self-directed learning. Thus, educators should not ignore the communication preferences of students who perceive the effectiveness of technology and visual artefacts to support their learning. As the flow of screen media increases for information, entertainment and educational purposes, the demand for a meaningful inclusion of these resources and the need for adjusting current pedagogical approaches to the media ecology are greater than ever.

The use of audiovisual media in MFL (L2) teaching to enhance teaching and students' learning is not new, yet the notion of how it may be implemented in lesson plans without putting too much strain on teachers and on curriculum constraints is not always well understood. This chapter examines findings from the *Teacher Training Project: Film, Languages and Pedagogy* and the *New Approaches to Transmedia and Language Pedagogy Project* (2014–21). These projects were led by the research group Film, Languages and Media in Education (FLAME) at Manchester Metropolitan University, with funding from the AHRC Open World Research Initiative (OWRI) 'Cross Language Dynamics: Reshaping Community'. Central to the AHRC's OWRI was the focus on language and community building by supporting language teaching at all levels and working closely with schools.[1] Therefore, vital to the impact of Modern Languages research was developing new approaches to the teaching of languages that could enhance the value of language learning. Given these priorities, the projects' main aim was to investigate the ways in which films could be integrated into the L2 curriculum to engage learners actively and creatively. For the purposes of these projects, 'film' was used as a broader concept to encompass films and other formats of screen media.[2] Although, as Herrero (2019b: 193) notes, 'the term "video" now encompasses a number of shifts that have taken place in contemporary media culture, moving away from rigid conceptions of television, film, digital media and video games'. The key objectives were to identify suitable pedagogical approaches; to evaluate current practices in teacher training and curriculum requirements related to the use of film; to assess and respond to teacher training needs regarding the use of visual and media culture in language teaching in UK secondary schools and higher education; and to design cutting-edge resources and teacher-training workshops that account for multimodal communication. This chapter presents the stages of the projects, as well as the pedagogical approaches and perspectives that underpin them. It also reports the key findings and outcomes and the steps taken to maintain their sustainability.

Key concepts and pedagogical approaches

With visual content at the forefront of digital content, it is particularly relevant to explore pedagogical approaches that account for the changes in literacy skills and the strong presence of the visual mode in education. These theories underpin the framework on how to introduce films and screen media effectively in the language curriculum to support a wide range of literacies, motivate students and enhance active learning. Language curriculum, digital literacies and film-based language pedagogy are the three fundamental concepts underlying the *Teacher Training Project*. This section presents a review of the literature that was gathered as a starting point for conceptualizing the theoretical framework for this study.

CEDEFOP (2011: 43) describes curriculum as the 'inventory of activities implemented to design, organize and plan an education or training action, including the definition of learning objectives, content, methods (including assessment) and material, as well as the arrangements for training teachers and trainers'. In the field of language education, Richards (2001: 2) sees language curriculum development as 'an interrelated set of processes that focuses on designing, revising, implementing and evaluating language programs'. Moreover, Narcy-Combes et al. (2019: 57) have stressed the importance of taking into consideration the inclusive nature of context during curriculum design: 'It goes beyond the learning environment [...] and includes the global sociolinguistics, cultural, social, even economic and political environment, while including didactic and pedagogical parameters that reflect the global environment'.

Since the 1970s, but more significantly so since the 1990s, different notions of 'literacy' have been proposed to respond to the demands of new communicative praxis (see Bateman 2021). Recognizing how the changes brought about by the development of globalization and technologies were affecting educational environments, the New London Group (1996) proposed a new framework of 'multiple literacies' and, subsequently, a new pedagogical approach.[3] In their proposal, they paid particular attention to changes in texts and communicative practices and how they were used in specific cultural and social situations. They put forward four multimodal components (Cope and Kalantzis 2000: 7): 'situated practice', 'overt instruction', 'critical framing' and 'transformed practice'. These were subsequently translated in the Learning by Design project into 'Experiencing', 'Conceptualizing', 'Analysing' (functionally, critically and creatively) and 'Applying' (Kalantzis et al. 2016: 82–3). 'Situated practice/ experiencing' focuses on the connections between meaning-making processes in real-world situations and the educational spaces with everyday experiences. 'Overt instruction/conceptualizing' involves learners developing an explicit metalanguage to describe 'design elements'. 'Critical framing/analysing' entails the capacity to critically analyse text functions and to interpret the power relationships involved in the communicative actions. 'Transformed practice/ applying' implies that learners become makers of texts in real communicative contexts. This framework provides an ideal model for articulating possible approaches for integrating and exploiting multimodal resources, such as film, in the L2 classroom. On the one hand, it encourages the development of learners' analytical skills and the production of multimodal materials making use of different semiotic resources. On the other hand, it helps teachers to understand the pedagogical and educational possibilities of multimodal resources in L2 learning. Thus, the framework facilitates a more comprehensive use of moving images as a tool to develop a wider range of skills and multimodal communication.

The 'multiliteracies' model highlights the crucial role of multimodality in today's communication; that is to say, the shift towards broadening the meaning-making processes in multimodal texts, which combine various semiotic resources or modes (Kress and van Leeuwen 2001; Kress 2003). The umbrella framework of multimodality recognizes how the semiotic resources of each mode are 'socially shaped and culturally specific' (Bezemer and Kress 2016: 25); and how the potential representation (affordances) of each of the available semiotic resources should be considered in the composition of multimodal digital texts. Thus, the concept of multimodal 'ensembles' (the combination of modes, i.e. image, layout, writing, etc.) has a direct potential application in education as 'communication and learning are meaning-creating practices' (Bezemer and Kress 2016: 143). In *Literacy in the New Media Age* (2003: 1), Kress also points to the 'dominance of the medium of the screen', which represents a major paradigm shift in the way ideas are communicated. However, Bateman has questioned the simplistic association of 'writing' with the 'book', and 'image' with the 'screen'; he interprets Kress's words as more of 'a suggestive metaphor of broader changes in sociocultural priorities' (Bateman 2021: 13). In any case, the value of 'multimodal literacy' for educational purposes cannot be disputed given the range of media practices beyond verbal and written literacies.

It is hardly surprising that the multiliteracies framework and the principles of multimodality have gained currency in the field of language education, although they are still underexploited (Kern 2000; Paesani, Willis-Allen and Dupuy 2016). Within the edutainment field, researchers and practitioners are rightly arguing for the use of film and screen media to integrate and develop multiple skills and multimodal practices in L2 (Chan and Herrero 2010; FILTA 2010; Elsner, Helff and Viebrock 2013; Thaler 2014; Donaghy and Xerri 2017; Viebrock 2016; Herrero and Vanderschelden 2019). Moreover, film literacy is a core component in twenty-first-century curricula. However, the potential of screen media for achieving what the language curriculum prescribes is still undervalued or seen as secondary to oral and written formats.

The principles of the multiliteracies framework call for schools and other educational institutions to support the development of a wider range of competences to keep up with the digital landscape. The so-called 'twenty-first-century skills' include, among others, communication, intercultural awareness, critical thinking, problem solving, creativity, teamwork, visual literacy and digital literacy. Given the weight of visual images in the current era, visual culture features prominently in several pedagogical models that give special emphasis to education in and with media: the 'pedagogy of the gaze' (Dussell and Gutiérrez 2006) and 'emotional education' through screens (Ferrés 2014). Faced with the saturation of images, Dussell and Gutiérrez urge educators to adopt a new pedagogy of the gaze. They defend the legitimacy of the image for the transmission of knowledge. Hence, they consider it to be imperative that this 'pedagogy of the image' questions the prevailing tradition of modern educational systems, in which the image has generally been disdained as an inferior form of representation to writing. Additionally, they argue in favour of approaching images with a critical perspective (political and ethical training), combined with audiovisual education. Equally, Joan Ferrés defends the educational value of screen products. He points out the emotional appeal of television and cinema as they provoke sensory stimulation with colours, moving images, music and soundtrack. All these components have an impact on the capacity of cinema to involve the spectator in the story being told and to provoke identification with the characters. Ferrés also highlights how the aesthetic value of cinema affects the emotion that the spectator feels. Hence, in our opinion, if film generates emotion and pleasure, it constitutes an ideal educational tool for L2 learning as it conveys concepts, ideas and knowledge and promotes meaningful learning.

Equally relevant for working with screen media is digital literacy, which should be understood as the ability to engage actively with digital technologies. According to Spires and Bartlett (2012: 8), it involves three processes: locating and consuming digital content; producing digital compositions by using a 'number of digital "reading" and "writing" techniques across multiple media forms' (words, texts, visual displays, motion graphics, audio, video, and multimodal forms); and communicating digital content. Furthermore, given that achieving effective communication is equally a priority, intercultural/transcultural competence and mediation take centre stage in L2 learning (Council of Europe 2001, 2018; Beacco et al. 2016). As the reach of digital and non-digital communicative situations expands, engaging with an extensive set of products and practices requires the broadening of the range of configurations (see Sindoni et al. 2019).

The shift towards multiliteracy is not just a question of terminology but a conceptual shift. Literacy theorists Lankshear and Knobel (2006: 60) consider them to be 'new' literacies because they are made of a different 'ethos stuff': 'they are more "participatory", more "collaborative" and more "distributed"'. Taking a similar stance, Jenkins (2006) adopts the concept of 'collective intelligence' (Lévy 1997) to define a participatory culture in which members believe in the importance of sharing their contributions and knowledge. Several pedagogical proposals have placed special emphasis on the role of the learner as an active agent in the situated learning processes that take place in face-to-face and online environments: pedagogy of participation (Piscitelli 2009), invisible learning (Cobo-Romani and Moravec 2010), the education of interactivity (Aparici and Silva 2012) and connected learning (Ito et al. 2013). Jenkins et al. (2009: 7) identify a series of participatory practices and new media skills that have potential applications in the educational sphere: play, performance, simulation, appropriation, multitasking, distributed cognition, collective intelligence, judgement, transmedia navigation, networking and negotiation. In the context of 'convergence culture', characterized by fragmentation and multiple entry points for both traditional and new media (Jenkins 2006), one of the most relevant skills for education is 'transmedia navigation', defined as 'the ability to deal with the flow of stories and information across multiple modalities' (Jenkins et al. 2009: 46). Also, focusing on this participatory practice, the European project *Transmedia Literacy* documents current strategies that can be deployed in educational interventions. Based on the research carried out as part of this large-scale initiative, Scolari (2018: 11) defines transmedia skills as 'a series of competences related to digital interactive media production, sharing and consumption'. These skills and informal learning strategies based on the media activities that young people (12–18 years old) carried out include problem-solving activities in an informal environment (for example, in video games); as well as the production, sharing and consumption of narrative content in social media and other digital platforms and transmedia pedagogy. Given the exponential growth of videos created for personal and professional purposes, student-generated videos for L2 learning are ideal tools to enhance language and digital skills and provide more authentic and engaging learning experiences.

Teachers' perspectives, praxis and curriculum requirements in the UK

Based on UX research, another of the main objectives of the project was to explore teachers' points of view on the advantages and drawbacks that may constrain the successful integration of film into language curriculum design. To gain the best knowledge and understanding of how films are used in L2 syllabi and to canvas the needs of language tutors, the project research team designed an online questionnaire that was distributed via the Film in Language Teaching Association's (FILTA) community website. FILTA is an online professional learning community, with more than 5,200 members from over one hundred countries, that encourages sharing examples of good practice and resources working as a community of practice (Herrero 2016). The qualitative sample collected from the thirty teachers who responded offered a valuable insight into training needs related to this field and on the value of the teaching materials available on the FILTA website (mostly study guides based on feature films). Most of those who responded were teaching Spanish (60 per cent), followed by those teaching English and French (38 per cent, respectively). Half of the educators (50 per cent) were teaching in the UK and the rest were working in

Spain, Germany, Ireland, Romania, Greece, Argentina, Italy, Canada and South Korea. Most of the respondents were practitioners in secondary education and higher education, but there were also language teachers involved in other sectors (primary, supplementary schools and language schools). The vast majority (97 per cent) had more than six years of teaching experience. More than half of those who completed the questionnaire had used the FILTA resources in the lessons (53 per cent), either in the current format or to complement other resources. In terms of relevance for their syllabus, 70 per cent of the respondents agreed that the materials were pertinent. The teachers considered that the resources had had a positive impact on learners' motivation (86 per cent) and learning process (89 per cent). The educators also indicated that these teaching materials had saved them time as reusable resources (89 per cent). In terms of professional learning needs related to the field of film and the moving image, the main areas were the following (listed in order of importance): workshops and resources on the 'grammar' of film; training on how to analyse films and the vocabulary to use; guidance on teaching critical analysis and how to use film to develop intercultural competence; ideas, resources and activities for the GCSE and KS3 curriculum; workshops on technology and film (editing, adding subtitles to videos); and accessing examples of using film for cross-media (literary adaptations) and interdisciplinary activities or modules (History, sociolinguistics, etc.).

The main challenges for an optimal approach to film were directly related to teaching conditions and curriculum constraints: the pressing need to balance content and language; the difficulties in reconciling the 'restrictive curriculum' with learning theories and teaching with authentic materials such as film; and the lack of time due to the extensive curriculum content that had to be covered. Another concern was the lack of experience in this interdisciplinary field (film analysis). In terms of support, there was a wide range of suggestions: more study guides and resources closely related to the curriculum; exchanges of ideas and resources within the FILTA community; seminars and webinars on specific topics of interest; promotion of educational research, examples of good teaching practice and links with practitioners and other educational institutions; organizing INSET days and CPD events to present inspiring ways of approaching this subject; outreach activities for schools; time-saving resources. Many of the opportunities that were already available in the FILTA community were mentioned: 'be a hub of resources, discussion and signposting' and 'providing access to a wide range of experiences and the opportunity for exchange on a general basis, as well as within specialised groups, in terms of both teaching practice and research'.

Overall, the results from the survey confirmed that films have something very special to offer to L2 learning. Teachers understood their value for learners as films are motivating and engaging authentic materials. Teachers' needs included providing adequate guidance and further training so they could feel confident when using film in the language classroom. It goes without saying that this support could be offered in many forms: teachers were interested in resources, empirical studies and examples of action research that have tested different methodologies and approaches for integrating film into L2 curricula.

The next stage of this project was to investigate existing practices related to the successful uses and positive impact of film and audiovisual media in the language classroom. The literature review highlighted the main strategies that have been used to integrate film into language curriculum design since the 1980s (see also Herrero, Suarez and Requena's chapter in this volume). Most of these works adopt communicative cultural models primarily applied to English, French and Spanish language teaching (Donaghy 2015; Thaler 2014 and 2017; Vanderschelden 2014; Junkerjürgen, Scholz and Alvárez Olañeta 2016; Viebrock 2016; Herrero 2018, 2019a; Herrero and Vanderschelden 2019) and, to a lesser extent, are extended to other European and non-European languages (Chan and Herrero 2010; Anderson and Macleroy 2016). Many practitioners advocate for integrating films into the L2 curriculum to develop learners' linguistic and cultural competences. Education specialists have also defended the value of using film and moving images to enhance inter-/transcultural competence and film/media literacy (Pegrum 2008; Vanderschelden 2014; Herrero and Vanderschelden 2019). New technologies offer exciting opportunities for teachers and students to make use of screen media as rich multimodal resources, including audiovisual translation activities and filmmaking (Keddie 2014; Goldstein and Driver 2015; Donaghy and Xerri 2017; Incalcaterra McLoughlin, Lertola and Talaván 2020). In my view, as a practitioner and researcher, the integration of film into L2 teaching and learning represents a communicative experience that can support the transfer of knowledge and content (e.g. grammar, concepts, culture) and trigger a stronger engagement with the learning process, as well as enhancing a wide range of skills (language, digital, media and film literacy). Particularly video-based learning, which is driven by the learner's interest and motivation, is becoming the norm in informal learning and, in formal settings, can contribute to an effective engagement with the target language.

Another objective of the *Teacher Training Project* was to identify curriculum requirements in MFL secondary education across the UK. The study of film is optional as part of the MFL curriculum at A-Level in England, as it is possible to study two literary works, or one literary work and one film from a list of prescribed titles. Although it is optional, the study of a film is a very popular choice. However, at a lower level, the provision at GCSE does not include an explicit reference to the study of film (see Goodwin's chapter in this volume). The recent Ofsted Curriculum Research Review for languages (Ofsted 2021) further marginalizes the cultural content of the GCSE curriculum. It proposes that an effective language curriculum should focus on phonics, vocabulary and grammar as 'the building blocks of language'. This narrow focus of the Ofsted new curriculum for languages has been questioned and criticized in a special issue of *The Language Learning Journal* (Pachler and Broady 2022). Several of the chapters included in this publication advocate for the central role of culture alongside linguistic provision. Porter et al. (2022: 213–14) emphasize that learners 'should experience cultural artefacts as well as develop critical evaluation of such artefacts'; and they highlight that 'creativity, challenge and culture' are essential elements in the modern languages classroom to foster engagement and motivation (214). Similarly, Woore, Molway and Macaro (2022: 149) state that 'learners can and should encounter the cultural riches of another language from the very beginning of the learning process' and challenging texts (including videos) 'may serve as a powerful motivator'. In the same vein, the case presented in this chapter argues for films as cultural artefacts of great value in L2 teaching as their use boosts student interest and engagement with the subject (see Goodwin's chapter in this volume).

Workshops, activities and resources

The following stage in the *Teacher Training Project* was intended to create a series of resources that could be relevant for all the languages and levels, and respond to needs, barriers and challenges identified in the FILTA teachers' responses: variety, adaptability and flexibility to different learning needs and to time restrictions. In 1989, Rick Altman, one of the pioneers of video pedagogy, opened the debate on how to integrate video into the curriculum by posing the following very pertinent questions: Will it [video] require similar impact and change to make a significant impact on educational practices? Can video materials be successfully integrated into existing courses without massive transformations of syllabi and resources? His 'integrated approach to video pedagogy' starts with two principles – context and control: 'Video is extraordinarily well suited to display the connections between language and the real world upon which comprehension depends. Video's striking ability to make these connections stems from its unique combination of two opposed qualities: *maximum contextualization* and *maximum control*' (Altman 1989: 8). Referring to the first advantage, he notes how '(n)ot only does the video medium provide an easily accessible combination of high-quality visual and aural materials, but it has the capacity to provide – through visual and aural channels alike – extremely faithful conditions of the world associated with the target language' (10); while the second merit allows the instructor to use the 'predictability of video' to prepare students (11). With these ideas in mind, a pressing need for the *Teacher Training Project* was finding films that could enhance learners' motivation and expose them to multimodal forms of communication while being integrated into existing syllabi and curricula easily, reducing the need for big changes. Likewise, it was essential to identify films that were available online that could be useful for different languages and levels to maximize the results and resources beyond the funding period. With all these requirements and given the many benefits of using short films in the language classroom (Chan and Herrero 2010; Donaghy 2014; Junkerjürgen, Scholz and Alvárez Olañeta 2016; Thaler 2017), the research team chose short films, particularly videos without dialogues for their potential applications to multiple languages. This was, in fact, one of the suggestions proposed by one of the members of FILTA to resolve the time constraints during the language classroom.[4]

The primacy of visual communication increases the relevance of media literacy in the educational arena, including in L2 education. The research team created a taxonomy that could illustrate the different approaches that comprise this interdisciplinary area of enquiry and practice. Figure 3.1 presents the relationship between screen media and language learning as the intersection of the two axes. The top right is the approach in which any project or lesson plan focuses on both developing language and media skills. On the top left-hand side of this axis, screen media is used as a tool for language learning per se. On the lower right-hand side of the axis, screen media is utilized as a product and the language component is only one of the semiotic modes. Finally, on the lower left-hand side, films or videos are used to convey general information, without any linguistic or media literacy engagement. Although all the approaches are valid, the *Film Teaching Training Project* was keen to develop materials and training teaching activities involving both language learning and media literacy.

As part of media education, film education comprises three dimensions: the 'level of understanding of a film, the ability to be conscious and curious in the

Integrating Screen Media into the Language Curriculum 57

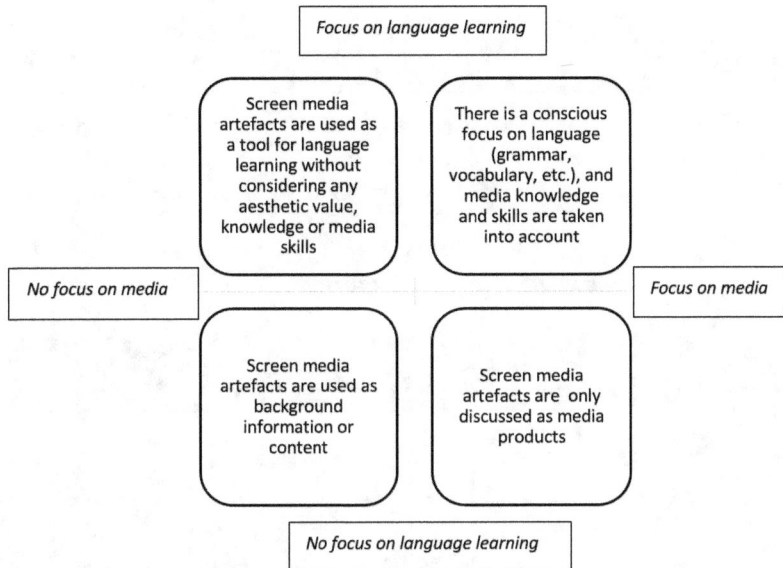

Figure 3.1 The intersection of screen media and language learning. Source: Author.

choice of films; the competence to critically watch a film and to analyse its content, cinematography and technical aspects; and the ability to manipulate its language and technical resources in creative moving image production' (British Film Institute 2013: 3) (see Figure 3.2).[5] Implicitly, there is a certain level of tension between the concept of film as an art form and other modes of screen media, which are often seen only as forms of entertainment and/or information. However, there is also an implicit recognition that both forms of literacy have similar aims and, in the current era of media convergence, its application in educational settings is more effective when they work together.

Each of the three dimensions of film education – Cultural, Critical and Creative – were used as a focal point for the first INSETs to support the integration of film literacy in the L2 learning processes and teaching.[6] The cultural approach means broadening the range of films that L2 students have access to so that they can connect with different groups of people with their stories and cultures. The critical approach focuses on being able to read critically screen media. The creative approach involves expanding in a practical way learners' knowledge and understanding of what film can do. It includes any creative task with media in L2 and activities involved in movie-making and remixing (e.g. creating a poster, designing a new version of a trailer, adding subtitles to a film clip, audiodescribing

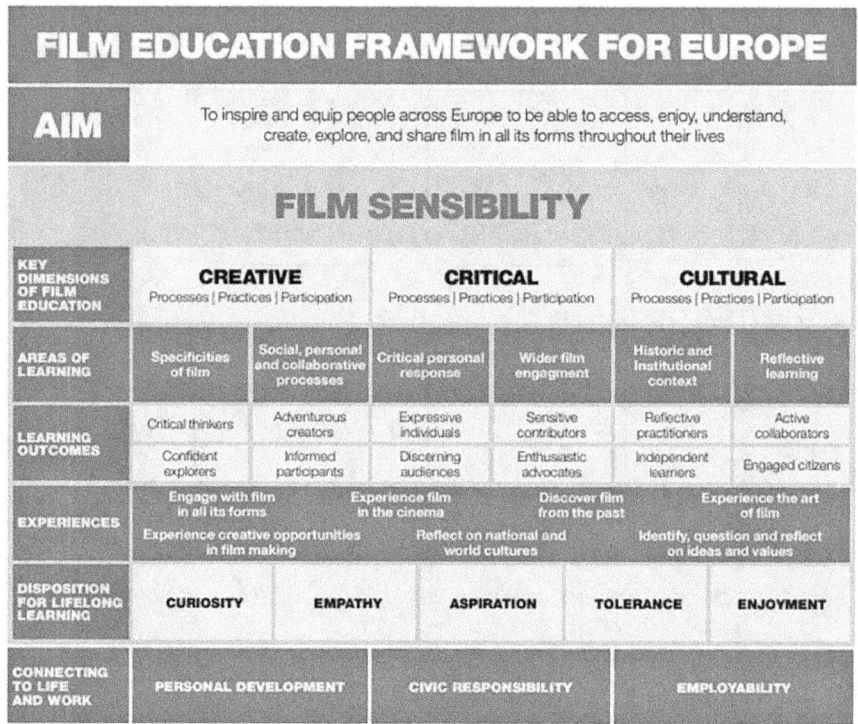

Figure 3.2 The Film Education Framework. Source: BFI 2015: 7.

a scene, or writing music and lyrics for the soundtrack of a scene). To test the pedagogical principles of the project, the team focused on designing a series of workshops to present hands-on activities and to offer the notions and concepts associated with film-oriented language teaching. One of the challenges was creating learning materials based on short films that could test and sample various approaches for different types of educational settings. At the same time, each of the workshops provided further opportunities for collecting more feedback on the teaching needs and practices of the language tutors who attended, to refine and improve the resources and activities offered at the next event. The evaluation during each of the training events (pre- and post-questionnaires) fed into the subsequent INSETs.

The first one-day INSET, 'Using the short film to develop language skills and intercultural competence in language learning (French/Spanish)', took place at Manchester Metropolitan University in July 2017.[7] Before attending the workshop, the participants completed a questionnaire to gather information regarding their own experience of teaching languages, the challenges encountered when they used film, television and moving image (short films, TV series, videos and commercials, among others) in the classroom, their perceived needs, and the type of support they felt they required. This survey was complemented with the evaluation of the training event (post-questionnaire) by the language tutors who attended the workshop. The main aim was to introduce the framework using short film in the language classroom to develop cultural and intercultural competences and multimodal and film literacies. A short film without dialogue was screened during the general session to guide the discussion on the integration of film into the language curriculum. Attendees were encouraged to develop exercises focusing on the connections between meaning-making processes in real-world situations and their educational contexts through a series of exercises designed to apply the analytical model of multimodality developed by Cope and Kalantzis (2000). In the second part of the INSET, other short films for French and for Spanish were screened to discuss further ideas and activities that could be easily transferable to a range of educational contexts. The workshop offered purpose-designed film study guides developed for this training session, as well as other resources (bank of materials, vocabulary, etc.). The study guides were based on the following films and languages: *Peripheria* (David Coquard-Dassault 2015) [silent short film, adaptable to any language, guide in English], *Hoy no estoy* (Gustavo Taretto 2007) [silent short film, guide in Spanish], *Les Crayons* (Didier Barcelo 2005) [short film, guide in French], *Maman(s)* (Maïmouna Doucouré 2015) [short film, guide in French] and *The Entire Journey* (Brunners 2017 [silent short film, guide in Spanish).

The second INSET, 'Using Short films for Critical Analysis in Language Teaching and Learning', took place at Manchester Metropolitan University in September 2018.[8] The integration of critical enquiry is particularly relevant for language instruction and is intrinsically linked to the second dimension of film literacy: critical personal responses and engagement with a wider range of films. On this day, the aim was to assess specific training in film analysis by using short films to enhance critical literacy in the language classroom. The interactive workshop responded to practitioners' needs for further development in critical thinking and writing on films for the new A-Level curriculum, as well as the integration of film analysis into the language classroom at GCSE to negotiate the transition. The workshop provided relevant key terminology and concepts of film analysis and examples to illustrate them. The event guided teachers on how to develop a series of practical tasks using formative exercises to promote critical analysis and visual literacy. The second part of the event proposed a range of activities for embedding film literacy and critical thinking into the language classroom using short films for teaching French and Spanish but could be adapted to other languages. This format was particularly effective to bring together teachers to share expertise and practice.

In addition to the teacher-training activities, the team co-organized events with Huw Baird College in Liverpool, our partner school for A-level students in 2018 and 2019. The focus for these events was developing language learners' film literacy and their critical skills working with the film *María, llena eres de gracia* (Joshua Marton 2004). The approach and resources were also tested in a series of Film Study Days for French and Spanish language students (GCSE and A-Level) organized by HOME Arts Centre between 2018 and 2020. These events comprised an introduction to a film, then the screening, followed by interactive activities based on the film.

Focusing on creativity, the third INSET theme was dedicated to 'Gaming and Storytelling in the Modern Foreign Language Classroom' (October 2018).[9] Video games are a relevant medium in the L2 classroom that can stimulate affect towards L2 acquisition. To incentivize its use in the foreign language, the research team suggested video games with a lot of storytelling, such as graphic adventures or role-playing games. There are also video games lacking oral or written language. This type of video game includes not only some puzzle games such as *Tetris* (1984), but also graphic adventures such as *Machinarium* (2009), *Botanicula* (2014) or *Chuchel* (2018), all created and published by the Czech developers Amanita Design. These are puzzle-ridden adventures with a point-and-click gameplay that lack any form of written narration or dialogues. They resort to visual, auditory, kinaesthetic and even tactile means (depending on hardware) to communicate the story and events to users from multiple cultural backgrounds. Thus, these games are accessible to all students, from A1 to C2 levels, and can be used for developing transcultural competence, too. Given the features of these non-verbal adventure games, the workshops (French and Spanish) focused on how to exploit these resources, as their content can be used to build teaching units for second language acquisition at all levels: from basic colours and shapes to complex storytelling (e.g. writing a short story). The session concentrated more specifically on the point-and-click game *Samorost* (Amanita Design 2003) and on the escape room game *Crimson Room* (Toshimitshu Takagi 2004). The advantage of these two free games, available online, is that tutors and students do not need to be experts in gaming. The workshop included a walk-through video of the point-and-click game *Chuchel* (Amanita Design 2018), which can be an alternative when tutors do not feel confident using video games. As in previous training sessions, the team collected information before and after the INSET about teachers' needs and the level of satisfaction with the framework, resources and activities. The main finding from this workshop was the fact that many of the teachers were uncomfortable with the use of video games in the L2 classroom. However, they were very interested in incorporating digital storytelling into their schemes of work.

The INSET on 'Gaming and Storytelling in the Modern Foreign Language Classroom' was part of the project *New Approaches to Transmedia and Language Pedagogy*, dedicated to transmedia education applied to L2 learning and teaching. This project was built on the opportunities and challenges offered by the participatory culture in formal and non-formal educational settings. The aim was twofold. First, given the growth of user-generated content and digital media-based work, the project endeavoured to take advantage of the potential of learners as 'knowledge producers and co-contributors to knowledge communities' with the aim of developing 'critical, creative and design thinking' (Kalantzis and Cope 2020: 54–5). For this purpose, the small-scale qualitative project *Open Education Resources for Students by Students* encouraged language learners to create digital artefacts based on their assignments and share them publicly under a Creative Commons licence (see Herrero 2021). The second aim was creating teaching materials based on a mix of non-verbal cultural artefacts (short films and video games, without dialogue) to broaden translingual and transcultural competences, creativity and storytelling skills. The final phase comprised a symposium ('Transmedia Theory and Practice in Teaching and Learning') and an international conference ('New Approaches to Transmedia and Language Pedagogy'), which took place in Manchester in April and June 2019, respectively. The objective of these events was to bring together experts on transmedia and L2 researchers and practitioners, as well as language teachers interested in new pedagogical approaches.

To disseminate the results of the project, all the presentations, worksheets and teacher resources were uploaded on the project's new website ('Transmedia in Education') and on FILTA. To ensure the sustainability of the project beyond the funding period, the team aimed at building a stronger community of practice (i.e. groups of teachers who wish to deepen their knowledge, expertise and practice in this field by sharing experiences, examples of good practice, tools and resources) (Wenger, McDermott and Snyder 2002; Herrero 2016). In February 2019, the team offered two workshops in Manchester and London aimed at trainee teachers on 'Using films creatively in the language classroom: Visual literacy and critical thinking'. In April 2019, a similar INSET was offered in collaboration with the Association of Teachers and Researchers of Portuguese

Language in the UK (TROPO), attended by Portuguese teachers of secondary and higher education. In collaboration with the ALL, the team offered two more webinars on 'New Approaches to Transmedia and Language Pedagogy'. The first one took place in January 2021 and was specifically designed for French and Spanish teacher trainees; whereas the second one, in June 2021, was aimed at Arabic teaching and was attended by higher education, secondary and supplementary school teachers. Overall, including the international workshops, over five hundred language teachers have attended the INSETs, seminars and webinars offered as part of the *Teacher Training Project* and the *New Approaches to Transmedia and Language Pedagogy Project*.

To sum up, based on UX research, the design team tailored teacher-training workshops, designed materials and study guides, and attended to changing needs by acting on participants' feedback. The projects responded to the ongoing shifts in media consumption and their impact on the learners as prosumers, which are opening up new avenues for integrating films and other types of screen media into the language curriculum in creative and engaging ways. The complex media ecosystem in which we are involved provides challenges and opportunities for revisioning language learning. In the current context, it makes sense to involve L2 learners not only as consumers of media but as producers and creators. The positive response to the materials and activities shared in these training activities should encourage more language teachers to adopt and develop interactive, engaging and creative learning strategies when using video in the L2 classroom (e.g. mobile learning, peer collaboration and video assessments) (Herrero 2919b).

Conclusion

This chapter has shown the prominent role of film in language-learning instruction. Rather than seeing film as a form of entertainment outside the classroom, it is time to value its real potential when bringing it into the classroom: enhancing language skills, developing traditional and new skills, comparing cultures, training students to feel empathy and fostering intercultural awareness, and showing multilingual communication features in action, among others. The different approaches adopted in the *Teacher Training Project* have demonstrated how films can be integrated into curriculum design moving beyond traditional literacy forms. The aim was to create a framework for easily and effortlessly embedding films in curricular design, making the most of the multimodal affordances of short films. Going further, integrating films into the L2 curriculum requires nurturing critical prosumers, who can understand the cultural references and create and share screen media artefacts. The *New Approaches to Transmedia and Language Pedagogy Project* focused on some of the ways in which educators could respond proactively to the challenges and opportunities provided by the digital media ecosystem to develop and/or apply innovative and effective approaches to L2 learning by embracing multimodal and transmedia approaches in language teaching.

The findings reported here are limited, as it would have been beneficial to follow up and evaluate the experiences of the many participants in the INSETs and webinars with their implementation of the multimodal and creative teaching strategies, as well as its impact on learner engagement and attainment. Hopefully, further research will respond to other questions related to the use of screen media as a rich multimodal input for L2 learning. While this study offers only a glimpse of the possibilities of transmedia education and practices applied to L2 learning and teaching, this is a work in progress as digital technologies continue to expand. Another research area to pursue relates to the role and contribution of communities of practice to teacher development and professionalization in this interdisciplinary domain of knowledge and practice (multiliteracies, multimodality, screen studies, transmedia studies and second language acquisition studies). After all, with the changes that have taken place in education since the onset of the COVID-19 pandemic, it is indeed vital to engage L2 researchers and practitioners with a wider understanding of communication, its potential and the challenges it presents.

Notes

1 Cross-Language Dynamics was a multidisciplinary programme led by the University of Manchester in partnership with Durham University and the School of Advanced Study, University of London, and several additional external partners. The project was funded by the AHRC and was part of the Open World Research Initiative (2016–21) https://www.ukri.org/what-we-offer/browse-our-areas-of-investment-and-support/open-world-research-initiative/.

2 In 2015 the British Film Institute proposed that '*film* refers to all forms of moving images with sound (and without!), irrespective of the medium, be that digital or analogue, TV, online or cinema' (BFI 2015: 3). In the 2022 BFI Strategy, the British Film Institute differentiates between film, television, animation and the moving image generally. The category of 'film' includes 'anything that tells a story, expresses

an idea or evokes an emotion through the art of the moving image, whilst honouring the platform for which the work was intended' (BFI 2016: 4).
3   The New London Group is a group of ten scholars who gathered in London, New Hampshire, in 1994 with the aim of discussing the future of literacy pedagogy: Courtney Cazden, Bill Cope, James Cook, Jim Gee, Mary Kalantzis, Gunther Kress, Allan Luke, Carmen Luke, Sarah Michaels and Martin Nakata.
4   See also Screening Languages, a two-year curriculum and professional development project funded by the Mayor of London's Schools Excellence Fund (2013–15) https://www2.bfi.org.uk/education-research/screening-languages.
5   See also Film Education Framework Group (2022).
6   The model, devised by Cary Bazalgette for the UK Task Force on Media Literacy, was adopted by the BFI 2008 in its Reframing Literacy campaign.
7   This INSET was led by Carmen Herrero and Isabelle Vanderschelden.
8   This training event was led by Carmen Herrero, Isabelle Vanderschelden and Marta Suarez.
9   This INSET was led by Daniel Escandell, Sophie Guingouain and Carmen Herrero.

References

Altman, R. (1989), *The Video Connection: Integrating Video into Language Teaching*, Boston, MA: Houghton Mifflin.

Anderson, J., and V. Macleroy (2016), *Multilingual Digital Storytelling*, London: Routledge.

Aparici, R., and M. Silva (2012), 'Pedagogía de la interactividad', *Comunicar*, 19 (38): 51–8.

Bateman, J. (2021), 'What Are Digital Media?', *Discourse, Context & Media*, 41 (100502): 1–16.

Beacco, J. C., M. Byram, M. Cavalli, D. Coste, M. E. Cuenat, F. Goullier and J. Panthier, (2016), *Guide for The Development and Implementation of Curricula for Plurilingual and Intercultural Education*, Strasbourg: Council of Europe Publishing.

Bezemer, J., and G. Kress (2016), *Multimodality, Learning and Communication: A Social Semiotic Frame*, London and New York: Routledge.

British Film Institute (2013), *Screening Literacy in Europe*, London: BFI.

British Film Institute (2015), *Framework for Film Education*, London: BFI.

British Film Institute (2016), *BFI 2022 Strategy*, London: BFI.

CEDEFOP (2011), *Glossary: Quality in Education and Training*. Luxembourg: Publications Office of the European Union. Available online: https://europa.eu/capacity4dev/iesf/document/glossary-quality-education-and-training-cedefop-2011.

Chan, D., and C. Herrero (2010), *Using Film to Teach Languages*, Manchester: Cornerhouse.

Cobo, C., and J. W. Moravec (2011), *Invisible Learning. Towards a New Ecology of Education*, Barcelona: Publicacions i Edicions de la Universitat de Barcelona.

Cope, B., and M. Kalantzis, eds (2000), *Multiliteracies: Literacy Learning and the Design of Social Futures*, London: Routledge.

Cross-Language Dynamics OWRI (2016–21), *Cross-Language Dynamics: Reshaping Community*. Available online: http://projects.alc.manchester.ac.uk/cross-language-dynamics/.

Council of Europe (2001), *Common European Framework of Reference for Languages: Learning, Teaching, Assessment*, Cambridge: Cambridge University Press.

Council of Europe (2018), *Common European Framework of Reference for Languages: Learning, Teaching, Assessment. Companion Volume with New Descriptors*, Strasbourg: Council of Europe Publishing.

Donaghy, K. (2015), *Film in Action: Teaching Language Using Moving Images*, London: Delta Publishing.

Donaghy, K., and D. Xerri, eds (2017), *The Image in English Language Teaching*, Malta: ELT Council.

Dussel, I., and D. Gutiérrez (2006), *Educar la mirada*, Buenos Aires: Ediciones Manantial.

Elsner, D., S. Helff and B. Viebrock, eds (2013), *Films, Graphic Novels and Visuals. Developing Multiliteracies in Foreign Language Education: An Interdisciplinary Approach*, Münster: LIT Verlag.

Ferrés, J. (2014), *Las pantallas y el cerebro emocional*, Barcelona: Gedisa.

Film Education Framework Group (2022), *Film Education: A User's Guide*. Available online: filmeducationframework.eu.

FILTA (2010), *Film in Language Teaching Association* (FILTA). Available online: http://www.filta.org.uk.

FLAME Research Group (2013), *Film, Languages and Media in Education* (FLAME). Available online: http://www2.mmu.ac.uk/languages/flame/.

Goldstein, B., and P. Driver (2015), *Language Learning with Digital Video*, Cambridge: Cambridge University Press.

Herrero, C. (2016), 'The Film in Language Teaching Association (FILTA): A Multilingual Community of Practice', *ELT Journal* 70 (2): 190–9.

Herrero, C. (2018), 'El cine y otras manifestaciones culturales en ELE', in M. Martínez-Atienza de Dios and A. Zamorano Aguilar (eds), *Iniciación a la metodología de la enseñanza de ELE* (vol. IV), 65–85, Madrid: EnClaveELE.

Herrero, C. (2019a), 'Medios audiovisuales', in J. Muñoz-Basols, E. Gironzetti and M. Lacorte (eds), *The Routledge Handbook of Spanish Language Teaching: metodologías, contextos y recursos para la enseñanza del español L2*, 565–82, London and New York: Routledge.

Herrero, C., (2019b), 'Conclusion: Present and Future Directions for Video, Film and Audiovisual Media in Language Teaching', in C. Herrero and I. Vanderschelden (eds), *Using Film and Media in the Language Classroom: Reflections on Research-led Teaching*, 188–97, Bristol: Multilingual Matters.

Herrero, C. (2021), 'La educación transmedia como estrategia innovadora para integrar lengua y cultura en la enseñanza de ELE', *Doblele. Revista de Lengua y Literatura*, 7: 50–66.

Herrero, C., and I. Vanderschelden, eds (2019), *Using Film and Media in the Language Classroom: Reflections on Research-led Teaching*, Bristol: Multilingual Matters.

Incalcaterra McLoughlin, L., J. Lertola and N. Talaván, eds (2020), *Audiovisual Translation in Applied Linguistics: Educational Perspectives*, Amsterdam: John Benjamins.

Ito, M., K. Gutiérrez, S. Livingstone, B. Penuel, J. Rhodes, K. Salen, J. Schor, J. Sefton-Green and S. C. Watkins (2013), *Connected Learning: An Agenda for Research and Design*, Irvine, CA: Digital Media and Learning Research Hub.

Jenkins, H. (2006), *Convergence Culture. Where Old and New Media Collide*, New York and London: New York University Press.

Jenkins, H., R. Purushotma, M. Weigel, K. Clinton and A. J. Robison (2009), *Confronting the Challenges of Participatory Culture: Media Education for the 21st Century*, Cambridge, MA: MIT Press.

Junkerjürgen, R., A. Scholz and P. Alvárez Olañeta, eds (2016) *El cortometraje español (2000–2015). Tendencias y ejemplos*, Madrid: Iberoamericana-Vervuert.

Kalantzis, M., and B. Cope (2020), 'After the COVID-19 Crisis: Why Higher Education May (and Perhaps Should) Never Be the Same', *Access: Contemporary Issues in Education* 40 (1): 51–5.

Kalantzis, M., B. Cope, E. Chan and L. Dalley-Trim (2016), *Literacies*, Cambridge: Cambridge University Press.

Keddie, J. (2014), *Bringing Online Video into the Classroom*, Oxford: Oxford University Press.

Kern, R. (2000), *Literacy and Language Teaching*, Oxford: Oxford University Press.

Kress, G. (2003), *Literacy in the New Media Age*, London and New York: Routledge.

Kress, G., and T. van Leeuwen (2001), *Multimodal Discourses: The Modes and Media of Contemporary Communication*, New York: Oxford University Press.

Lankshear, C., and M. Knobel (2006), *New Literacies: Everyday Practices and Classroom Learning*, Maidenhead: Open University Press.

Lévy, P. (1997), *Collective Intelligence: Mankind's Emerging World in Cyberspace*. Cambridge: Perseus.

Narcy-Combes, M.-F., J.-P. Narcy-Combes, J. McAllister, M. Leclère and G. Miras (2019), *Language Learning and Teaching in a Multilingual World*, Bristol: Multilingual Matters.

New London Group (1996), 'A Pedagogy of Multiliteracies: Designing Social Futures', *Harvard Educational Review*, 66 (1): 60–92.

Ofsted (2021), *Curriculum Research Review Series: Languages*. Available online: https://www.gov.uk/government/publications/curriculum-research-review-series-languages.

Paesani, K., H. Willis-Allen and B. Dupuy (2016), *A Multiliteracies Framework for Collegiate Foreign Language Teaching*, Upper Saddle River, NJ: Pearson.

Pachler, N., and E. Broady (2022), 'Language Policy, Evidence-Informed Practice, the Role of Regulatory Bodies and Teacher Agency', *The Language Learning Journal*, 50 (2): 135–41.

Pegrum, M. (2008), 'Film Culture and Identity: Critical intercultural Literacies for the Language Classroom', *Language and International Communication*, 8 (2): 136–54.

Piscitelli, A. (2009), *Nativos digitales, dieta cognitiva, inteligencias colectivas y arquitecturas de participación*, Montevideo: Editorial Santillana.

Porter, A., S. Graham, F. Myles and B. Holmes (2022), 'Creativity, Challenge and Culture in the Language Classroom: A Response to the Ofsted Curriculum Research Review', *The Language Learning Journal*, 50 (2): 208–17.

Richards, J. C. (2001), *Curriculum Development in Language Teaching*, Cambridge: Cambridge University Press.

Scolari, C. (2018), *Transmedia Literacy on The New Media Ecology: White Paper*. H2020 TRANSLITERACY Research Project, Barcelona: Universitat Pompeu Fabra.

Sindoni, M. G., E. Adami, S. Karatza, I. Marenzi, I. Moschini, S. Petroni and M. Rocca (2019), *The Common Framework of Reference for Intercultural Digital Literacies*. EUMade4ll. Available online: https://www.eumade4ll.eu/wp-content/uploads/2019/09/cfridil-framework-MG3_IM_4-compresso.pdf.

Spires, H. A., and M. E. Bartlett (2012), *Digital Literacies and Learning: Designing a Path Forward*, Raleigh: Friday Institute for Educational Innovation, North Carolina State University.

Thaler, E. (2014), *Teaching English with Film*, Paderborn: Schöningh.

Thaler, E. (2017), *Short Films in Language Teaching*, Tübingen: Narr Francke Attempto.

Transmedia in Education (2018), 'Transmedia in Education: New Approaches to Transmedia and Language Pedagogy', FLAME. Available online: http://www.transmediaineducation.com.

Vanderschelden, I. (2014), 'Promotion de l'interculturel par le film dans la classe de langue au 21e siècle: une approche multimodale', in A. Lachkar (ed.), *Langues Cultures et Médias en Méditerranée*, 222–36, Paris: L'Harmattan.

Viebrock, B., ed. (2016), *Feature Films in English Language Teaching*, Tübingen: Narr Francke Attempto.

Wenger, E., R. McDermott and W. Snyder (2002), *Cultivating Communities of Practice*, Boston, MA: Harvard University Business School Press.

Woore, R., L. Molway and E. Macaro (2022), 'Keeping Sight of the Big Picture: A Critical Response to Ofsted's 2021 Curriculum Research Review for Languages', *The Language Learning Journal*, 50 (22): 146–55.

4

Bridging the Gaps Left by Boredom and Sociocultural Misperceptions: Does Foreign-Film Pedagogy Hold the Answer?

Mark Goodwin

Introduction

Despite reassurances from the British government that the number of MFL students in England has seen a gradual increase in recent years, there are 45 per cent fewer GCSE MFL students overall in England (and Wales and Northern Ireland) than in 2002 (Long and Danechi 2018; Jeffreys 2019). Enquiry into potential sources to blame uncovers a plethora of large-scale concerns. The difficulty level continues to be a significant barrier (Weale 2013). Simultaneously, achievement in lessons is ranked lower in MFL when compared to other subjects (Ofsted 2015, cited in Long and Danechi 2018: 9). Harsh grading, particularly at A-Level, lingers on as a core obstruction (Bawden 2019). Similarly, the advantages of the EBacc remain highly questionable (BBC News 2011; Long and Danechi 2018: 3). Finally, the impact of Brexit is deemed by many to be significantly damaging for MFL learning (Tinsley 2019: 18; Collen 2021), not least due to the UK's departure from the highly successful Erasmus Programme, although a new scheme – the Turing Scheme – has subsequently been launched by the British government. Moreover, the DfE's (2021) GCSE overhaul proposals put forward in March of that year have come as a great disappointment for many MFL educators due in part to a continued failure to address cultural learning and associated assessment adequately.

Spanish, meanwhile, at further and higher education levels, has enjoyed a relatively healthy growth over the past few decades. One of the most notable factors in the enhancement of the subject's popularity can be attributed to the evolvement and rising popularity of the study of Spanish-speaking cinema.

Davies (2010: 1) observes that the previous two decades have seen a rise to greater prominence of Spanish film studies. At the same time, young people are engaging more and in greater numbers with technological advances in popular media and are developing the skills and confidence in navigating spaces, such as those afforded by film (or video, more generally, particularly via the internet). Despite this, Ofsted (2011, cited in Long and Danechi 2018: 8) highlights a lack of intercultural understanding in the majority of MFL lessons, because students do not have good opportunities to develop it. This chapter captures the core findings of a PhD project completed in February 2020 that examines whether film pedagogy (related to all MFL, often using Spanish examples as a demonstration of success and specific analysis) is best placed to address and alleviate the obstacles outlined above. Specifically, the chapter outlines arguments in favour of film studies to combat the barriers in the current MFL curriculum content, long-standing issues with motivation, and inadequate intercultural exposure and understanding. The first section highlights several areas where statutory guidance and specifications fail to provide GCSE and A-Level students with a sufficiently consistent and broad curriculum related to film pedagogy. The second section reflects on where foreign-film studies aptly address the much-cited problem of boredom and poor motivation related to MFL learning. In large part, this relates to a combination of unstimulating material and resources, and the well-documented perception of languages being so challenging to learn – arguably, a significant (mis)conception that, in turn, deters and disengages students prematurely, where they then rapidly (incorrectly) associate a lack of confidence with a lack of interest.

Film in the MFL curriculum in England

Although limited in some areas, in recent times there was significant scope for learning MFL through film, according to the MFL curriculum in England, as referenced via DfE documentation and two of the most popular exam boards for England's GCSE and A-Level specifications, AQA and Edexcel. The 2008 framework for KS3 specifies the necessity of 'appreciating the richness and diversity of other cultures [and] recognising that there are different ways of seeing the world' (DfE 2007: 165). The 2014 national curriculum for KS3 adds that students should 'understand and respond to [...] a variety of authentic sources' (DfE 2014: 98). Despite these references, it fails to include any direct mention of film. There is, however, some direct referencing within core KS3 resources. Describing different film genres and giving opinions on them is a common topic at Year 8/Year 9 (12- and 13-year-olds), and appears in many popular KS3 MFL textbooks, such as *Mira 2* (Heinemann) for Spanish. Such topic areas and activities provide a worthy opportunity to make use of clips to initially expose (KS3) students to directors, actors, regions of the target-language countries, national history, etc. The reformed AQA GCSE specification (AQA 2016a: 10) explicitly mentions 'cinema' within 'free-time activities'. The equivalent Edexcel specification (Edexcel 2016a: 8) explicitly refers to 'film' (and television) within the context of 'Identity and culture'. The same specification notes that students should 'respond to a rich range of authentic [...] material' and 'develop awareness and understanding of the culture and identity of the countries and communities where the language is spoken' (Edexcel 2016a: 6).

The reformed AQA A-Level specification (2017: 10) states that there is a 'focus on how the Spanish-speaking society has been shaped socially and culturally', and that studies should include 'aspects of artistic life' via the use of authentic spoken resources. It is suggested to link certain topic areas with films from the prescribed list, although direct links are not included. There is the option to study two literary works or one literary work and one film. Examiners' reports from the first two years' exam series (2018–19) suggest that one of each is by far the most popular model, which confirms the demand for film pedagogy at this level, at the very least to complement and offer an alternative to the study of literature. If the study of a film is chosen, students complete an essay within Paper 2, worth 20 per cent of the A-Level (10 per cent per essay). Students can also explore Spanish film within 'artistic culture'. The most specific reference to film in the topic-based work is 'film stars'; however, there are additional listed topics where film provides an ideal basis for contextual study related to 'traditions and customs', 'cultural heritage', etc. The reformed Edexcel specification is largely similar. Paper 2 requires students to write an essay on a film and a book (or two books). Students should 'engage critically with intellectually stimulating [...] films' (Edexcel 2016b: 7). Students are also encouraged to 'develop knowledge about matters central to the society and culture, past and present' (Edexcel 2016b: 7). It is evident that KS3 teachers and students must rely on their own ideas and those within published resources for engaging with film in MFL lessons. This is unlikely to encourage educators who are sceptical about film study to explore its pedagogical possibilities, as professional experience suggests that school priorities are naturally given to subjects, skills and topics explicitly highlighted within official schemes of work. At GCSE, there is a tradition of topics offering good scope for the inclusion of film and, previously, teachers took the opportunity afforded by the controlled assessments (legacy GCSE) to describe and review film plots, characters, etc. (AQA 2014). There is yet to be, however, a component of the GCSE that is explicitly dedicated to the study of film, or any cultural text, apart from brief, isolated extracts of literary sources within the reading papers; an issue that is unlikely to improve, should the most recent DfE (2021) proposals be approved. This prevents students from having the opportunity to build the necessary skills related to film analysis which often forms a significant part of the A-Level and, indeed, MFL degrees. At A-Level, the two exam boards discussed appear to be largely on the same page, seemingly directed by the DfE and Ofqual. Film study remains optional, but has proven to be popular, and is able to enhance deeply several aspects of learning about 'Spanish'. This overview confirms that the opportunity for film-based work is very much there at all levels of MFL education, although it is much more directly referenced at KS5. This raises several questions about an imbalanced curriculum, conflicting perspectives on the importance and place of film as a learning tool and, consequently, how well students and teachers are prepared for the demands of foreign-film analysis at higher levels.

At the beginning of the twenty-first century, much discussion surrounded the worrying fact that nine out of ten students in the UK stop learning a language at 16 years of age (Hawkins 2002; Jeffreys 2019). The Nuffield Report (2000) warned that the UK was heading towards being a minority clinging to monolingualism. Earlier publications, such as CILT's *Thirty Years of Language Teaching*, had placed the blame on the MFL curriculum, which had a 'badly leaking roof' and 'insecure foundations' (cited in Hawkins 2002: 23–4). Similarly, Pachler and Field (2001: 303) criticized 'the emphasis on formal grammatical accuracy characterising GCE and CSE examination syllabi', which 'has been said to have contributed to a lack of pupils' success in MFL and a lack of popularity of the subject'. Such comments suggest that, for some time, there has been a dominant focus on linguistic accuracy and significantly less on more appealing topics, such as cinema. Such aspects of studying MFL are often regarded as the most enjoyable, where students become substantially more motivated to engage in other tasks connected to the language after the study of the film(s), particularly if interlinked with history, society or culture. It is fair to say that the renewed emphasis on culture within the cultural topic of the legacy A-Level arrived without any directed provision for preparation at GCSE (AQA 2014); a problem that continues, where neither the legacy specifications, the reformed series nor the current proposals include any candid encouragement to include Spanish film study (Adams and Badwens 2022). Thorogood and King (1991: 2) had earlier pointed out that with the 'A/AS level being much less teacher-centred and instead reliant on more independent learning, it seems that [...] the GCSE [is] fail[ing] to prepare the learner for the next stage up'. With no units specifically focused on Spanish culture, history or aspects of society in the GCSE course, it is both illogical and unfair that students (and teachers) have then been expected to succeed with such demands at the next Key Stage.

Researchers have long posited a lack of confidence as one of the main disincentives of studying MFL post-GCSE (Horwitz and Young 1991; Arnold 1999). In his role as Education Officer at the BBC, Fawkes (cited in Chambers 2001: 72) notes that the combination of visuals and audio 'reassures the learners that they are able to understand the foreign language'. The incorporation of film (or any visually supported listening exercise), then, can help alleviate the perception of listening as one of the most challenging skills. There are also grounds to claim that listening to understand dialogue in a film has an obvious and defined purpose – that is, to understand the story and the characters within it. This broad exercise sits apart from many other traditional listening exercises, often more transactional in style, where the principal objective may be to get as many marks as possible or 'fill in the blanks', for example. Is it not time to introduce some form of moving image media, feature film or otherwise, to the assessed listening component at GCSE and A-Level?

The study of foreign cinema not only provides an ideal platform for broader studies related to literature, fictional narrative and the learning processes involved in moving image media, but it also provides an ideal basis for language enhancement and an ideal context on which to base history-, society- or culture-based work. To cite the most commercially and, arguably, critically successful Spanish director of all time, Smith (2000: 194) observes 'Pedro Almodóvar's increasing engagement with social issues', while Allinson (2001: 48) notes a change in the Spanish society portrayed in the director's films after the 'hedonistic 1980s'. A study of Almodóvar's later films is likely to give a stronger impression of a modern, complex but cohesive society, where people from a variety of backgrounds and experiences work together and largely successfully.

Although the written word has for some time no longer been considered by many as the only element in literacy education (Sherman 2003; Knobel and Lankshear 2008; Álvarez 2009; Herrero and Valbuena 2010), statutory requirements and government-led initiatives continue to disregard the vast potential of the moving image, including film, in literacy education and, indeed, in improving literacy standards (see Ofsted 2013). Therefore, it has been a disappointment that the National Strategies (1997–2011) (DfE 2011), introduced by the then Labour Government, omitted film or any form of media or the arts non-specific to the written word from its direction. It is equally disappointing that the current national curriculum (DfE 2014), implemented by the Conservatives, does not offer any substantial encouragement to incorporate audiovisual resources within the development of literacy in MFL. However, it does stipulate that 'the writing [students] do should include narratives, explanations, descriptions, comparisons, summaries and evaluations' (DfE 2014: 10), all of which lend themselves very well to foreign-film analysis and critique. Meanwhile, the A-Level has for many years expected students to learn to 'communicate confidently, clearly and effectively in the language for a range of purposes' (AQA (legacy) 2014: 19). The reformed A-Level (AQA 2016b: online) requires students to 'engage critically [with] films [...] in the original language, developing an appreciation of sophisticated and creative uses of the language and understanding them within their cultural and social context'.

In 1999, the BFI (2004: 4) stated that being literate in the present day means students attaining 'a wider range of critical and creative competencies than has been adequate in the past'. At the launch of the Charter for Media Literacy in 2005, Anthony Minghella (cited by Available Light Advisory 2012: 6) remarked that, considering 'the way in which moving images can manipulate us, allow us to inhabit many differing points of view, take us on journeys to other times, places and cultures [...], surely it's time for our education system to hold the teaching of the sentence we watch as no less important and crucial than the teaching of the sentence we read'. The Media Literacy Task Force (cited by the BFI 2013: 6) provides a model that centres on 'the three C's'; critical, cultural and creative, praising the popularity of 'TV, DVDs and videos [for ensuring that] four- and five-year-olds arrive in school with a wider grasp of [such] key concepts [and with an] understanding of narrative, genre, character, setting and time' (see also Available Light Advisory 2012: 8). Such competences are of significant benefit to the early development of essential skills in literacy (across all story-based art forms) needed at primary level, thus providing a solid basis for learning at secondary. Questions aimed at developing students' ability to read a film (BFI 2013: 6) are reminiscent of the GCSE in MFL subject content, where students are expected to 'deduce meaning from [...] authentic material' and to 'draw inferences in context and recognise implicit meaning where appropriate' (DfE 2015: 6). Using film in the MFL classroom carries benefits to fulfil such statutory expectations, although, as pointed out previously, the official subject content fails to make any mention of film or the moving image. When students are exposed to films and filmmakers that they would perhaps not otherwise know about, they are empowered to 'engage with the widest possible range of people, stories and cultures' (BFI 2013: 6). Specific sections of the subject content (DfE 2015: 3) touch upon such areas as key to learning at GCSE, for example, where 'students should develop their ability and ambition to communicate with native speakers', and where the GCSE course should 'encourage [students] to step beyond familiar cultural boundaries and develop new ways of seeing the world'. Therefore, the DfE guidance cited above and, indeed, the most recent GCSE proposals (DfE 2021) focusing on vocabulary, phonics and grammar continue to cause confusion and a lack of confidence for teachers and students of MFL.

The ability to be both visually literate and visually critical is a vehicle for raised attainment (BFI 2013). Marsh and Bearne (2008: 20) note further positive evidence citing that, two weeks after completing a unit of film-related work, the number of children writing in one class at Level 4 (the expected level for their age group at the time) had risen from 29 per cent to 75 per cent. During this time, the children had extended their vocabulary and were able to write for a variety of purposes with greater confidence. Such an impact has resonance for GCSE and A-Level assessments, where many pupils especially struggle under the pressure of assessed speaking. Some of this is due to a general lack of confidence to speak in a foreign language, although with the removal or reduction of the amount of direct, fixed-answer questioning offered by discussing a film, students are given greater flexibility to use the language they are most comfortable with. A vital attribute of the critical analysis of any artistic product lies in an understanding of there being 'no right or wrong answer'. If this is accepted, then there is a good argument for such a message being made even clearer to help reduce the declining numbers of MFL students referred to in the introduction. Results and examiners' reports from the reformed GCSE suggest that students are losing marks primarily because of not understanding the bullet points. However, an additional problem is that, within legacy and reformed specifications, pieces of writing have often been based around overused and unstimulating topics, such as 'daily routine' or 'describing my bedroom'. From professional experience, film reviews, character descriptions and alternative plot endings make for some of the most interesting, and often, best quality, examples of written and spoken work.

Being visually literate allows for a greater understanding of other forms of media and other forms of literacy in the fields of cultural studies, art and literature. In a world surrounded by so many complex forms of imagery and sound, the development of visual literacy skills is essential to interpret the vast range of visual metaphors presented to audiences via multiple forms of media (Forceville 2016). Metaphors serve many functions in prose and poetry and can therefore serve similar functions when using film as a teaching tool. They clarify complex thoughts, bring vividness to abstractions, magnify a thought for dramatic effect, and gain insight (Champoux 1999). A vital function of metaphor is the expression of imagination and stimulating imaginative images in a reader or listener; 'a metaphor does not distort the facts described; it offers a new way of experiencing those facts' (Hawkes 1972: 34). The encouragement of imagination, the incorporation of novel teaching and learning methods, and the cementing of information in students' memories are, arguably, three of the most highly sought-after objectives for MFL teachers. Combined with the evidence presented so far, it can be concluded that teaching students to interpret artistic strategies such as metaphors, as part of developing their skills in visual and film literacy, is likely to be both a stimulating and highly effective strategy for the development of students' understanding of varying perceptions of what constitutes 'Spanish', 'French', 'German', etc. as languages, as nationalities and as academic subjects. It has been argued that the study of authentic visual media and, in particular, target-language cinema, is well equipped to fill significant learning gaps left by such omissions, in a subject which is meant to inspire students to access, interpret and enjoy all aspects of (inter)national languages, cultures and identities.

Film pedagogy as a tool to enhance motivation

Since the 1970s, educationalists experienced in using film as a teaching tool have urged its adoption by others (Maynard 1971, 1977; Culkin 1970; Wegner 1977). Films are a comfortable, familiar medium to contemporary students; one that can keep students' interest in the theories and concepts under discussion; 'in more than a figurative sense, theories and concepts "leap from the screen"' (Champoux 1999: 11). The power of media has shifted from communication to education to the point where it has become an 'essential tool in the teaching of foreign languages' (Álvarez 2009: 1). In fact, there are few other art forms of which teachers can be so confident that pupils will already have substantial experience with stories in audiovisual format from a young age. The result is that by the time they get to school, children have gained a repertoire of skills for interpreting narrative texts, such as inference, prediction, recognition of genres and character types, and the ways in which narratives can manipulate time (Bazalgette 2009).

In addition to gaining the aforementioned skills via traditional forms of storytelling, children now gain the vast majority of their awareness and understanding of narrative and culture via screens. The New London Group (1996: 10) highlights the increasing invasion of private spaces by mass media culture, global commodity culture, communications and information networks, and the collective impact on (child) audiences. In the modern-day world, childhood cultures are made up of interwoven narratives and commodities, including the internet. As a result, teachers find that monocultural and linguistic messages are losing power and relevance as they compete with these global narratives.

Collectively, the above claims point towards the necessity to establish how these various texts are best negotiated, understood and exploited within education. Increased exposure globally to the moving image underlines a growing need to create a more 'cineliterate' audience (Bazalgette 2006: 1). The BFI (1999: 2) predicted previously that the importance of recognizing critical and creative moving image skills would be a key element of literacy in the twenty-first century, given the then existing 'lack of recognition of the potential of moving image education [MIE] across the curricula'.

More recent evidence points to film's motivational factor due to it being something of a novelty and/or something different to the norm. Conversely, it may be considered a medium with which students are comfortable and highly familiar. The combination of novelty, comfort and familiarity constitutes an excellent asset for teachers as it 'stimulates' and motivates students in the learning process (The New London Group 1996; Bazalgette 2009). Learning through media, such as film, involves, engages and motivates students, and gives them control over their own learning (Wilkinson, Head and McConnell 2010; Available Light Advisory 2007; BFI 2013).

Setting the scene for how foreign cinema can be an ideal platform for linguistic development, Ortí, García and Bendriss (2011: 1) highlight the dominance of the visual image in today's world and suggest that the use of visual imagery is likely to appeal to a younger audience. The authors claim that film can increase communication among students by promoting the exchange of opinions, interests and personal experiences. They take inspiration from Ontoria (2007) and Urpí (2000) in classifying cinema as a fitting teaching resource because it influences the development of imagination, sensitivity and the psyche of the spectator by combining linguistic, sound and visual elements. English subtitled versions can be used in the classroom to ensure that the dialogue and overall content of the film(s) are grasped as well as possible. However, subtitles also have the potential to enhance a range of basic language-learning skills. Hearing new words while reading the English translation offers itself well to a general expansion of vocabulary and expression. The combination of foreign audio and English subtitles is direct training and practice in translation, a significant requirement of the reformed GCSE. The removal and/or manipulation of subtitles can be used to assess listening progress, whereby students have to either demonstrate understanding from the audio alone or add the correct subtitles (by interpreting the audio), as noted by Sánchez-Requena and Alonso-Pérez (2018) or Sánchez-Requena (2018).

The experiences afforded by foreign cinema study encompass a wide variety of linguistic, cultural, social and historical references via a multimodal relationship between the spectator and the work. As noted by Stephens (2001: 2), with its ability to pack a two-hour period with plot, emotion, drama, events, images and ideas, a film draws attention to ethical boundaries, conceptual frameworks, national memory and identity, and the use of language and idioms. Films can be regarded as 'a globalised discipline' (one that can usefully be split into three categories: linguistic, paraverbal and cultural (Castiñeiras and Herrero 1998: 1). These three categories set out clear areas of study and provide a valuable framework for the planning of learning objectives in relation to foreign-film analysis; studying foreign films is not just about one specific element, such as 'language', but rather it involves a combination of a number of elements that include various forms of communication (such as looks or gestures), learning about Spanish cinema as a national art form, and the integration of cross-curricular work (Castiñeiras and Herrero 1998: 1–2) (my own translation). *El laberinto del fauno* (Guillermo del Toro 2006), a dominant work on the Spanish A-Level course, provides a clear context on which broader and stimulating studies of genre and any form of (inter)cultural mechanism can conveniently be executed via the study of foreign film in MFL.

Beyond the visual, other senses are stimulated within the development of literacy through foreign-film study. Film is a multisensory medium that offers students more than listening comprehension (Swaffar and Vlatten 1997: 175). It is an incorrect assumption that the principal purpose of incorporating foreign cinema in the MFL is to enhance listening skills, despite the clear benefits to listening. The many different cognitive and critical functions involved in the film viewing process extend the visual and the audio into the development of multiliteracies, inherent to foreign-film pedagogy, as film is 'multimodal in nature' (Pegrum, Hartley and Wechtler 2005: 55). Film brings together a large variety of modes, increasingly important in the 'new media age' (Kress 2010: 30).

The growing necessity, and demand, for students to develop skills in recognizing, understanding and interpreting the various elements involved in multisensory-, multimodal- and multiliteracy-based processes in the technology-age society is highly evident.

Films for intercultural appreciation

MFL studies naturally lend themselves exceptionally well to learning about the various elements that define, evolve or, perhaps, distort perceptions of national identity. Moreover, as Chan and Herrero (2010: 11) note, 'films are perfect vehicles for introducing students to different types of popular culture and engaging them with critical questions about the relationship between information and power through the critical analysis of socio-political issues and intercultural relationships'. Additionally, foreign-film study facilitates 'intercultural communicative competence' (Byram 1997; Herrero, Fuentes and Doblas 2014; Tomlinson 2019; Herrero 2019). Research from the past two decades has pinpointed cultural learning (via film) as a successful method for developing skills in communication within and across countries. As Pachler and Field (2001: 147) note, for example, the ability to understand the cultural context of foreign language use can be 'key in leading to effective communication in the target language'. It is the images of cinema that allow for the comprehension of linguistic messages and the development of sociolinguistic and pragmatic competence (Ortí, García and Bendriss 2011: 1). The development of such skills begins with the unique property of film to make one see and grasp things which only the cinema is privileged to communicate (Kracauer 1973, cited in Champoux 1999: 1). Collectively, such observations not only support arguments in favour of foreign film being a substantial resource to help linguistic development, but they also provide an important reminder of additional elements involved in domestic and international communication.

Despite this, many experts signal inadequacies in the teaching and learning of foreign culture within MFL studies. Byram (cited in Swarbrick 2002: 84) signals that the effect of language teaching on British students' perceptions of and attitudes towards other cultures has been 'negligible'. Castiñeiras and Herrero (1998: 1) speak of the 'complexity of cultural experience', supporting the notion that culture is a hugely broad and diverse subject, particularly when attributed to a whole nation (such as France) or group of nations (such as French-speaking countries) or, indeed, the UK. Culture is also remarkably complex to teach to a foreign audience due to the difficulty of defining it, partly because of the fluidity of its actual meaning. Many have argued that foreign-film pedagogy supplies excellent potential to expose students to varying aspects of foreign culture directly. Ortí, García and Bendriss (2011: 2) specify 'the knowledge of customs of "material culture" (clothes, housing, objects etc.) which are presented within the storyline'. Stephens (2001: 2), however, advises that educators have an obligation to move students beyond a 'mere tourist knowledge of foreign cultures'. Similarly, Pachler and Field (2001: 147) summarize that the development of cultural awareness is essential to understand that there are other ways of life in order to tackle stereotypes. Cinema is especially recommendable in the teaching of a foreign language because it 'ties together the elements of language and culture [in a] "natural way"' (Santos 2007, cited in Ortí, García and Bendriss 2011: 1). Nevertheless, educators are urged to proceed with caution and not to make assumptions when it comes to their students' ability to perceive any aspect of a foreign film in a 'natural way' or, indeed, to see fiction film itself as 'natural', as it is, of course, a scripted creation. Oliveras (2000: 38) labels this capability as 'intercultural competence', which he defines as 'the ability of a person to act in an appropriate and flexible way when faced with actions and expectations of people from other cultures'. The extent to which students are interculturally competent or, indeed, equipped to process a combination of linguistic and intercultural elements cannot be assumed.

The central concept of intercultural literacy, and its inherently associated benefits for language understanding and acquisition, is explicitly referenced in the CEFR (Council of Europe 2001: 22: 98). It is also interesting to note the CEFR's more recent updates on the processes of 'pluricultural competences', including online interaction and responses to cultural texts (including film) (Council of Europe 2018). Echoing the implicit value of directly combining language and cultural learning, Ortí, García and Bendriss (2011: 2) declare that cinema allows for the development of communicative competence and intercultural consciousness, as it 'permits the understanding of similarities and differences between one's own culture and the culture represented in the film'. Much recent investigation has centred on the concept of 'interculturality', rather than simply 'culture'. Fuentes (in Herrero, Fuentes and Doblas 2014) suggests that the main purpose of showing foreign films to non-mother-tongue students is to expose them to the 'other' – that is, the target-language country itself. Fuentes draws attention to how the intercultural value of cinema lies in its unique ability to capture multiple aspects of culture at once, and indeed, the complexities of cross-culture identities. In terms of how intercultural conflicts may be taught or incorporated into classroom activities, Fuentes (in Herrero, Fuentes and Doblas

2014) puts forward strategies of 'contextualization', 'description', 'analysis' and 'students' own recording'; and he concludes that interculturality allows for the 'break-through of linguistic, economic and anthropological barriers', and that 'film provides one of the most useful models for this breakthrough'.

Baddock (1996) notes that cinema offers an ideal means of introducing real-life situations and language. However, the author's claim fails to sufficiently define what is meant by 'real life' and such discussion raises vital questions about students' ability to process any concept of a foreign, or domestic, nation-related 'reality'. It presents the equally crucial question(s) of to what extent students are equipped to comprehend perceptions of reality and, indeed, any forms of theorized and intended cinematic realism. A pursuit to uncover aspects of 'real' France/Germany/Spain, or what the French, Germans or Spaniards might 'really' be like, is often synonymously associated with the incorporation of so-called 'authentic materials'. These authentic resources, such as films, offer teachers the opportunity to expose pupils to 'material produced for "real", out-of-classroom contexts and for specific purposes' (Pachler and Field 2001: 147). Film may be as close to 'real' France/Germany/Spain or French/German/Spanish as some students can get. While most films are fiction, they can offer powerful experiences that students are unlikely to have in a classroom (Champoux 1999: 12). A further reason for developing students' cultural awareness is to learn to empathize with speakers of other languages (Pachler and Field 2001: 148).

Studies of national cinemas are of great benefit when attempting to demonstrate, explain or better understand 'other' nations and peoples – at least, that is, from the subjective perspective of the filmmaker(s). However, it is essential to consider where and to what extent particular filmmakers and particular works, both individually and collectively, create the image of the nation itself, viewed from both within and outside of its borders. Established auteurs and younger generations of filmmakers have harnessed cinematic language towards a commentary on the nation-state and the politics of historical and cultural memory. Spanish filmmaker, Pedro Almodóvar – to return to him – has become an international trademark, whose work and success spanning Europe, Asia and the Americas has further served to generate interest in Spanish film products (Delgado 2013: 1–2). In which case, Almodóvar may be to thank for some of the extended academic interest in Spanish cultural studies at both school and university level in recent years. With the popularity of other modern languages, most notably German, in fairly consistent decline, it is more significant than ever to look carefully at all factors behind such shifts in subject choices, and the associated concerns for the future of British linguists, arguably even more so in a post-Brexit context. It is pertinent to consider the debate spanning the same period highlighting the specific implications of popular Spanish works for interpretations of national identity, for example. In the context of Spain, discourse has largely focused on the works' content, artistic designs, genres, the professional and personal identities of the filmmakers, and their transnational identity appeal. Most interestingly, often such discourse is tied directly to perceptions of a nation that had for so long struggled to freely portray itself in all artistic forms due to the heavy censorship imposed by the Francoist dictatorship. On the reverse side, there is a significant and increasing demand for Spanish culture – including from foreign audiences – to contain broader and more diverse thematic preoccupations than those offered currently.

Conclusion

Recent, current and proposed policies, statutory guidance and specification details contain admirable intentions. Still, they expose a host of inconsistencies and significant weaknesses in cross-Key-Stage transition. Much can be learned from the relative success story of Spanish and, in particular, the extent of its increasing popularity attributed to increased global interest in Spain's national cinema and wider popular culture. Similarly, the successes of both the legacy and reformed A-Levels' attempts to enhance students' (inter)cultural awareness via, first, the (legacy) cultural topic and, then, the 'Paper 2' (reformed A-Level) requirements to have studied a film (and a book, or two books) ought to be emulated at GCSE, where the continued insistence on the comprehension and production of (largely transactional) language remains an unhelpful and discouraging obsession.

MFL remains behind in terms of appealing to and directly targeting today's moving image media-reliant/proficient younger generation. The facilitation of multimodal and multiskilled MFL learners is limited by overly challenging, language-central assessments, instead of capitalizing on the vast range of multimedia cultural texts available. It is hoped that this chapter encourages teachers to embark on their own foreign-film pedagogy journey to fill the gaps left by the inconsistencies/inadequacies of the curriculum and appropriately address the (difficulty-associated) boredom factor. In a post-Brexit environment, and looking ahead to a post-pandemic world, the values of international engagement, intercultural literacy and an educational strategy far beyond politics have never been so important. Not only may such commitments provide a vehicle to explore concerns regarding future political, economic and diplomatic relationships, but most importantly, they also ensure that learners are provided with the most appropriate and fruitful platforms on which to base their own interpretations about British, French/German/Spanish, European, simply 'foreign' identities. Film pedagogy in MFL does not provide the only key to unlocking each of the aspirations explored above, but, if sufficiently appreciated and well executed, it does provide at least some of the solutions to the ever-present conundrum of languages education in the UK.

References

Adams, R., and A. Badwens (2022), 'Plan for Pupils to Learn 1,700 Words for Language GCSEs Gets Go-Ahead', *The Guardian*, 11 January. Available online: https://www.theguardian.com/education/2022/jan/14/plan-pupils-learn-1700-words-language-gcse-go-ahead.

Allinson, M. (2001), *A Spanish Labyrinth: The Films of Pedro Almodóvar*, London: I.B. Tauris.

Álvarez Mennuto, A. (2009), '¿Cómo puedo usar material audiovisual auténtico con principiantes?', in R. Bueno Hudson, M. Abad and A. Valbuena (eds), *Actas de las II Jornadas Didácticas del Instituto Cervantes*, Manchester: Instituto Cervantes.

AQA (2014), 'GCSE [legacy] Spanish specification'. [No longer available online.]

AQA (2016a), 'GCSE Spanish Specification 8698. Specification for First Teaching in 2016', *AQA*. Available online:https://filestore.aqa.org.uk/resources/spanish/specifications/AQA-8698-SP-2016.pdf.

AQA (2016b), 'A-Level Spanish. Scheme of Assessment', *AQA*. Available online: https://www.aqa.org.uk/subjects/languages/as-and-a-level/spanish-7692/scheme-of-assessment.

AQA (2017), 'A-Level Spanish Specification 7692. Specification for First teaching in 2016', *AQA*. Available online: https://filestore.aqa.org.uk/resources/spanish/specifications/AQA-7692-SP-2016.pdf.

Arnold, J., ed. (1999), *Affect in Language Learning*, Cambridge: Cambridge University Press.

Available Light Advisory (2012), 'Integrating Film into Education – Advocacy Report', *BFI*. Available online: https://www.bfi.org.uk/sites/bfi.org.uk/files/downloads/film-21st-century-literacy-advocacy-report.pdf.

Baddock, B. (1996) *Using Films in the English Classroom*, London: Prentice Hall.

Bawden, A. (2019), 'Modern Language Teaching "under Threat from Tough Exams"', *The Guardian*, 11 May. Available online: https://www.theguardian.com/education/2019/may/11/modern-language-teaching-under-threat-from-tough-exams.

Bazalgette, C. (2006), *Making Movies Matter -Seven Years On*, London: BFI.
Bazalgette, C. (2009), *Impacts of Moving Image Education: A Summary of Research*, Glasgow: Scottish Screen.
BBC News (2011), 'Divided opinion: English Baccalaureate', *BBC News*, 12 January. Available online: https://www.bbc.co.uk/news/education-12160738.
British Film Institute (1999), *Making Movies Matter*, London: BFI.
British Film Institute (2004), *Making Movies Matter: A Wider Literacy*, London: BFI.
British Film Institute (2013), *Reframing Literacy*, London: BFI.
Byram, M. (1997), *Teaching and Assessing Intercultural Communicative Competence*, Bristol: Multilingual Matters.
Castiñeiras, A., and C. Herrero (1998), 'Más allá de las imágenes: El cine como recurso en las clases de español', in M. Franco, C. Soler, J. de Cos, M. Rivas and F. Ruiz (eds), *Nuevas perspectivas en la enseñanza del español como lengua extranjera*, 375–83, Cádiz: ASELE and Universidad de Cádiz.
Chambers, G. (2001), *Reflections on Motivation*, London: CILT.
Champoux, J. E. (1999), 'Film as a Teaching Resource', *Journal of Management Inquiry*, 8 (2): 240–51.
Chan, D., and C. Herrero (2010), *A Teachers' Toolkit for Educators Wanting to Teach Languages Using Film in the Classroom*, Manchester: Cornerhouse.
Collen, I. (2021), 'Language Teaching in Primary and Secondary Schools in England', *British Council*. Available online: https://www.britishcouncil.org/sites/default/files/language_trends_2021_report.pdf.
Council of Europe (2011), *The Common European Framework for Languages*. Available online: http://www.coe.int/t/dg4/linguistic/Source/Framework_EN.pdf.
Council of Europe (2018), *Common European Framework of Reference for Languages: Teaching, Learning, Assessment: Companion Volume with New Descriptors*. Available online: https://rm.coe.int/cefr-companion-volume-with-new-descriptors-2018/1680787989.
Culkin, J. M. (1970), 'Films Deliver', in A. Schillaci and J. M. Culkin (eds), *Films Deliver: Teaching Creatively with Film*, 19–29, New York: Citation Press.
Davies, A. (2010), *Spain on Screen: Developments in Contemporary Spanish Cinema*, Basingstoke: Palgrave Macmillan.
Delgado, M. (2013), 'Introduction', in M. Delgado and R. Fiddian (eds), *Spanish Cinema 1973–2010: Auteurism, Politics, Landscape and Memory*, 1–20, Manchester: Manchester University Press.
Department for Education (2007), 'Key Stage 3 National Curriculum for Modern Foreign Languages', *The National Archives*, 15 February 2011. Available online: https://webarchive.nationalarchives.gov.uk/20110215120931/http:/curriculum.qcda.gov.uk/uploads/QCA-07-3340-p_MFL_KS3_tcm8-405.pdf.
Department for Education (2011), 'The National Strategies 1997–2011: A Brief Summary of the Impact and Effectiveness of the National Strategies'. Available online: https://assets.publishing.service.gov.uk/government/uploads/system/uploads/attachment_data/file/175408/DFE-00032-2011.pdf.

Department for Education (2014), 'The National Curriculum in England: Key Stages 3 and 4 Framework Document'. Available online: https://assets.publishing.service.gov.uk/government/uploads/system/uploads/attachment_data/file/381754/SECONDARY_national_curriculum.pdf.

Department for Education (2015), 'Modern Foreign Languages GCSE Subject Content'. Available online: https://assets.publishing.service.gov.uk/government/uploads/system/uploads/attachment_data/file/485567/GCSE_subject_content_modern_foreign_langs.pdf.

Department for Education (2021), 'GCSE MFL Subject Content Review'. Available online: https://consult.education.gov.uk/ebacc-and-arts-and-humanities-team/gcse-mfl-subject-content-review/supporting_documents/GCSE%20MFL%20subject%20content%20document.pdf.

Edexcel (2016a), 'GCSE Spanish Specification', *Pearson Edexcel*. Available online: https://qualifications.pearson.com/content/dam/pdf/GCSE/Spanish/2016/specification-and-sample-assessments/Specification-Pearson-Edexcel-Level-1-Level-2-GCSE-9-1-Spanish.pdf.

Edexcel (2016b), 'A-Level Spanish Specification', *Pearson Edexcel*. Available online: https://qualifications.pearson.com/content/dam/pdf/A%20Level/Spanish/2016/Specification%20and%20sample%20assessments/Specification_GCE_A_level_L3_in_Spanish.pdf.

Forceville, C. (2016). 'Visual and Multimodal Metaphor in Film: Charting the Field', in K. Fahlenbrach (ed.), *Embodied Metaphors in Film, Television and Video Games: Cognitive Approaches*, 17–32, London: Routledge.

Hawkes, T. (1972), *Metaphor*, London: Methuen.

Hawkins, E. (2002), 'Drop Out from Language Study at 16+: A Historical Perspective', in A. Swarbrick (ed.) (2002), *Teaching Modern Foreign Languages in Secondary Schools*, 23–43, London: Routledge.

Herrero, C. (2019), 'Conclusion', in C. Herrero and I. Vanderschelden (eds), *Using Film and Media in the Language Classroom: Reflections on Research-led Teaching*, 188–97, Bristol: Multilingual Matters.

Herrero, C., R. Fuentes and B. Doblas (2014), 'Uso didáctico del cine en el aula', Summer Course, Fundación Ortega y Gasset, Madrid (7–9 July).

Herrero, C., and A. Valbuena (2010), 'Trailers y teasers en la clases de español', in M. Abad, R. Bueno Hudson and A. Valbuena (eds), *III Jornadas Didácticas de ELE Instituto Cervantes de Manchester/ 3rd Conference of Teaching Spanish as a Foreign Language*, 67–72, Manchester: Instituto Cervantes.

Horwitz, E. K., and D. J. Young (1991), *Language Anxiety: From Theory and Research to Classroom Implications*, Englewood Cliffs, NJ: Prentice Hall.

Jeffreys, B. (2019), 'Language Learning: German and French Drop by Half in UK Schools', *BBC*, 27 February. Available online: https://www.bbc.co.uk/news/education-47334374.

Knobel, M., and C. Lankshear (2008), *Digital Literacies: Concepts, Policies and Practices*, New York: Peter Lang.

Kress, G. (2010), *Multimodality. A Social Semiotic Approach to Contemporary Communication*, London: Routledge.

Long, R., and S. Danechi (2018), 'Language Teaching in Schools (England)', House of Commons Briefing Paper (No. 07388), *House of Commons Library*. Available online: https://researchbriefings.parliament.uk/ResearchBriefing/Summary/CBP-7388#fullreport.

Marsh, J., and E. Bearne (2008), *Moving Literacy On: Evaluation of the BFI Lead Practitioner Scheme for Moving Image Media Literacy*, Sheffield: The University of Sheffield/UK Literacy Association.

Maynard, R. A. (1971), *The Celluloid Curriculum: How to Use Movies in The Classroom*, New York: Hayden Book Company Inc.

Maynard, R. A. (1977), *Classroom Cinema*, New York: Teachers College, Columbia University.

New London Group (1996), 'A Pedagogy of Multiliteracies: Designing Social Futures', *Harvard Education Review*, 66 (1): 60–92.

Nutfield Foundation (2000), *The Nuffield Languages Inquiry. Languages: The Next Generation*, London: The Nuffield Foundation.

Ofsted (2013), 'Improving Literacy in Secondary Schools: A Shared Responsibility', April. Available online: https://assets.publishing.service.gov.uk/government/uploads/system/uploads/attachment_data/file/413182/Improving_literacy_in_secondary_schools.pdf.

Oliveras, Á. (2000), *Hacia la competencia intercultural en el aprendizaje en una lengua extranjera*, Madrid: Edinumen S.A.

Ontoria, M. (2007), 'El uso de cortometrajes en la enseñanza de ELE', *RedELE*, 9. Available online: http://www.mepsyd.es/redele/revista9/MercedesOntoria.pdf.

Ortí Teruel, R., M. A. García Collado and N. Bendriss (2011), 'El desarrollo de la competencia intercultural a partir del cine', *Comprofes*. Available online: http://comprofes.es/sites/default/files/slides/garcia_collado_angeles.pdf.

Pachler, N., and K. Field (2001), *Learning to Teach Modern Foreign Languages in the Secondary School*, London: Routledge.

Pegrum, M., L. Hartley and V. Wechtler (2005), 'Contemporary Cinema in Language Learning: From Linguistic Input to Intercultural Insight', *Language Learning Journal* 32 (1): 55–62.

Sánchez-Requena, A. (2018), 'Audiovisual Translation in Teaching Foreign Languages: Contributions of Dubbing to Develop Fluency and Pronunciation in Spontaneous Conversations', *Porta Linguarum*, 26: 9–21.

Sánchez-Requena, A., and R. Alonso-Pérez (2018), 'Teaching Foreign Languages Through Audiovisual Translation', *Applied Language Learning*, 28 (2): 1–24.

Santos Asensi, J. (2007), 'Cine en español para el aula de idiomas', *Actas del Encuentro de Profesores de Español de Nueva Zelanda*, Consejería de Educación en Australia y Nueva Zelanda, Ministerio de Educación y Ciencia.

Sherman, J. (2003), *Using Authentic Video in the Language Classroom*, Cambridge: Cambridge University Press.

Smith, P. J. (2000), *Desire Unlimited: The Cinema of Pedro Almodóvar*, 2nd ed., London: Verso.

Stephens, J. (2001), 'Teaching Culture and Improving Language Skills Through a Cinematic Lens: A Course on Spanish Film in the Undergraduate Spanish Curriculum', *ADFL Bulletin*, 33 (3): 22–5.

Swaffar, J., and Vlatten, A. (1997), 'A Sequential Model for Video Viewing in the Foreign Language Curriculum', *Modern Language Journal*, 81 (2): 175–88.

Swarbrick, A., ed. (2002), *Teaching Modern Foreign Languages in Secondary Schools*, London: Routledge.

Thorogood, K., and L. King (1991), *Bridging the Gap: GCSE to A Level*, London: CILT.

Tinsley, T. (2019), 'Language Trends 2019. Language Teaching in Primary and Secondary Schools in England (Survey Report)', *British Council*. Available online: https://www.britishcouncil.org/sites/default/files/language-trends-2019.pdf.

Tomlinson, B. (2019), 'Multilingualism, Intercultural Awareness and Competence', in C. Herrero and I. Vanderschelden (eds), *Using Film and Media in the Language Classroom: Reflections on Research-led Teaching*, 19–29, Bristol: Multilingual Matters.

Urpí, C. (2000), *La virtualidad educativa del cine a partir de la teoría fílmica de Jean Mitra (1904–1988)*, Eunsa: Pamplona.

Weale, S. (2018), 'Stress and Serious Anxiety: How the New GCSE is Affecting Mental Health', *The Guardian*, 17 May. Available online: https://www.theguardian.com/education/2018/may/17/stress-and-serious-anxiety-how-the-new-gcse-is-affecting-mental-health.

Wegner, H. (1977), *Teaching with Film*, The Phi Delta Kappa Educational Foundation.

Wilkinson, J. E., G. Head and F. McConnell (2010), *Evaluation of the Moving Image in Education Project: Final Report*, Glasgow: University of Glasgow.

5

Teaching Languages to Generation Z Students: The Impact of the Use of Audiovisual Materials in the Spanish Classroom

Nazaret Pérez Nieto and Ares Llop Naya

Introduction

This chapter provides an overview of the use of different audiovisual resources within the university-level Spanish-language classroom to assess these activities' impact on students' motivation and attitudes towards learning a second language in HE contexts. In order to explore the potential of these resources, a classroom-based study was carried out to gather learners' opinions regarding their interests and motivation. The first part of this chapter presents the theoretical framework that serves as the basis for our proposal, while the second part describes the methods and analyses the data. Within the discussion of the theoretical framework, the first part includes a brief overview of film education, its intersection with language learning and teaching, the descriptors for audiovisual reception and mediation at the European level, and a review of studies involving students' motivation in the context of the so-called 'Generation Z' (Gen Z). The audiovisual activities developed during this study and a summary of the perceptions that they motivated in students are included in the second part, where this chapter also describes the methods and the data analysis. The final section comprises the conclusions, limitations and proposals for further research.

The UK's exit from the European Union is already impacting its relationship with its European counterparts and other countries beyond Europe. In this context, languages are strategically vital for the future of the UK to forge wider commercial and other links. A report published by the British Academy, ASCL and the APPG on Modern Languages to the Comprehensive Spending Review (British Academy 2021) suggests that the current language skills deficit could cost the UK economy up to 3.5 per cent of GDP per annum as a result of overdependence on anglophone export markets. Thus, the study concludes that 'urgent, concerted and coordinated action to address the inadequate, longstanding, and worsening supply of the language skills is needed by the UK to meet future needs' (British Academy 2021: 2).

In this regard, Tinsley and Board (2017: 6) stated that intercultural and international awareness and capability are increasingly essential skills within the UK. The ability to function in professional and personal spheres in more than one language is not simply considered as 'enabling a basic transaction but as a vital component of a set of skills, attributes and knowledge required for success' that young UK learners need to acquire (Tinsley and Board 2017: 6).

This view contrasts with the current state of languages in Britain, with only just over one in three British people stating they are able to hold a basic conversation in another language (British Council 2017). Recent reports on the uptake of languages at GCSE level suggest that this situation will continue. For example, the BBC reported in February 2019 drops of between 19 per cent and 50 per cent in numbers taking GCSE language courses since 2013 across the UK (Jeffreys 2019). In England alone, A-level entries in MFL subjects from 1996 to 2020 dropped from approximately 39,000 to 23,000 (Tinsley and Doležal 2018: 4; Collen 2021: 20).

In HE, the language landscape is similar. Between 2011 and 2021, there was a 36 per cent decrease in the number of students partaking (Baker 2021). In this regard, there seems to be a clear correlation between the drop in pupils taking languages in secondary school and students taking up languages at university level, responding to claims from academics pointing out that exams are graded too severely and that languages are perceived as difficult compared with other subjects at secondary school (Bawden 2019). This perception, together with the commitment from HEIs to recruit and support students' learning experience, highlights the need for new strategies and resources to address language learning.[1]

Despite the challenging situation for language learning in the UK, it is important to highlight that within language intakes, the number of students interested in studying Spanish as a foreign language is growing every year. In the *Languages for the Future* report published by the British Council (Tinsley and Board 2017), Spanish was identified among the five most valuable languages in the UK. Furthermore, according to the Joint Council for Qualifications' report (2019), Spanish became the most popular modern foreign language in England on record for the first time in the 2019 A-level exams.

In recent years, a range of audiovisual entertainment platforms, such as streaming television platforms and the availability of on-demand services from abroad, have increased broadcasted material in the Spanish language. These materials constitute a unique tool for Spanish-language teachers, as they provide instructors with resources that reflect daily life, in which grammar and vocabulary are used in context, and where the use of visual images aids students in their learning. Given the promotion of student-led learning in HE contexts, language teachers must find creative and dynamic approaches to the contemporary model of the HE language classroom. This approach can be achieved by incorporating materials that encourage students to continue learning and challenging themselves outside the classroom. The use of audiovisual resources, specifically TV series, films and music video clips, can play an important role in students' motivation. These resources contribute to creating a more engaging teaching environment. Audiovisual texts stimulate more active student engagement, in contrast to traditional text-based activities.

Theoretical background

Audiovisual literacy has been recognized and promoted by a substantial number of initiatives and programmes at European level.[2] For example, the Creative Europe Programme (2014–20), funded by the European Union, was created with the aim of fostering film literacy and contributing to increasing audiences' knowledge of European audiovisual works, particularly among young people. Similarly, the BFI report *Screening Literacy in Europe: Film education in Europe* (British Film Institute 2013) provided an experts' study on film literacy in Europe and recommendations to inform policymaking within the Creative Europe Framework. Finally, the *Framework for Film Education in Europe* (British Film Institute 2015) was released with the aim of supporting film educators in their teaching practice and to serve as 'a model of film education for Europe, including appreciation of film as an art form, critical understanding, access to national heritage, world cinema and popular film' (British Film Institute 2015: 3). Another report undertaken at European level by Lardoux (2014: 44), *For a European Film Education Policy*, states the need to foster learning foreign languages through film by 'organising and greatly expanding the provision of film education combining the artistic and linguistic approaches'. As evidenced by Brooks, Cooper and Penke (2012: 6) and Herrero and Vanderschelden (2019), the use of film in primary and secondary schools by teachers and students across the UK has a clear positive impact on motivation, learning engagement, students' understanding of the world and other cultures, and attitudes towards tackling challenging subjects and tasks. Furthermore, both studies concluded that there is an evident desire on the part of teachers and students alike to see an expansion of the use of these resources in the classroom.

Addressing the decline in the uptake of languages in formal education, Herrero (2016: 192) remarks that 'the perception of languages as difficult and the use of uninspiring methods in schools demotivating pupils' can be tackled through pedagogical and curricular changes involving the use of film.[3] In fact, research indicates that foreign-language films in language learning increase motivation levels and enhance intercultural understanding (Herrero 2016; Viebrock 2016; Alonso-Pérez 2019; Goodwin 2019; Seeger 2019; Tomlinson 2019). In this sense, Herrero (2016: 192) indicates that the use of film applied to foreign-language teaching responds to the 'increasing importance of a wider range of literacies which include multimodal literacy and media literacy' and it also relates to the identification of media education and digital literacy as top priority skills for the twenty-first century by UNESCO and the European Union.

Some of the positive benefits identified on the impact of multimodal audiovisual texts on language learning correspond with the skills currently in demand within the UK in this current climate and include improving language skills and visual and media literacies, nurturing critical thinking, cultural understanding and intercultural communication, and supporting lifelong language learning (Herrero 2018; Goodwin 2019; Herrero and Vanderschelden 2019; Herrero and Escobar 2020).

At a linguistic level, audiovisual resources used in language learning comprehension activities have also been recognized as a descriptor since the publication of the *Companion Volume to the Common European Framework of Reference for Languages* created by the Council of Europe (2018). With regard to audiovisual comprehension, for which the framework provides one scale (watching TV and Film), it includes a specific reference to 'the user who watches TV, video, or a film and uses multi-media, with or without subtitles and voiceovers' (Council of Europe 2020: 47). The descriptors for audiovisual comprehension for intermediate and advanced levels include the following: grasping changes of topic and identifying main points; recognizing details, nuances and implied meaning; being able to handle a good number of slang and idiomatic expressions. The full table of descriptors for all levels can be found in the companion volume referenced above.

A new addition to the CEFR, which is relevant to our study and the activities proposed, is the introduction of scales for areas not illustrated in the original framework, particularly the concept of mediation, broadly understood as 'the process to enable communication between individuals who are unable to communicate with each other'. According to the document (Council of Europe 2020: 250), mediation is not limited to passing on information in another language (cross-linguistic mediation) but also incorporates social and cultural mediation. Special emphasis is given to the descriptors for translating a written text in writing, which do not aim to relate to the activities associated with professional translators' training but intend to provide a functional description of the language ability necessary to reproduce a source text in another language. In the scale, Language A and Language B may be two different languages, two varieties of the same language, two registers of the same variety, or any combination of the above (Council of Europe 2020: 250).

The students for whom this initiative is designed are part of Gen Z. Gen Z is formed by those students born between the mid-1990s and early 2000s. According to a report by Pearson Publishing (2018: 16), technology influences their 'educational expectations' as an 'integral part of life' and 'Generation Z expects experiences both inside and outside the classroom that are more rewarding, more engaging and less time consuming'.[4] The report notes that 44 per cent of Gen Z members spend three or more hours per day on YouTube and that 55 per cent of these members declare this platform as contributing to their education and knowledge, with another 44 per cent of participants claiming to watch films online every week. Vision Critical (2019) conducted another survey with American teenagers and young people, noting that they are the first generation fully immersed in multi-platform and online-video consumption. However, even if Gen Z students are engaged with technologies and online sources as new or non-traditional methods to achieve knowledge, 78 per cent still rank teachers and professors as the most influential agents for their personal and professional development; and 57 per cent value more in-person learning by means of directed activities in class, rather than self-directed learning, which is preferred by only 22 per cent of them. Quite conclusively, Stoller (2017) indicates that the 'connection between digital engagement and student experience' must be integrated naturally into the language classroom. Doing so means adapting lessons to students' needs and catering to the expectations of a new generation – one that is already in our classrooms and will enter the professional world in the near future. The activities suggested as part of this study have been designed taking into account this generational interest in audiovisual content.

The rationale behind this study is based on the idea that the use of media and the increased exposure to audiovisual input enhances student motivation in foreign-language learning processes (Chan and Herrero 2010; Talaván 2013; Alonso-Pérez 2019). Growing interest in Spanish language and culture has coincided with the proliferation of audiovisual productions, including film, TV series and music in the Spanish language. Global online entertainment platforms are now producing and displaying TV series, documentaries and films in Spanish in their repositories, and Latin music is now more popular than ever before. Some clear examples of this success include the Spanish TV show *La casa de papel* (*Money Heist*) (2017–21), which became the most-watched non-English language series on Netflix of all time (Armstrong 2019), and the song *Despacito* (Luis Fonsi 2017), which broke a global streaming record in YouTube with 4.6 billion views in July 2017 (Savage 2017). This increased interest and demand for audiovisual resources in Spanish offers an excellent opportunity to expand Spanish-language provision of materials for teaching and learning by making use of audiovisual resources that not only are attractive and motivating for the younger generations but also reflect the 'real' use of Spanish language and culture in context.

Madrid and Pérez Cañado (2001) define motivation as 'an internal state of the individual influenced by certain needs and/or beliefs which generate favourable attitudes and interests towards a goal, as well as a desire which moves him/her to attain it with dedication and continued effort because (s)he likes it and feels satisfied each time (s)he obtains positive results' (2001: 333). Motivation studies focus on the cause of an increase in positive attitudes and desire to achieve a specific goal, which was established in advance. Specifically, when dealing with L2 learning, according to Dörnyei and Ottó (1998: 65) motivation is defined as 'the dynamically changing cumulative arousal in a person that initiates, directs, coordinates, amplifies, terminates and evaluates the cognitive and motor processes whereby initial wishes and desires are selected, prioritised, operationalised and (successfully or unsuccessfully) acted out' (see also Dörnyei and Ushioda 2021).

According to Madrid and Pérez Cañado's (2001) review of the different approaches to motivation, there are three main reasons to explain people's engagement with certain activities (which can be applied to the L2 learning process). First, in line with Freud's psychoanalysis, stress reduction is crucial. Secondly, as established by Weiner (1989) and drawing on foundational theories by Rotter (1954) and Atkinson (1957), what determines learners' motivation are the individual's expectations of attaining success and the incentives to reach the goal. The third group of reasons to explain students' motivation relates to those approaches linking motivation with self-development – that is, motivation is also fuelled by those growth processes which involve understanding yourself and your surroundings.

According to the factors influencing students' motivation in the process of learning a foreign language, the study presented in this chapter focuses on the role of audiovisual materials as a teaching and learning tool that provides the following benefits: a) it reduces students' stress when exposure to linguistic stimuli; b) it challenges learners to improve their linguistic and cultural knowledge as well as to achieve different communicative goals in an interactive, natural and engaging way; and c) it qualifies students as proficient and socioculturally conscious users of the language in question.

In order to test the impact of didactic activities involving audiovisual materials on students' motivation there are three stages at which factors affecting motivation can be studied, according to Madrid and Pérez Cañado (2001). The authors approach the notions of 'pre-action' or 'initial motivation' to reflect 'the subject's mental state when (s)he is affected by possible personal needs [...], and by his/her previous experiences, beliefs, opinions, and perceptions' (Madrid and Pérez Cañado 2001: 334). Concerning the students taking part in this study, we begin from an assumption of their initial desire to become proficient Spanish speakers and their interest in achieving a high command of both the language and its cultural context, as they are pursuing a degree in Spanish Studies. The second stage, 'action motivation', is the period in which 'the motivational states undergo the greatest changes, increasing, sustaining themselves, or diminishing, depending on the types of teaching-learning processes that the individuals experience' (Madrid and Pérez Cañado 2001: 334). For this study, testing the impact of the usage of audiovisual materials on action motivation is vital, as it shows how beneficial the inclusion of such materials in the language classroom can be. The third stage of the approach to motivation in the classroom is related to the impact of the achievement (or not) of the initial goal (in this case, improving their linguistic skills and their sociocultural knowledge). 'Post-action motivation', as it is called, acts as the emotional evidence of the increment, maintenance or diminishment of students' motivation. In our study, the post-action motivation stage is tested using an evaluation tool, defined later in the chapter.

Method

Participants

This classroom-based study involved nineteen Spanish Studies undergraduate students from Cardiff University, Wales. Their ages ranged from 19 to 21, from Wales and England. All of them were taking the second-year compulsory module 'Ex-Advanced Spanish', which aims to prepare students thoroughly for their period of study abroad, both linguistically and culturally. If using the scale of the CEFR for Languages, their level of Spanish ranged from B2 to C1 (Council of Europe 2020).

The need to motivate young UK learners in foreign-language learning in the twenty-first century, the establishment of new audiovisual policies at the European level, and the changes introduced to the CEFR for languages emphasize the need for new curricular and pedagogical changes within foreign-language learning programmes. This is the case for the modules offered to second-year advanced students of Spanish within the Hispanic Studies department at Cardiff University, which are the focus of our study.

This paper has the dual purpose of presenting a sample of language teaching activities involving audiovisual materials as well as assessing how these activities impact our students' attitudes towards learning Spanish. In order to do so, in this section we start by characterizing the set of activities. Subsequently, we comment on the survey created to assess how these activities impact our students' attitudes towards learning Spanish.

First, we created a set of different activities making use of audiovisual resources to engage advanced Spanish students and aid them in preparing them linguistically and culturally for their year abroad. Each activity is accompanied by a description of the type of audiovisual source used, its aims and the competencies and linguistic/discursive/cultural elements studied.

Instruments

A mixed-methods approach was used to analyse the impact of audiovisual resources and materials, based on the students' responses in terms of successful and significant learning and motivation. A qualitative survey was developed to collect feedback on the impact of the activities created and students' attitudes towards learning Spanish. The ten-item questionnaire comprised six closed-ended and four open question items to allow participants to add further details and comments. The online software used to create and administer the questionnaire was Survey Monkey. Question 1 aimed to explore students' awareness of audiovisual materials being used in the language classroom. Questions 2, 3 and 4 were related to the usefulness of these resources for their learning, while questions 5, 6 and 7 explored the students' perceptions on how motivating they found the activities. Questions 8 and 9 included the students' preferences on the different audiovisual resources and learning activities. Finally, question 10 sought to determine whether the students wished more audiovisual resources to be incorporated into the syllabus. The results of the survey are presented in the data analysis section.[5]

Procedures

This study was carried out during the academic course 2018–19. The module 'Ex-Advanced Spanish' is taught three hours per week. In order to ensure that students are linguistically and culturally equipped while engaged with their learning at the appropriate level, audiovisual resources (TV series, films and music video clips) were designed, compiled and exploited within the course. The development of skills required in the current teaching and learning context and the students' needs and profile were considered during the selection of audiovisual resources and activities creation. The audiovisual sources were selected based on their recognition and success in the Spanish-speaking world and globally, and on the narrative and elements presented in their plot, allowing students to develop a wide range of intellectual, practical and transferable skills. These include the development of critical thinking and creativity skills, enhancement of aural, oral and audiovisual skills, improvement of language ability, grammar and vocabulary, development of cultural understanding and linguistic and cultural mediation, as well as translation skills, awareness of registers, accents and pronunciation. The activities tested in this study were designed to intellectually and creatively engage advanced undergraduate Spanish learners by selecting and incorporating specific audiovisual resources into their language classes. Through the deployment of audiovisual materials, students are invited to be actively involved in their learning process. This practice encourages students to continue their learning outside the classroom by raising awareness of the wide range of resources that students can explore and utilise.

Materials and activities

As previously discussed in this chapter, television series and films represent a highly valuable resource for language learning, mainly because the target language is used naturally and presented in daily-life situations that students can relate to while being exposed to a wide range of different accents and registers in the target language. Additionally, the video element aids students in their understanding of the language and exploring the sociocultural elements being present.

The films and series selected for this study, which were made available to students so that they had asynchronous access to them, have intertwined storylines that are challenging for students aiming to discover the historical and contemporary social and cultural reality of Spanish-speaking territories. For example, the series *Las chicas del cable* (*Cable Girls* 2017–20) portrays the struggle of women to attain their dreams in the context of the social and historical transformations of 1920s Spain. *La casa de papel* (2017–21) focuses on contemporary social changes, dealing with themes such as political corruption, wealth inequality and precarious employment. In relation to films, *Ocho apellidos vascos* (*Spanish Affair* 2014) depicts the persistence of stereotypes among different historical Spanish regions (in this case, the Basque Country and Andalucía); and *Perdiendo el norte* (*Off Course* 2015) explores issues such as youth unemployment and economic migration after the 2008 financial crisis. Furthermore, audiovisual resources constitute a valuable tool to develop students' mediation and intercultural skills through the use of translation. In our study, we enhance students' social and cross-cultural skills as they act as language and cultural mediators, having to consider the cultural and linguistic implications of their translations and dealing with challenging linguistic and cultural aspects throughout. For instance, due to its humoristic nature, the series *Friends* (Crane and Kauffman 1994–2004) serves as the ideal resource to illustrate to students how humour is represented differently in other languages and cultures, while enabling students to work with specific aspects of the target language through translation (Romero Fresco 2006; Frumuselu 2019). In addition, music videos represent a rich and useful resource as they are shorter than television series and films, yet they are rich in audiovisual content while still telling a story. For the activities proposed, we have chosen two songs from well-known Spanish musicians whose message fosters women's empowerment (*Lo malo* by Aitana Ocaña and Ana Guerra, and *Pienso en tu mirá* by Rosalía).[6] The next section shows examples of pre-, while- and post-viewing activities catering for the learning objectives mentioned above for each of the film, series and music videos used as part of this classroom-based study.

Friends

The pre-viewing and while-viewing activities introduce students to a specific topic using a short clip in the original language. Students are encouraged to identify potential challenging structures and expressions they will have to translate into Spanish. Students are also instructed to pay particular attention to intonation and body language in order to understand the communicative situation fully. The post-viewing activities focus on the analysis of the transcript and translation process. After watching the clip, students are given a copy of the full transcript with the dialogue of the video for them to analyse. Then, they are divided into teams (three to four students each) and are asked to translate the text, identifying translation issues and strategies to overcome them. Students depend on their knowledge of the formal and informal registers, grammar structures, vocabulary, colloquial expressions and idioms to capture the nuances of the script. To conclude the session, one of the groups is selected to present their translation to the class, justifying their translation choices and explaining the strategies adopted. The aim of this activity is to generate a debate among the students, exchange ideas and share knowledge.

Las chicas del cable

The pre-viewing activities included a discussion on television series and genres. Students were given a handout containing pictures of contemporary television series and vocabulary they might need. All students were asked to discuss in groups what they thought of television series in general and if they followed any television series in particular, identifying the genres of the series provided on the handout. The trailer was used to develop students' translation and aural comprehension skills, an activity also applied to *Perdiendo el norte*, for which students worked specifically with idioms. The trailer of *Las chicas del cable* helped to introduce students to the theme of the series, presenting new vocabulary and grammatical structures. It was played in Spanish with English subtitles, so they could identify and match some of the structures in both languages. Afterwards, students were given a full transcript of the dialogues in English, to be translated into Spanish. In the transcript, all the verb tenses were highlighted in different colours for the students to pay special attention to how to translate these into the target language. After having done the translation, students watched the trailer again to compare their translations with the official version. In order to provide students with some historical background, students they were provided with a list of definitions and terms for relevant historical events and characters of the 1920s. For the while-viewing activity, students answered some comprehension questions on the content of the first episode of the show. Students were presented with multiple-choice questions to ensure a holistic understanding of the episode. The first after-viewing activity focused on the analysis of key scenes. Students were presented with screenshots that corresponded to different moments of the episode with accompanying dialogue. In groups, they discussed each scene, put them in the correct order, and matched the images to the appropriate dialogue. Once the students had an integral understanding of the plot of the episode, they were asked to analyse the main characters and themes presented in the episode. A picture of the four protagonists was displayed together with four characteristics that defined them. They discussed how each character represented certain values and behaviours. Finally, they were also encouraged to answer questions related to the role of women at the time and whether the problems portrayed in the show still exist in the society of today. This activity helped the students deepen their knowledge of the characters' perspective and compare it to their own cultural values.

La casa de papel

As a pre-viewing activity, students were asked to watch the trailer of the TV series twice. The aim of the first visualization was to get an overview of the plot and characters. The second viewing focused on vocabulary using the full transcription of the trailer with gaps that they had to fill in (key words related to the themes). The while-viewing activity concentrated on characters. Pictures of all the main characters were presented to students together with a list of adjectives which described them. In the follow-up activity, students in groups had to associate at least two adjectives to each character and explain their role in the development of the story.

The first post-viewing activity aimed at discussing and analysing the content of the first episode. Students had to answer some multiple-choice questions on the content of the first episode of the show. As some of the options were very similar, students had to pay special attention to the wording. Another post-viewing activity focused on the narrative structure. Students were presented with images that corresponded to different moments of the episode. In groups, they commented on each scene taking the visual input into consideration and put the images in the right order. Once the students had worked to develop a holistic understanding of the plot, they were asked to reflect in a debate on whether they thought the characters were going to be successful in their endeavours, the boundaries between what is right and what is wrong, and how Spanish society was portrayed in this first episode.

Perdiendo el norte

The first post-viewing activity focused on the study of the characters. Students had to match a sample of adjectives with a character of the film. After that, they were given time for an interactive negotiation (accompanied by a sample of model questions) with their colleagues to lengthen the list with other adjectives. There was also a guided metalinguistic approach to the adjectives given when students were asked about the metaphorical (or non-literal) uses of some of the linguistic items. In the follow-up activity to the previous oral exercise, students were requested to write a short description of the different characters of the film. By doing so, they systematized and made a significant use of the exponents already worked and discussed. Once the context of the film and the characters had been revised, the students discussed the plot in small groups. First, they had to title and put in order the different scenes of the film. This activity helped them to deepen their knowledge of the plot and the main themes of the film. Idioms and instances of colloquial speech were discussed, and they also had to correct and students corrected a list of expressions used in the film that had been modified to include minor mistakes. In order to make those expressions significant for students, they had to use them during a role-play activity based on daily life in a Spanish-speaking context. Finally, students put into practice all the knowledge acquired in a guided free-speech debate about work and unemployment in Spain and the challenges faced by those who migrate to another country.

Ocho apellidos vascos

As a warm-up dynamic and gap-filling activity, students were introduced to language variation in Spain, working with vocabulary that they might encounter during their year abroad and, thus, might be useful for effective and successful communication in different regions of Spain. Aspects regarding variation in pronunciation were also introduced at this point. Once students had watched the film, they were asked to identify cultural and social references related to the Basque and Andalusian cultures presented in the film (for example, artists, traditions, sports, drinks, etc.). This activity was designed not only to enrich students' knowledge of different areas of Spain, but also to allow them to share what they already knew. The final post-viewing activity aimed at exploring, discussing and reflecting on stereotypes from a linguistic and a sociocultural point of view. Students were asked to watch four excerpts from the film, each depicting a different topic about stereotypes, as well as a broad characterization of assumed differences related to the particular regions depicted and ideas of national identity linked to the historical regions. This was addressed with examples related to behaviours, modes of flirting, dressing, attitudes towards life, etc. This activity provided an opportunity to reflect on similarities and differences in greater detail. The study of kinesics (the meaning of gestures) in different languages was also addressed in this exercise.

Music video clip 1: 'Lo malo'

The pre-viewing activity contextualized the song within Spanish society. Students were given a piece of news in Spanish that was related to the content of the song, discussing in groups the relevance of this problem. The while-viewing activity focused on listening comprehension. The music video clip was played twice. During the first visualization, students were asked to pay attention to the image and the lyrics in order to fully understand the communicative situation. In the second, students were given an incomplete transcription of the lyrics and they had to fill in the gaps. In the post-viewing activity, after the lyrics were completed by students, some guided questions prompted students to reflect on the key themes – for example, to think about why the lyrics from *Lo malo* were used in International Women's Day demonstrations across Spain and whether feminism is perceived in the same way in different countries. Other questions considered students' musical preferences, sexism in the music industry, and particularly their perceptions of *machismo* in music.

Music video clip 2: 'Pienso en tu mirá'

Pre-viewing activities are suitable for speculating about the text. In this case, we gave students the title of the song and we asked them to guess the theme. Since the song is about jealousy and a toxic relationship, the title is consciously misleading ('I Think About Your Gaze') and invited dynamic conversations. We took this opportunity to discuss how the pronunciation and spelling of certain words in Spanish may change depending on their regional use. In the while-viewing activity, students were asked to pay special attention to the images and references included, which can be associated with the themes of the song. In the first post-viewing activity students had to analyse them in groups and discuss the point of view and voice in the story, as well as the importance of this positioning. In the analysis of the lyrics, students were asked to identify the parts that describe jealousy and control, as well as the grammatical structures used to express them. As a final activity, the students were given the opportunity to film and edit their own vlog (3–4 minutes long) in Spanish with two topics to choose from: either an analysis of *machismo* in the music industry and misogynist lyrics in Spanish; or the function of stereotypes in society, whether these can be offensive or positive, and a description of stereotypes associated with their own regions/countries and whether these are justified.

Data analysis

The quantitative data obtained was divided into positive and negative answers, with a view to exploring our students' opinions on the impact of audiovisual materials used in class. The intention was to evaluate if the students found them useful for learning Spanish and increasing their motivation, as well as assessing their preferences for activities based on audiovisual sources.

First, regarding learners' awareness of the inclusion of audiovisual materials in the class, the majority of students, almost 95 per cent, reported that they were aware of their usage (see Figure 5.1). This confirms that the students acknowledged the efforts made by the tutors to include these new resources in the module.

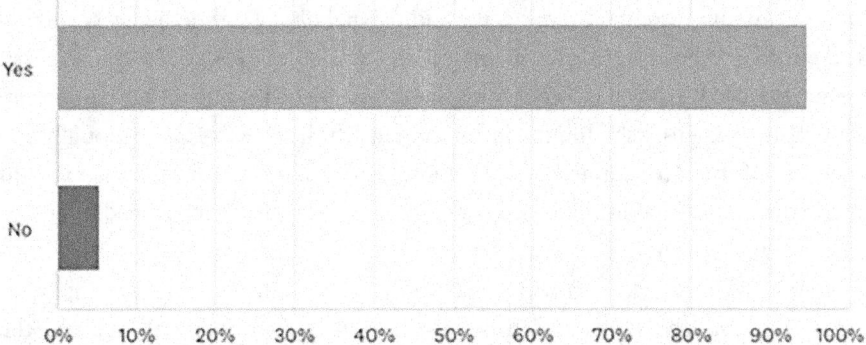

Figure 5.1 Awareness of the usage of audiovisual materials in the Spanish class. Source: Authors.

The data analysis also revealed that 94.74 per cent of students found the audiovisual materials useful for learning Spanish.

What is particularly interesting about this high reliance of students on audiovisual materials as a tool for language learning is the analysis of the reasons posed by students in favour of such strategies. Eleven students emphasized how audiovisual materials are engaging and enjoyable and how using them in class fostered their photographic memory and helped them focus. One student highlighted the importance of diversifying the dynamics of the language class, indicating that 'such strategies create a third-party interaction that helps the brain break the same thought pattern between student and teacher'.

Focusing on linguistic skills, twelve students commented that these materials helped them to feel more exposed to and surrounded by the target language; thus, they could learn how to use vocabulary and structures in a contextualized practice or what some of them call 'real-life application'. Some students recalled the improvement of listening skills they had experienced (thanks to the tips given by multimodal sources) as well as the challenge of being exposed to natural speed of speech, new accents and different registers. Moreover, some learners appreciated the opportunity to work with translations in the subtitles.

One of the central questions of the survey was about how motivating students found audiovisual materials. The analysis shows that 94.74 per cent of students felt highly motivated by this type of material.

The reasons given by students for being more motivated aligned with the fact that this kind of input opens a broader range of topics to be addressed in the language classroom, connected to their interests and the reality they might find at their destinations during their year abroad. In particular, one student stated how useful they were in terms of visual thinking and mental organization, pointing out that 'the visual materials give me a focus-point and allow me to start a train of thought on the specific audiovisual object, immediately springing ideas into my head, resulting in me having valuable ideas that I can express'. Being engaged with the input presented, students find it easier and more enjoyable to identify the linguistic component studied in class. Additionally, the majority of students claimed that the audiovisual materials gave them an insight into what native colloquial language sounds like and encouraged them to improve their pronunciation and fluency.

Many students stated that after having worked on the audiovisual inputs in class, they realized they liked this new learning tool because it changed the dynamics of the course; they were not supposed to take notes all the time and were asked to focus their attention on their own ideas. Moreover, they were inspired to continue watching trailers, films, series and music videos at home. In a nutshell, as stated by one individual, they fuelled 'students' passion for languages as well as their desire to learn more'.

As for the types of activities preferred, Figure 5.2 reveals that discussions and activities based on movies and series were the most valued ones. While translation exercises were also appreciated as a learning strategy by almost 60 per cent of the students, activities related to music videos were the lower-rated item (35.29 per cent). Apart from the impact that students' musical preferences may have on these responses, translation exercises and discussion activities based on TV series and movies were preferred as they involved a longer exposure to a breadth of contextualized grammar structures and lexical items, which students identified as meaningful and, hence, acquired more readily.

The results clarified that the variety of sources selected and activities proposed were suitable for engaging and motivating all students and covered all their expectations and preferences. Students were particularly interested in those activities that implied not only the presentation of linguistic input, but also the production and exploration of the linguistic and cultural contents of the audiovisual sources.

Interestingly, Figure 5.3 shows that when students were asked to select as many resources as they wished in terms of their preference for audiovisual resources, the most valued ones were those that allowed students to continue enjoying by themselves after the lessons – that is, movies (58.82 per cent) and TV series (64.71 per cent).

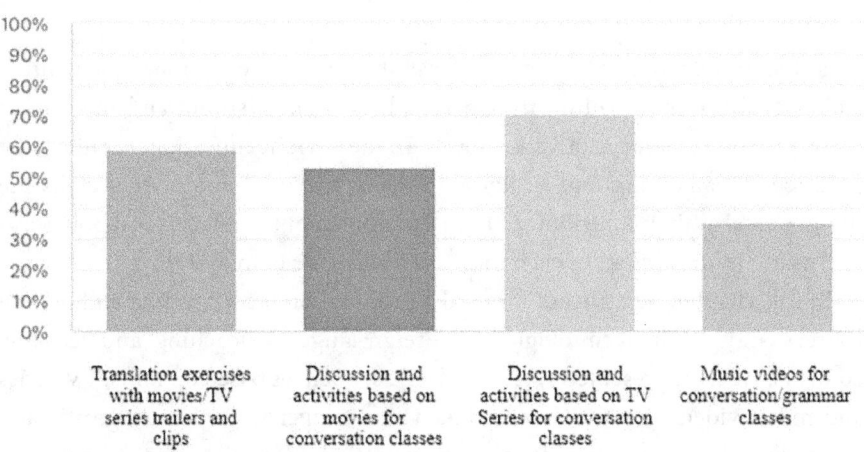

Figure 5.2 Types of exercises preferred by students. Source: Authors.

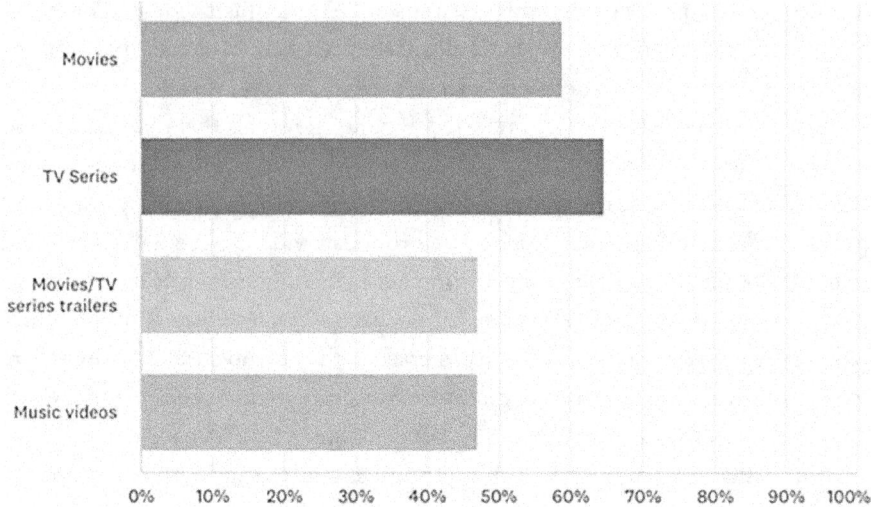

Figure 5.3 Types of audiovisual materials preferred by students. Source: Authors.

Finally, when asked to state whether they would like to see more audiovisual resources used in language classes, 84.21 per cent agreed on the value of working with audiovisual material. This highlights that the use of audiovisual materials constitutes a valuable tool to engage students with formal learning activities inside the classroom and encourage them to continue the learning process outside the classroom.

Conclusions

This chapter intended to explore the feasibility and strategies for implementing audiovisual resources within the Spanish-language classroom and the impact these have on students' motivation levels. In the current educational context, the processes of analysing and exploiting Gen Z students' audiovisual skills are fundamental as they contribute to both the adjustment of educational policies as well as the improvement of each individual student's employability.

In this chapter, we have put forward a proposal on incorporating audiovisual sources and digital technologies in foreign-language teaching and learning contexts. We have presented several didactic sequences based on films, TV series and music video clips which were taken as a trigger to explore linguistic and sociocultural contexts. In order to demonstrate the feasibility of this approach, we assessed the influence of the designed activities on students' motivation, attitudes and beliefs towards learning a second language.

The findings align with the positive results reported in studies undertaken in the same field and with students in secondary and HE settings (Alonso-Pérez 2019; Seeger 2019). The present study reveals that students are aware of the use of audiovisual resources in the classroom and they value their usage both in relation to usefulness and motivation towards their learning. In terms of usefulness, the analysed data show that students engage more with resources, such as films and TV series, which after being studied in class provide the opportunity to continue their exposure to the input and their consolidation of specific aspects of the target language (registers, language variation, idiomaticity, etc.). For similar results, see Alonso-Pérez (2019: 120–1). Although embracing the authenticity of the sources, some learners stated that they found them challenging in terms of comprehension.

In terms of motivation, the qualitative comments from students confirm Tomlinson's (2019: 27) observations about how audiovisual materials foster learners' interest in the social and cultural panorama of other cultures along with enhancing their intercultural and mediation skills (see Seeger 2019: 44–5 for similar results in the teaching of German as a foreign language).

If developed further, some of the limitations of the current study would need to be addressed. First, the number of participants should be increased to present a quantitative rather than a qualitative approach to the results. Subsequently, more research should involve a quantitative study of the correlation between the motivation level and the improvement of second-language skills. Additionally, for future replications of the study, special attention should be drawn to the adaptation of those audiovisual materials that were considered as more challenging by students. Equally, it would be very beneficial for the purpose of this study to assess the impact that subtitling exercises using the L2 may have on the results, following the research done by Bravo (2008), Incalcaterra (2009), Sokoli, Zabalbeascoa and Fountana (2011), Talaván, Ibáñez and Bárcena (2016) and Alonso-Pérez (2019).

Nonetheless, the results obtained through this preliminary study revealed the importance of symbiotic relationships between teachers and learners, with the latter providing feedback on how to adapt and improve the activities designed. This is the way forward to continue researching how to implement didactic practices to engage students with the target language and foster them to acquire the sociocultural knowledge required to master it.

Notes

1. For more information on these initiatives, see the UCML reports available online: https://university-council-modern-languages.org/languages-education/621-2/.
2. For a definition and a more detailed characterization of media and film/audiovisual literacy, see Commission of the European Communities (2007) and visit the EKOME, National Centre of Audiovisual Media and Communication website (National Centre of Audiovisual Media and Communication 2022).
3. Here and throughout this paper, the word '"film" refers to all forms of moving images with sound (and without) irrespective of the medium, be that digital or analogue, TV, online or cinema' (British Film Institute 2015: 3).
4. Although the percentages in this study correspond to US citizens, we take the information presented as data which contributes to a general characterization of the generation to which our students belong. The collection of data regarding the profile of our students as audiovisual consumers remains pending for a future extended version of this study.
5. For a full overview of the structure and the questions asked to students, see Appendix.
6. Aitana Ocaña and Ana Guerra became finalists in the most popular Spanish singing contest of all time in 2017, while the Latin Grammy-winner Rosalía has revolutionized the Spanish music industry with her reinterpretation of flamenco. Both songs were chosen because of their impact in Spanish society and culture. In 2018 *Lo malo* received five platinum certifications and *Pienso en tu mirá* received a nomination as best pop song in the Latin Grammy Awards.

References

Alonso-Pérez, R. (2019), 'Enhancing Student Motivation in Foreign Language Learning through Film Subtitling Projects', in C. Herrero and I. Vanderschelden (eds), *Using Film and Media in the Language Classroom. Reflections on Research-Led Teaching*, 108–26, Bristol: Multilingual Matters.

Armstrong, J. (2019), '*La Casa de Papel*: Setting the Bar for Global Television', *BBC*, 13 March. Available online: http://www.bbc.com/culture/story/20190312-la-casa-de-papel-setting-the-bar-for-global-television.

Atkinson, J. W. (1957), 'Motivational Determinants of Risk-taking Behaviour', *Psychological Review*, 64: 359–72.

Baker, S. (2021), 'Languages Decline Sees Numbers Drop to Zero at UK Universities', *Times Higher Education*, 24 February. Available online: https://www.timeshighereducation.com/news/languages-decline-sees-numbers-drop-zero-ukuniversities.

Bawden, A. (2019), 'Modern Language Teaching under Threat from Tough Exams', *BBC News*, 11 May. Available online: https://www.theguardian.com/education/2019/may/11/modern-language-teaching-under-threat-from-tough-exams.

Bravo, C. (2008), 'Putting the Reader in the Picture: Screen Translation and Foreign-Language Learning', PhD thesis, Department of English and German Studies, Universitat Rovira i Virgili. Available online: https://www.tesisenred.net/handle/10803/8771.

British Academy (2021), 'The future of Languages in the UK Submissions by the British Academy, ASCL and the APPG on Modern Languages to the Comprehensive Spending Review', *The British Academy, and Association of School and College Leaders*. Available online: https://www.thebritishacademy.ac.uk/documents/3510/British_Academy-ASCL-APPG-Modern_Langagues-Budget-Languages.pdf.

British Council (2017), 'Parlez-vous English? British Holidaymakers Embarrassed by Poor Language Skills', *Populus Survey for the British Council*, 3 August. Available online: https://www.britishcouncil.org/organisation/press/british-holidaymakers-embarrassed-poor-language-skills.

British Film Institute (2013), *Screening Literacy in Europe*, London: BFI. Available online: https://op.europa.eu/en/publication-detail/-/publication/cbc5f0fb-3a04-4b44-898b-8b61b0b1c520.

British Film Institute (2015), *A Framework for Film Education*, London: BFI. Available online: https://www2.bfi.org.uk/sites/bfi.org.uk/files/downloads/%20bfi-a-framework-for-film-education-brochure-2015-06-12.pdf.

Brooks, R., A. Cooper and L. Penke (2012), *Film: 21st Century Literacy. Teaching Using Film – Statistical Evidence*, London: 21st Century Literacy and BFI. Available online: http://www.bfi.org.uk/sites/bfi.org.uk/files/downloads/ film-21st-century-literacy-teaching-using-film-statistical- evidence.pdf.

Chan, D., and C. Herrero. (2010), *Using Film to Teach Languages*, Manchester: Cornerhouse. Available online: https://goo.gl/oP4t3A.

Collen, I. (2021), 'Language Trends 2021. Language Teaching in Primary and Secondary Schools in England'. *British Council*. Available online: https://university-council-modern-languages.org/wp-content/uploads/2021/07/i5EDPR-language_trends_2021_report.pdf.

Commission of the European Communities (2007), 'Communication from the Commission to the European Parliament, the Council, the European Economic and Social Committee and the Committee of the Regions. A European Approach to Media Literacy in the Digital Environment, *Eur-Lex. Access to European Union Law*. Available online: https://eur-lex.europa.eu/LexUriServ/LexUriServ.do?uri=COM%3A2007%3A0833%3AFIN%3AEN%3APDF.

Council of Europe (2018), *Common European Framework of Reference for Languages: Learning, teaching, assessment – Companion Volume with New Descriptors*, Strasbourg: Council of Europe Publishing. Available online: https://rm.coe.int/cefr-companion-volume-with-new-descriptors-2018/1680787989.

Council of Europe (2020), *Common European Framework of Reference for Languages: Learning, Teaching, Assessment – Companion Volume*, Strasbourg: Council of Europe Publishing. Available online: http://www.coe.int/lang-cefr.

Creative Europe Programme (2012–), *Culture and Creativity. European Commission*. Available online: https://culture.ec.europa.eu/creative-europe.

Dörnyei, Z., and I. Ottó (1998), 'Motivation in action: A Process of Model L2 Motivation', *Working Papers in Applied Linguistics*, Thames Valley University, London, 4: 43–69.

Dörnyei, Z., and E. Ushioda (2021), *Teaching and Researching Motivation*, New York: Routledge.

Friends (1994–2004), directed by D. Crane and M. Kauffman [TV Series]. US: Warner Bros.

Frumuselu, A. (2019), 'A Friend in Need Is a Film Indeed: Teaching Colloquial Expressions with Subtitled Television Series', in C. Herrero and I. Vanderschelden (eds), *Using Film and Media in the Language Classroom: Reflections on Research-led Teaching*, 92–107, Bristol: Multilingual Matters.

Goodwin, A. (2019), *Media Literacy and English*, London: Routledge.

Guerra, Ana; Aitana (2018). *Lo malo*. Spain: Universal Music. Available online: https://www.youtube.com/watch?v=MqnVeBR118I.

Herrero, C. (2018), 'El cine y otras manifestaciones culturales en ELE', in M. Martínez-Atienza de Dios and A. Zamorano Aguilar (eds), *Iniciación a la metodología de la enseñanza de ELE. IV. Literatura, cine y otras manifestaciones literarias*, 65–82, Madrid: enCLAVEELE.

Herrero, C. (2016), 'The Film in Language Teaching Association (FILTA): A Multilingual Community of Practice', *ELT Journal*, 70 (2): 190–9.

Herrero, C., and M. Escobar (2020), 'A Pedagogical Model for Integrating Film Education and Audio Description in Foreign Language Acquisition', in L. Incalcaterra McLoughlin, J. Lertola and N. Talaván (eds), *Audiovisual Translation in Applied Linguistics: Educational Perspectives*, 31–55, Amsterdam: John Benjamins.

Herrero, C., and I. Vanderschelden, eds (2019), *Using Film and Media in the Language Classroom: Reflections on Research-led Teaching*, Bristol: Multilingual Matters.

Incalcaterra McLoughlin, L. (2009), 'Inter-Semiotic Translation in Foreign Language Acquisition: The Case of Subtitles', in A. Witte, T. Harden and A. Ramos de Oliveira Harden (eds), *Translation in Second Language Learning and Teaching*, 227–44, Bern: Peter Lang.

Jeffreys, B. (2019), 'Language Learning: German and French Drop by Half in UK Schools', *BBC News,* 27 February. Available online: https://www.bbc.co.uk/news/education-47334374.

Joint Council for Qualifications (2019), 'GCE A Level & GCE AS Level, Results Summer 2019', *JCQ*, 15 August. Available online: https://www.jcq.org.uk/examination-results/a-levels/2019/main-results-tables.

La casa de papel (Money Heist) (2017–21), directed by A. Pina [TV Series]. Spain: Netflix.

Lardoux, X. (2014), 'For a European Film Education Policy', [report] *CNC*. Available online: https://www.cnc.fr/web/en/publications/for-a-european-film-education-policy--a-report-by-xavier-lardoux_227382.

Las chicas del cable (Cable Girls) (2017–20), directed by R. Campos, G. R. Neira and T. Fernández [TV Series]. Spain: Netflix.

Madrid, D., and M. L. Pérez Cañado (2001), 'Exploring the Student's Motivation in the EFL Class', in E. García Sánchez (ed.), *Present and Future Trends in TEFL,* 321–64, Almería: Secretariado de Publicaciones de la Universidad de Almería.

National Centre of Audiovisual Media and Communication (2022), 'Welcome to Ekome', *National Centre of Audiovisual Media and Communication – EKOME*. Available online: https://www.ekome.media.

Ocho apellidos vascos (*Spanish Affair*) (2014), directed by E. Martínez Lázaro [Film]. Spain: Universal.

Pearson Publishing (2018), 'Beyond Millennials: The Next Generation of Learners', *Pearson*. Available online: https://www.pearson.com/content/dam/one-dot-com/one-dot-com/global/Files/news/news-annoucements/2018/The-Next-Generation-of-Learners_final.pdf.

Perdiendo el norte (*Off Course*) (2015), directed by N. G. Velilla [Film]. Spain: Warner Bros.

Romero Fresco, P. (2006), 'The Spanish Dubbese -A Case of (Un)Idiomatic Friends', *Journal of Specialised Translation*, 6: 134–51.

Rosalía (2018). *Pienso en tu mirá*. Spain: Sony. Available online: https://www.youtube.com/watch?v=p_4coiRG_BI.

Rotter, J. B. (1954). *Social Learning and Clinical Psychology*, New York: Prentice Hall.

Savage, M. (2017), 'Despacito Breaks Global Streaming Record', *BBC,* 19 July. Available online: https://www.bbc.co.uk/news/entertainment-arts-40642701.

Seeger, I. (2019), 'Addressing "Super-Diversity" in the Language Classroom through Multilingual Films and Peer-generated YouTube Content', in C. Herrero and I. Vanderschelden (eds), *Using Film and Media in the Language Classroom: Reflections on Research-led Teaching*, 30–47, Bristol: Multilingual Matters.

Sokoli, S., P. Zabalbeascoa and M. Fountana (2011), 'Subtitling Activities for Foreign Language Learning: What Learners and Teachers Think', in L. Incalcaterra McLoughlin, M. Biscio and M. Á. Ní Mhainnín (eds), *Audiovisual Translation Subtitles and Subtitling. Theory and Practice*, 129–242, Oxford: Peter Lang.

Stoller, E. (2017), 'How Digital Engagement Enhances the Student Experience', *HEA 2017 Annual conference: Generation TEF.* Available online: http://ericstoller.com/blog/tag/student-experience/.

Talaván, N., A. Ibáñez, and E. Bárcena (2016), 'Exploring Collaborative Reverse Subtitling for the Enhancement of Written Production Activities in English as a Second Language', *ReCALL*, 29 (1): 39–58.

Talaván, N. (2013), *La subtitulación en el aprendizaje de lenguas extranjeras*, Barcelona: Octaedro.

Tinsley, T., and N. Doležal (2018), 'Language Trends 2018. Language Teaching in Primary and Secondary Schools in England. Survey Report', *British Council*, June. Available online: https://www.ciol.org.uk/sites/default/files/British%20Council%20-%20Language%20Trends%202018.pdf.

Tinsley, T., and Board, K. (2017), 'Languages for the Future, the Foreign Languages the United Kingdom Need to Become a Truly Global Nation', *British Council*, November. Available online: https://www.britishcouncil.org/sites/default/files/languages_for_the_future_2017.pdf.

Tomlinson, B. (2019), 'Developing Intercultural Awareness through Reflected Experience of Films and Other Visual Media', in C. Herrero and I. Vanderschelden (eds), *Using Film and Media in the Language Classroom: Reflections on Research-led Teaching*, 19–29, Bristol: Multilingual Matters.

Viebrock, B. (2016), *Feature Films in English Language Teaching*, Tübingen: Narr, Francke, Attempto.

Vision Critical (2019), 'The Everything Guide to Generation Z', *Vision Critical*. Available online: https://www.visioncritical.com/resources/the-everything-guide-to-gen-z.

Weiner, B. (1989), *Human Motivation*, Mahwah, NJ: Lawrence Erbaum Associates.

Appendix: Students' survey

Question 1: Are audio-visual materials (e.g., films, videos) used in your Spanish classes? Y/N

Question 2: Do you find audio-visual materials useful? Y/N

Question 3: If yes, how are they useful? (Open question)

Question 4: If no, why do you think they are not useful? (Open question)

Question 5: Do you find audio-visual materials motivating? Y/N

Question 6: If yes, how do they motivate you? (Open question)

Question 7: If no, why do they not motivate you? (Open question)

Question 8: What type of audio-visual materials do you find more interesting? (Select as many options as you wish)

- Movies
- TV Series
- Movies/TV Series trailers
- Music videos

Question 9: What type of exercises do you find more motivating? (Select as many options as you wish)

- Movies
- TV Series
- Movies/TV Series trailers
- Music videos

Question 10: Would you like to see more audio-visual activities in class? Y/N

6

Language Education at the BBC: Past, Present and Future

Steven Barclay

Introduction

Audiovisual materials have a long history in language education. This chapter looks at the central part of that history – educational broadcasting – in the context of politics and pedagogy in the UK. It explains the structural, social and political factors that influenced the success of this large-scale and long-running audiovisual education project and suggests that the lessons learned can be extrapolated to other projects and future policy. To explain the causal factors of the development of language teaching with broadcasting, it is necessary to consider the broader history of educational broadcasting. BBC educational broadcasting encompassed radio and television programmes and accompanying publications for use in education in the UK (a parallel service on television was produced by the UK's commercial television service, ITV). Educational broadcasting began in the 1920s and reached a peak of output in the 1980s. A decline in production and use started after the Broadcasting Act of 1990, which led to the cessation of ITV's school broadcasting service, and the Education Reform Act of 1988, which introduced the new national curriculum limiting the freedom of curriculum resource providers. The BBC's educational output continues to this day on a smaller scale with a basis on online resources. The focus of this chapter is mainly on the 1960s and 1970s, when several of the most important current trends in audiovisual pedagogy began. This chapter uses a historical methodology for two reasons. First, to understand the present, it is necessary to understand the past. The same long-term causal factors that have determined educational broadcasting development will continue to affect the development of audiovisual educational resources in the future. Secondly, the past can provide examples that can contrast with and shed light on possibilities for the present and future.

The chapter begins with an overview of BBC educational broadcasting. It then considers the most important causal factors in its history from the 1920s to the 1990s. The next part of the chapter explains the BBC's response to the various challenges and opportunities that these factors entailed and how a thriving educational broadcasting sector was built. Following this, the chapter examines in more detail some BBC foreign-language series and the influences behind them. The last part of the chapter explores the recent history of educational broadcasting in the statutory environment after 1990 and indicates possible future lines of development. These four sections build a picture of the main factors influencing the development of the audiovisual language education resources sector, what made the BBC successful, and explain some of its future course's fundamental limits and potential.

An overview of BBC educational broadcasting

The BBC is a public service broadcaster whose legal rights and responsibilities are set out in a royal charter, renewed every ten years. Its guiding principles are generally regarded as being: political independence, distinctive programming, universal funding and universal responsibility (Clementi 2020). The BBC is financed by an annual licence fee paid by audiences who watch BBC content, and it is committed to providing content and services to the entire UK population. The BBC was founded in 1922 and granted a royal charter in 1927, giving it a legal monopoly to broadcast on radio and television. This monopoly was broken in 1955 with the advent of commercial television (ITV). The BBC's current royal charter states as one of the BBC's public purposes: 'To support learning for people of all ages' (Department of Culture Media and Sport 2016).

The first BBC programmes for schools were broadcast in 1924, and the service expanded steadily on radio and on television from 1957. By the late 1970s, the BBC was producing over one hundred and forty different series across primary (4- to 11-year-olds) and secondary (12- to 16-year-olds) schools, covering all areas of the curriculum, including MFL. Over 90 per cent of UK schools were using it regularly, with usage particularly high in primary schools. School broadcasting series were produced in a similar way to other BBC series. However, these series were commissioned and approved by an advisory body of representatives from the educational world, the School Broadcasting Council

(SBC), rather than by BBC controllers. The programmes were broadcast during the day on normal BBC channels, which all schools could receive for free. Almost all of the series had both an accompanying students' book and a teacher's book with notes and instructions on how to use the broadcasts. The publications were sold to schools at competitive prices. All publications were sold at the same price so that the popular series could subsidize the minority ones.

The BBC's educational service for adults, BBC Further Education, also began in the 1920s and expanded onto television with the advent of the Further Education Advisory Council (FEAC) in the 1960s. Subjects were generally based around practical life skills, with language teaching series forming a prominent part of the output. The BBC also produced higher education programmes for the OU from the 1970s. Therefore, during the peak of the service from the mid-1970s to the early 1990s, the BBC was providing an extensive educational broadcasting service, from pre-school to university level. However, while the OU marked the height of the expansion of educational broadcasting, it also represented its limit, as unlike for school and further education series, the broadcaster was not responsible for the actual content of OU programmes, a power that was given to the OU itself. The OU still uses resources produced by the BBC.

Educational broadcasting had particular characteristics. First, the BBC was essentially an educational resource provider, comparable to an educational publisher, rather than a provider of education as such. However, unlike educational publishers, it was dedicated to audiovisual methods and had the extensive facilities, resources and cultural cachet necessary to produce such resources at a considerable scale. Secondly, because of its aims, it departed from broadcasts made for general audiences and was designed to be purposely educational, even though educators and students might have also used this other general programming as learning tools. Thirdly, because at the end of the day it was still broadcasting, the BBC was tied to a particular form of distribution with its own technological and statutory characteristics. In the current digital era, this form has changed considerably.

Long-term causal factors in the history of educational broadcasting

Four long-term causal factors can be identified as having particular significance in determining the course of the history of educational broadcasting. Each has affected events differently in this history; therefore, this section is not a linear narrative. These factors are: the essential characteristics of the national education system; technological developments; the statutory environments around education and broadcasting; and the state of educational theory and practice towards educational broadcasting.

First, the essential condition affecting the use of audiovisual material in education is that a national education system based around schools and teachers was already in place when broadcasting was invented in the 1920s. Universally available free state education dates from the 1870s in the UK, but by 1939, attendance at school for most children was only to the age of 14 (Simon 1991). A privileged few attended fee-paying private schools, from which most of the political and intellectual elite were drawn. There were also 'grammar' schools for the more affluent middle and working class, some of which charged fees or offered scholarships. When radio broadcasting began in the 1920s, some sought to use this new technological means of communication in the education system, including the BBC's first director-general John Reith. Early BBC producers of school programmes were inspired by the new possibilities of radio: it could pool and concentrate expertise and reach a vast audience (Cain and Wright 1994). But because the target audience had to attend schools during the day, school broadcasting had to be incorporated into schools. School attendance meant (and still means) spatial and temporal confinement within a hierarchical social order. In other words, children have lessons in school classrooms during the day, where they are under the command of adult teachers. Radio broadcasting tended towards upsetting this system: it could be heard only where a radio was tuned; its schedule did not necessarily fit that of a particular school; and broadcasts tended to usurp the teacher as the single source of knowledge. This mismatch between the school's material and conceptual conditions and the broadcast strongly influenced the course that educational broadcasting would take.

The education system had another basic condition that affected educational broadcasting. While schools and teaching were essentially state or publicly run institutions, many ancillary parts of the education system, such as resource provision, were commercial enterprises. Traditionally, resource providers were publishers such as Longman, Collins and E. J. Arnold. The BBC joined these firms as an educational resource provider, but unlike them, it had public funding. These two funding systems could coexist while broadcasting was only technologically and legally possible for large dedicated companies like the BBC or the ITV franchises, and there was little question of unfair competition.

The second crucial long-term factor was technological development. Although audiovisual technology was steadily improving and becoming increasingly available, these improvements ran to a timeline unrelated to educational needs. Before the 1960s, schools could not record programmes for use later; and even after audiotape recorders became commercially available, copyright laws prevented schools from keeping the recordings for more than three years. Video recording was expensive and did not become common practice until the 1980s. In this context, for most of the era of BBC school broadcasting, classes had to tune in at the appointed time of day if they wanted to use a broadcast – potentially a severe limitation on its usefulness. This was easier in primary schools, because pupils stayed in the same class all day; in secondary schools, it was more challenging because the classes were timetabled by subject.

A third crucial long-term factor concerns the statutory environments around education and broadcasting. The main educational reform of the twentieth century was the 1944 Education Act. The act introduced free universal secondary schooling and divided the school system into two: primary schools for children up to the age of 11, and secondary schools for those between the ages of 11 and 15 (raised to 16 in 1972). The act provided three (tripartite) types of secondary school: technical, grammar and secondary modern. A second meaningful reform came relatively soon after the first. During the 1960s, the tripartite system was largely abandoned in favour of non-selective, unitary secondary schools called 'comprehensives'. Until 1988 there was no government-determined national curriculum. Teachers, head teachers and local education authorities (LEAs) were responsible for deciding what was taught in their schools. In this situation, educational resource providers, including educational broadcasters, played an important role as innovators in the curriculum. Some innovative BBC language programmes are described later in this chapter. The Education Act of 1988 was the most decisive over conditions in the present day as its introduction of a national curriculum began a trend towards a lesser importance for resource providers (Department of Education and Science 1988).

The final important causal factor was the state of educational theory and practice and its attitude towards educational broadcasting. From the 1920s to the 1970s, the cutting edge of pedagogical methods was 'progressivism' (Selleck 1972; Cunningham 1988), a set of practices and principles, theorized by figures such as John Dewey (1938), who proposed a 'democratic' education system, and Jean Piaget (1955), who researched the developmental psychology of learning. Many teachers and teacher trainers followed and disseminated progressivism, whose influence grew until the 1970s. Progressivism was partly a reaction to the classroom methods that had prevailed since Victorian times, such as rote learning and strict discipline. The ideals that progressivists aspired to enact were freedom, discovery, experience, creativity and activity. What this meant for classroom methods was group work, project work, and a view of the teacher as a manager rather than an oracle. Perhaps the best-known phrase to emerge from the movement is 'child-centred'; the progressives thought that this, rather than 'subject-centred' alternatives, characterized true education (Cunningham 1988).

School broadcasting faced two big problems in this context. First, progressive and traditional teachers alike suspected that broadcasting would usurp their authority (Cain and Wright 1994). Secondly, asking students to listen to or watch broadcasts seemed to contradict the central progressive notion of 'activity'. This is the idea that people learn by doing and engaging with the world through direct experiences, rather than by 'passive' absorption from the teacher. Broadcasting seemed to offer a predominantly passive learning experience (Bates 1984).

The effect of this view persisted mainly in the most influential parts of the educational world, such as teacher trainers and theorists. As late as the 1960s, the SBC struggled to interest progressive teacher trainers (whom an SBC report referred to as 'discovery protagonists' (Gilbert 1967: 1)) in adopting school broadcasting. During a conference at the London Institute of Education in 1967, the SBC found that it was orthodox to view 'first-hand experience as the sole basis for primary education' (Gilbert 1967: 2). Teacher training colleges and universities continued to ignore educational broadcasting (Grant 1976; Bates 1984; Moss 2000). Its popularity lay with the grassroots of teachers rather than the educational establishment.

BBC's responses to these challenges

To help integrate school broadcasting with the school system, the BBC created the School Broadcasting Council (SBC). It comprised a set of panels across age ranges and some specialist panels, including a Modern Languages Advisory Panel. The SBC conferred legitimacy on the output of the BBC as 'teacher approved'. In addition to the expertise and experience of its council members, the SBC had a permanent staff of education officers, whose job was to visit schools, liaise with teachers and check how broadcasts were being used. This effective feedback structure helped the BBC provide usable and popular school resources and avoid flops (Fawdry 1974).

The BBC and the SBC also worked hard to overcome negative teacher attitudes towards school broadcasting, and attempted to ally themselves with the emerging doctrine of progressivism. In a book written by department members, teachers were told: 'Listening is an activity' and, 'A broadcast is . . . an experience for the children on which the teacher can build' (Palmer 1947: 42). As we have seen, 'activity' and 'experience' were keywords in the progressive movement. The BBC consistently emphasized the role of the teacher in adapting and drawing out the full use of the broadcasts. Producers steered away from 'direct teaching'; instead, the term used was 'enrichment'. The broadcasts were meant to provide a stimulus to further work and not replace anything the teacher could do (Bailey 1957).

The part of the school system that was most difficult for the BBC to overcome was one of its most contingent aspects: the commercial nature of the resource provision market. The BBC's operation in this market was questionable and eventually proved to be politically impossible, a subject returned to in the section on 'Recent History' below.

Statutory conditions did not at first hinder educational broadcasting. The BBC's charter did not require it to produce any educational broadcasting in a specific sense, nor did it limit the BBC's freedom in this regard. In some ways, the effects of the 1944 Act and its subsequent revision were to provide opportunities for resource providers: new curricula and practices could be established in the new types of schools. Grammar and private schools were more conservative and exam-focused, and had less desire for innovative methods. Secondary moderns and comprehensives were more responsive to innovation.

Technological development worked gradually in favour of educational broadcasting, as distribution technology improved by stages. The 1960s was a time of great optimism in the development of audiovisual methods, later referred to as 'audio-visual euphoria' (Escoffey 1980), as an investment in television, film projectors, slide and film-strip projectors and audio-cassette recorders was starting to bear fruit.

An advantage of broadcasting as a method of distribution was its low cost per programme viewed. There was no limit to the amount of broadcasting a school with a television and a licence could use for free. This also meant that a physical distribution system of selling ready-made copies (as was the case with educational film) was never developed, even after the commercial videotape market took off in the 1980s, as it was more cost-effective for schools to make copies themselves.

A further strength of educational broadcasting was that it could address a vast audience with a small staff and resources. Therefore, it could provide for subjects that were prohibitively expensive for individual schools to offer by themselves. A significant early success was music programmes, as radio was especially suited to providing music education and many primary schools lacked qualified music teachers. Another gap filled by the BBC was providing resources for primary school French, which will be returned to in the next section.

While television was still relatively new as a cultural phenomenon, senior broadcasters linked its offer of the 'visual' with the idea of 'concrete' knowledge (Scupham 1967). This led to the idea that television was especially appropriate for secondary modern pupils, who supposedly dealt less easily with abstractions. The controller of educational broadcasting at the BBC, John Scupham, was asked to contribute to the Newsom Report, a government investigation into education for pupils 'between the ages of 13 and 16 of average or less than average ability' (Newsom Report 1963: xv). The report recommended the use of television for such pupils' education. However, it may have been detrimental to the prestige of innovations, such as educational television, in the long run as they came to be associated with teaching lower achievers rather than those destined for elite universities and occupations.

Further education broadcasting was in a different situation to school broadcasting for various reasons. First, it did not need institutions in order to reach learners. Most viewing and listening were by adults privately in homes. This meant that it was not obliged to avoid direct teaching and could provide comprehensive courses. The downside of this was that far more perseverance and motivation were required on the part of the learner in order to complete the course – leading to unreliable outcomes. However, by the late 1970s, FEAC's education officers were increasingly successful in building institutional support in adult education agencies, where the use of BBC materials became a feature of course design (Innes, Sheila. Interview with the author, [8 February] 2018). Secondly, in order to reach their target audience, further education programmes had to be broadcast in the evenings. (School programmes were broadcast during the day when there was no competition for airtime). Further education producers had to persuade channel controllers to schedule their series even though they were unpopular with viewers compared to general programmes. This meant that further education broadcasting struggled to secure a foothold within the BBC. Having explained some of the long-term influences on the development of educational broadcasting as a whole, we can now look in more detail at their effect on language education programmes.

BBC foreign-language education

The BBC's foreign-language broadcasting producers sought to design a series with a balance between material that had an intrinsic appeal and took advantage of what broadcasting could offer, while still remaining relevant as language pedagogy. As a general principle, the audiovisual content of foreign-language school television was intended as a guide and a motivation to understand the surrounding linguistic content, rather than as a direct teaching and learning method. This translated into three main types of series. The earliest technique used was dramatization, in which the motivation for learners to comprehend the language lay in an enjoyment of the story, character and atmosphere. The next development was a move towards a kind of language-controlled documentary, depicting real or semi-real 'actuality' events. This was intended to motivate learners through their identification with real people and situations. The third development was less connected to audiovisual pedagogy, but was permitted by the greater use of recorded video. It was a change to a modular format for programmes, with self-contained topics and segments, rather than continuous series.

The SBC did not at first advise that television should be used for languages at all, in preference to radio. However, when primary schools began teaching French in the 1960s, the SBC decided to follow this trend as part of a new expansion into primary school television. It had been a long-standing principle of BBC school broadcasting that target learning was preferably presented in a dramatized or narrative format. For example, history programmes would feature dramatized scenes from history played by actors (e.g. *Stories from World History* (1940–66)), and geography programmes would feature a speaker narrating a personalized story of experiences abroad (e.g. *Travel Talks* (1925–65)). This was to avoid encroaching on the teacher's domain while playing to broadcasting's traditional strength of 'enrichment', and also because young children were thought to prefer information to be presented in this way (Palmer 1947: 81).

The BBC began foreign-language school television with a live-action drama serial. *La Chasse au Trésor* (1968–70) was written in the style of contemporary children's adventure serials, with a plot involving children searching for lost treasure and a villain. Written by Michel Faure, it was set in the French town of St Pourçain-sur-Sioule and shot on location, on black-and-white film, in eight episodes of 15 minutes. It was intended for children of around 10 with up to two years' experience learning French. The series was well-received by teachers, but filmed on-location drama was one of the most expensive ways of making television and was not a sustainable template to follow.

The next series was for secondary school pupils and, again, its character was tied to curriculum change (Fawdry 1974). With the introduction of comprehensive secondary schools, foreign languages were taught much more widely in the 1960s. Traditionally, languages had been taught as an intellectual exercise to relatively willing pupils in grammar and private schools only, with an emphasis on the comprehension of written texts. According to producer John Prescott Thomas (2019), things began to change during this period:

> ... the raising of the school leaving age ... and languages across the ability range ... (meant that) kids of fourteen plus in comprehensive schools who previously hadn't necessarily learned languages at all, became part of the game. And teachers were frequently quite pressed because they hadn't really taught this kind of clientele before ... (and) were still working from inheritance of the older method.
>
> Interview with the author, [15 March] 2019

The need to address the new range of abilities would entail emphasizing the grounding of language in real life: 'It was trying to get over the fact that the language you were learning ... was a tool which kids just like you used to live their lives' (Interview with the author, [15 March] 2019).

Indeed, this idea of language as a tool was related to new theories of language learning. Academics such as Michael Halliday (1961) began to view language as a system of communication for achieving tasks in the social world. This was partly a reaction to the cognitive view of language as a reflection of brain activity that was only incidentally connected with communication (such as that of Chomsky 1957). The new theory came to be known as functional linguistics or sociolinguistics. It describes language as a set of systems for performing different functions and was particularly useful for explaining the difference between different sorts of text and speech styles appropriate for different contexts (Sampson 1980: 126–7). It was connected to applied linguistics, another contemporary movement that wanted to put language learning on a more practical and sound pedagogical foundation (Mitchell 1997). These research trends influenced practice in classrooms. In language learning, the emphasis shifted towards achieving communicative competence rather than absolute accuracy in speech, with a view to producing speakers who could at least 'get by' when visiting foreign countries. This influence merged with the new enthusiasm for audiovisual methods as a solution to new educational challenges. The government's Newsom Report in 1963 had argued for the relevance of televisual methods for pupils:

> ... of average or below-average ability [...] just at the time when the demand for teachers of foreign languages may rise sharply, there have been striking advances in teaching techniques based on the use of audio-visual aids ... These methods, which put an emphasis on lively communication through speech, as opposed to an analytical, textbook approach, could have special significance for our pupils.
>
> Newsom Report 1963: 163

Tout Compris (1973–7), produced by Prescott Thomas, who was advised by the academic Ted Neather, was a significant innovation in this direction. It was shot on location in the town of Saint-Aignan-sur-Cher, featuring teenagers from the town who were chosen for their fluency and articulacy. They were filmed going about their everyday lives and pursuing their interests, such as fishing, playing in a band or celebrating Bastille Day. In separate audio interviews, they were asked carefully phrased questions to elicit an explanation of each activity. The audio voiceover and visuals were edited together to create the programme. It was intended that British teenagers would identify with the protagonists and realize that foreign languages could be relevant to them. This successful format was repeated and adapted for German (*Treffpunkt Deutschland* (1977–85)), Italian (*Appuntamento in Italia* (1978–85[1])) and Spanish (*Descubra España* (1981–7)).

Technological developments continued to be an important determiner of pedagogical forms. During the 1970s, video recording became more widely used.[2] The ability to pick the desired programme 'off-the-shelf' vastly improved the utility of broadcasts and permitted series to be designed accordingly. It meant a new modular format in which it was expected that some programmes could be used selectively or skipped, rather than in series with a continuous structure. These modular series (*Dès le Début* (1979–88), *Dicho y Hecho* (1981–8) and *Alles Klar* (1982–5) focused on basic skills, combining sketches and language explanations taped in studio and actuality exchanges shot on location. A modular approach with a basis in functional language continued to guide the BBC's foreign language output into the 1980s and 1990s. Once a stock of series for various languages was in circulation, the BBC also returned to pure drama serials, including *La Marée et Ses Secrets* (1984–93) and *Le Café des Rêves* (1992–2007).

BBC Further Education broadcasting was also influenced by changes in theory and research into modern language pedagogy. Prior to the 1960s, the pattern of foreign languages for adults on BBC radio had been a mixture of cultural talks, grammar lessons and readings from literature. A move towards a more digestible teaching method was aided by the advice of John Trim, a lecturer in phonetics at Cambridge University. *Parliamo Italiano* (1963–7) was the first foreign-language further education television series. It was a series of separate sketches based on ordinary life situations, shot in studio. The syllabus was based on structures that could be easily adapted to different situations. BBC Further Education benefited from greater integration between its radio and television departments, allowing a multimedia approach with linked television, radio and textbook kits.

Like *Tout Compris* for schools, the further education series *Kontakte* (1974–8) marked a move away from the contrivance of studio-based actors to actuality documentary-style filming. It also marked a step forward in integrating further education series with outside institutions, as the University of Cambridge Local Examinations Syndicate devised an optional achievement test around the series (Innes, Sheila. Interview with the author, [8 February] 2018). BBC Further Education language programmes gained popularity throughout the 1970s and a peak of success was reached with *Russian Language and People* (1980–9), whose peak-time transmission slot helped it earn an audience of 1.25 million viewers.

Recent developments and considerations

The popularity of BBC School programmes declined in the 1990s. Again, the long-term causal factors mentioned above were crucial to events. Perhaps most important was the overall political statutory environment. It is likely that the introduction of the national curriculum in 1988 negatively affected the service for two reasons. First, it meant less interest on the part of teachers. This was more evident in primary schools, which had traditionally been more varied in their approaches to the curriculum and the keenest users of school broadcasting. School broadcasting had frequently been understood as 'enrichment' – that is, a learning tool without the directly observable results of core teaching and learning. Yet, it was not extra-curricular in the way that enrichment has come to mean in current educational structures. As the curriculum was now prescribed and standardized nationally, there was less opportunity for teachers to use innovative curriculum resources, with their more variable outcomes. Secondly, it seems likely that it caused less interest on the part of BBC producers, as the prescription of content reduced the chance for a creative approach to production.

The national curriculum also negated the need for an advisory body, and so BBC School Broadcasting lost its external voice when the SBC was disbanded in 2000.

The statutory environment for broadcasting also precipitated changes. The 1990 Broadcasting Act meant an effective removal of ITV's public service obligations, and a new responsibility for the BBC to commission a percentage of its programming from independent production companies. This process should be seen within a broader trend of removing privileges from public service broadcasters across Europe and America in the neoliberal media market reforms of the 1980s and 1990s (Donders, Pauwels and Loisen 2014). In a newly competitive environment, it is arguable that the BBC deprioritized its educational mission. Further education programmes in particular, which had never been great rating winners, became increasingly marginalized.

Trends in educational theory and research also had detrimental effects. From the 1970s, policymakers and popular opinion began to turn away from curriculum innovation. The reasons for this are complex and partly political. In educational research methodology, large-scale, empirical, outcomes-based testing methods attained greater rigour and validity (Bennet 1977). This type of research came to dominate research departments and influence policymaking (Lowe 2007; Biesta 2015). When educational broadcasting was tested in this way, it seemed to have doubtful overall effects on attainment (Bates 1984).

The interplay between the statutory environment and technological developments dictated what happened next. The most important development in BBC School Broadcasting of the late 1990s and 2000s was the gradual move from television and radio to online. There had been increasing enthusiasm in the 1990s among educational policymakers for the use of computers and the internet in schools, and it seemed clear to many that what were then long-standing educational media – print and broadcasting – would be supplemented or even replaced by this new method of distribution (Moss 2000). In 1998 the BBC launched Bitesize, a website conceived as a self-study tool, particularly for students aged 15 and 16 facing exams (BBC 2020d). The process of change from broadcast to online provision culminated in a proposal to introduce a new service known as the BBC Digital Curriculum (later called BBC Jam) in 2002. The core of the Digital Curriculum was a virtual learning environment to support individual learning, which could be used in schools and homes (BBC 2000). Here, the regulatory status of the BBC as a publicly funded public service broadcaster was crucial to events. A lobby of commercial educational resource providers, led by the publisher Pearson, protested to the government that the BBC's proposal would constitute unfair competition in a potentially lucrative emerging market and lodged a complaint to the European Commission. Though this complaint was dismissed, the Digital Curriculum was approved by the Commission and the UK government only on the conditions of 'complementarity' and 'distinctiveness', and extensive restrictions were set to minimize market impact (EC 2003). For example, it was permitted to cover a maximum of half the learning outcomes in the national curriculum that were amenable to ICT learning. However, after a soft launch in 2006, the service was again alleged by a government report and commercial providers to have failed to comply with the regulations. In response, the BBC Trust, the BBC's new governing body, suspended the Digital Curriculum in 2007 and formally closed it down in 2008. This outcome remains contentious among BBC staff and media policy experts. Michalis (2012: 952) argues that 'there is lack of convincing evidence establishing a clear correlation between BBC Curriculum and market displacement'. The predicted investment by commercial firms in online resource provision did not emerge on a scale comparable to the BBC's proposals.

The present

The withdrawal of the Digital Curriculum left the BBC's educational output in a state of uncertainty. Ironically, it was just at the time that the technological problem that had plagued educational broadcasting, its distribution system, had finally been solved by online video streaming – BBC iPlayer was launched in 2008 – that the ability to take advantage of this solution became politically impossible. Now all of BBC Education's output is through the Bitesize and Teach websites. Educational audiovisual content featured is typically only a few minutes in length. The aftermath of the dispute between the BBC and commercial providers was a lingering uneasy relationship in which the BBC is careful not to be seen competing too directly. The current directorate responsible for educational output, Children's and Education, commissions some material from independent production companies and the Teach website links to a large number of commercial providers, including Pearson but also Espresso, a provider bought recently by Discovery, the multinational media corporation behind the Discovery Channel (BBC 2020b).

The conditions for educational broadcasting changed unexpectedly during the global COVID-19 pandemic, when in March 2020 the government ordered a national closure of schools. One week before the closure was announced, the government asked the BBC to provide remote learning for the school students who would be sent home. Five weeks later, school programmes returned temporarily to broadcast television during weekday mornings and afternoons in strands including *Bitesize Daily*, *BBC Live Lessons* and a *Celebrity Supply Teacher* (BBC 2020a), including a beginners' Spanish lesson from former footballer Gary Lineker (BBC 2020e). While the government had initially suggested that the programmes feature teachers presenting to camera, and pursued this in a separate venture, the Oak Academy (Oak National Academy 2022), the BBC was able to use its broadcasting resources to produce a cross between this format and normal children's programmes. The BBC's offer was attractive to schools partly because it was free. Most commercial audiovisual educational resource providers, such as Thisislanguage (Thisislanguage 2020), require a paid subscription for users to proceed beyond the basic version. The BBC was able to provide a vital educational resource during the national lockdowns, though it must be made clear that even this increase in provision was far less extensive an operation than educational broadcasting had been at its peak. All popular foreign languages were covered, but apart from the new initiative to put educational programmes on television, most of the core resources, including the Bitesize revision materials, remained the same.

The future

It is likely that in the future, changes to BBC educational broadcasting will continue to be linked to conditions and curriculum in schools, technological developments, the statutory framework of education and broadcasting, and the state of educational theory and pedagogy as it pertains to audiovisual methods.

Academic research into educational theory and pedagogy connected to audiovisual resources continues to accumulate, to the point that teachers' attitudes are probably more favourable now than ever. However, that is not to say that the typical practices of schools reflect the importance of digital and online communication to young people's lives and cultures (Buckingham 2014). Educational broadcasting in the particular political and cultural form that was so successful up until the 2000s has largely ceased. Research into the theory of its use has also ceased without ever having developed to a high degree of sophistication (Moss 2000).

The basic conditions of the education system – schools and their curricula – have been static now for some time. They currently seem unlikely to undergo reforms of similar magnitude to those between the 1920s and 1970s, which allowed the opportunity for an innovation like educational broadcasting to flourish. However, the recent pandemic and lockdown circumstances meant a temporary alteration of these conditions, which highlighted the degree to which technological change has the potential to alter basic educational conditions.

Online distribution can provide audiovisual resources to students' homes, enhancing the potential of remote learning and negating the spatio-temporal and hierarchical limitations of the traditional school. But any move towards more remote learning for school students does not seem likely in the near future. Concepts like the 'flipped classroom' are probably of more relevance to HE (Abeysekera and Dawson 2015). In many ways, national lockdowns during the COVID-19 pandemic were a disaster for education. The provision of remote learning by individual schools varied widely, and some children did little or no schoolwork at all while they were at home (Green 2020). Technology requirements mean that access to remote learning is unequal across socioeconomic groups. More affluent schools and students typically have greater access to devices like personal tablets. Historically, universal free schooling has been a leveller of socioeconomic opportunity, but this depends on physical attendance at school where teaching and resources are accessed. Political attitudes towards education have so far not favoured remote learning. Nor has there been any indication of a reversal of the trend towards curriculum prescription and testing regimes that initially helped reduce the power of educational broadcasting.

At the time of writing, it is too early to say if the role played by the BBC during the closure of schools in 2020 and 2021 will mean a significant lasting change for BBC Education. However, there are signs that it caused an improvement in its relationship with the commercial sector, as the *Bitesize Daily* strand involved increased commissioning from independent production companies. The BBC will likely proceed more cautiously than it did with the Digital Curriculum, aiming to build markets rather than lead them. It now tries to take initiatives in education with partnerships with other commercial and public organizations, including educational publishers Pearson (BBC 2020c).

The rise of digital television and broadband internet has altered the potential for audiovisual resources in classrooms and arguably forged the way for a newly effective educational broadcasting service. At the moment, the potential of the BBC to take advantage of these changes depends most on the statutory framework for broadcasting, which has lagged behind the pace of technological change (Barnett and Seaton 2010; House of Lords Select Committee on Communications and Digital 2019). The BBC has traditionally been restricted to television and radio activities, but recently the advent of on-demand video and audio streaming has erased the distinction between broadcasting and the internet (Grainge and

Johnson 2018). It is argued by some that the light touch applied to the regulation of the internet until now has been a mistake, and public service principles, like the ones that once governed broadcasting, should be applied to the online world as well (Fuchs and Unterberger 2021). A smaller body of academic opinion, usually grounded in economic theory, does not consider the continuation of universal publicly funded public service broadcasters justifiable any longer (Booth 2020; Sieg and Stühmeier 2015).

A change to the way the BBC is currently funded seems likely in the medium term. This may accompany changes to its charter, which is due for renewal in 2027, and therefore its statutory obligations and permissions. It is conceivable that the future of the BBC might include an increasing emphasis on its educational programmes, but this would contradict a long-standing trend.

Conclusion

What can we learn about the social and political conditions that favour audiovisual education from the history of language education at the BBC? First, it is clear that the cultural, statutory and technological characteristics that allowed public service broadcasting to flourish were also crucial to the health of educational broadcasting. While the BBC was not part of the state education system, its public service remit gave it the obligation and opportunity to build an extensive educational offer. The success of educational broadcasting was safeguarded by its having a political shield and an effective feedback mechanism through its advisory bodies: SBC and FEAC. The technology of television and radio broadcasting offered extensive access to schools. Although the school system was set and the government never directly supported educational broadcasting through legislation or funding, changes to the statutory environment for education from the 1940s to the 1960s largely worked in educational broadcasting's favour. The BBC benefited from and participated in a broader movement of curriculum innovation in this period. Its independence allowed it to engage with educational research with results that solved real educational problems.

However, several factors limited its success as an education provider. As the main business of education, schools, teachers and classrooms did not naturally translate into the use of broadcasting. This was especially the case before recorded use of programmes became widespread. Pedagogical orthodoxy traditionally promoted teacher authority, and the new theory and practice of progressivism prioritized direct experience of the world and activity. Neither was conducive to the use of broadcasting. Most seriously, the BBC's public status left it with ambiguous legitimacy as an educational resource provider, a market traditionally served by commercial companies.

The BBC's language education television came in several different forms, which exploited the strengths of the audiovisual and of broadcasting, while using different pedagogical strategies to motivate learners. The BBC was capable of producing foreign-language drama serials to a high standard. Documentary or actuality methods were cheaper and corresponded more closely with functional and social theories of language learning. The modular approach was made possible by the spread of recording and playback technology. A rich tradition was built up, as were a range of approaches and resources across television, radio and publications by the 1980s. The scale of the BBC's resources and its cultural cachet and access made this possible.

BBC educational broadcasting declined in the 1990s after changes to the statutory climate for education and broadcasting. Public service broadcasting itself became politically threatened. The introduction of the national curriculum in 1988 had diminished the value of unique curriculum resources and educational broadcasting suffered from accusations of ambiguous effects on attainment. Audiovisual resources had earned an accepted status in classrooms but the idea of educational broadcasting as an independent force had not. For further education for home learners, an audiovisual element is now expected from all providers, but broadcasters are absent. This means there is no provider able to produce these resources on the scale and with the level of professionalism the BBC possessed.

The online and digital era and the globalization of television through subscription video-on-demand services have caused a decline in the BBC's cultural power and rendered it a medium-sized player in a crowded market. As the content of Britbox proves, educational broadcasting is of little relevance to an international commercial video content market. The BBC's move of its educational provisions online and off broadcast was necessary and relatively successful. Still, the protests of commercial providers against the Digital Curriculum resulted in a much-reduced provision overall. The BBC's national status and access made it the natural choice to provide a remote teaching service during a sudden closure of schools, indicating that the BBC retains strategic importance for the UK's education system. In the future, the BBC will likely continue to work in a mixed economy in partnership with commercial providers. A return to the depth and breadth of educational provision which once existed is unlikely.

Notes

1   Compiled from library film rather than specially shot material.
2   Though in 1980 still only 9 per cent of primary schools and 83 per cent of secondary schools had video recorders, with an average of 1.2 and 2.0 per school, respectively (BBC 1980: Annex B).

References

Abeysekera, L., and P. Dawson (2015), 'Motivation and Cognitive Load in the Flipped Classroom: Definition, Rationale and a Call for Research', *Higher Education Research & Development*, 34 (1): 1–14.
Bailey, K. V. (1957), *The Listening Schools*, London: BBC.
Barnett, S., and J. Seaton (2010), 'Why the BBC Matters: Memo to the New Parliament about a Unique British Institution', *The Political Quarterly*, 81 (3): 327–32.
Bates, T. (1984), *Broadcasting in Education: An Evaluation*, London: Constable.
BBC (1980), 'Educational Broadcasting Policy 1975–85. Summary of Report by Future Policy Group 1980' (WAC R99/323/1) *BBC Written Archive*, Internal Report, September 11th.
BBC (2000), *A Digital Curriculum: Have Your Say*, London: BBC.
BBC (2020a) 'April BBC to Deliver Biggest Push on Education in its History', *BBC News*, April. Available online: https://www.bbc.co.uk/mediacentre/latestnews/2020/coronavirus-education.
BBC (2020b), 'About BBC Teach', *BBC Teach*, 21 October. Available online: https://www.bbc.co.uk/teach/about-teach/znhhbdm.
BBC (2020c), 'BBC Education Commissioning', *BBC Commissioning*. Available online: https://www.bbc.co.uk/commissioning/online/articles/learning.
BBC (2020d), 'Home – BBC Bitesize', *BBC Bitesize*. Available online: https://www.bbc.co.uk/bitesize.
BBC (2020e), 'Celebrity Supply Teacher Series 1:6 Gary Lineker – Spanish', *CBBC*. Available online: https://www.bbc.co.uk/programmes/m000k4pp.
Bennett, N. (1977), *Teaching Styles and Pupil Progress*, London: Open Books.
Biesta, G. J. (2015), *Good Education in an Age of Measurement: Ethics, Politics, Democracy*, London: Routledge.
Booth, P. (2020), 'The Future of Public Service Broadcasting and the Funding and Ownership of the BBC', *Economic Affairs*, 40 (3): 324–43.
Broadcasting Act 1990 (c42), London: HMSO.
Buckingham, D. (2014), 'Guest Editorial: The Success and Failure of Media Education', *Media Education Research Journal*, 4 (2): 5–18.
Cain, J., and G. B. Wright (1994), *In a Class of its Own: BBC Education 1924–1994*, London: BBC Education.

Chomsky, N. (1957), *Syntactic Structures*, The Hague/Paris: Mouton.
Clementi, D. (2020), 'Speech to the Voice of the Listener and Viewer Autumn Conference', *VLV*. Available online: https://www.vlv.org.uk/recent-events/vlv-autumn-conference-2020/.
Cunningham, P. (1988), *Curriculum Change in the Primary School Since 1945: Dissemination of the Progressive Ideal*, London: Falmer Press.
Dewey, J. (1938), *Experience and Education*, New York: Simon & Schuster.
Donders, K., C. Pauwels and J. Loisen, eds (2014), *The Palgrave Handbook of European Media Policy*, Basingstoke: Palgrave Macmillan.
EC (2003), 'State aid No. N 37/2003', *United Kingdom BBC Digital Curriculum*, Brussels: European Commission.
Education Act 1944 (c31), London: HMSO.
Education Reform Act 1988 (c40), London: HMSO.
Escoffey, R. (1980), 'Radio Language Broadcasts for Schools: The General Strategy', *British Journal of Language Teaching*, 18 (2, 3): 61–7.
Fawdry, K. (1974), *Everything but Alf Garnett: A Personal View of BBC School Broadcasting*, London: BBC.
Fuchs, C., and K. Unterberger, eds (2021) *The Public Service Media and Public Service Internet Manifesto*, London: University of Westminster Press.
Gilbert, L. A. (1967, April 3rd), Plowden & School Broadcasting Conferences – the "Science" day [Education officer report] BBC Written Archive (WAC R16/629/1), Caversham: BBC Written Archive.
Grainge, P., and C. Johnson (2018), 'From Catch-up TV to Online TV: Digital Broadcasting and the Case of BBC iPlayer', *Screen*, 59 (1): 21–40.
Grant, F. (1976), 'Educational Television: Context and Content', *Journal of Educational Television and Other Media*, 2 (2): 53–6.
Green, F. (2020), 'Schoolwork in Lockdown: New Evidence on the Epidemic of Educational Poverty', *LLAKES Research Paper*, 67: 135–51.
Halliday, M. A. K. (1961), 'Categories of the Theory of Grammar', *Word*, 17 (2): 241–92.
House of Lords Select Committee on Communications and Digital (2019), *Public service Broadcasting: As Vital as Ever*, London: House of Lords.
Lowe, R. (2007), *The Death of Progressive Education: How Teachers Lost Control of the Classroom*, London: Routledge.
Michalis, M. (2012), 'Balancing Public and Private Interests in Online Media: The Case of BBC Digital Curriculum', *Media, Culture & Society*, 34 (8): 944–60.
Mitchell, R. (1997), 'Notes on the History of the British Association for Applied Linguistics 1967–1997', *BAAL*. Available online: https://www.baal.org.uk/wp-content/uploads/2017/01/history_of_baal_2017d.pdf.
Moss, R. (2000), Closing a Window on the World: Convergence and UK Television Services for Schools, *Cultural Trends*, 10 (40): 1–27.
Newsom Report (1963), *Half Our Future: A report of the Central Advisory Council for Education*, London: HMSO.

Oak National Academy (2022), 'About Oak', *National Academy*. Available online: https://www.thenational.academy/about-oak.

Palmer, R. (1947), *School Broadcasting in Britain*, London: BBC.

Piaget, J. (1955), *The Child's Construction of Reality*, London: Routledge & Kegan Paul.

Prescott Thomas, J. (2019) 'Interview' [Personal communication. Interview with the author], 15 March.

Royal Charter for the Continuance of the British Broadcasting Corporation (2016, c6925), London: HMSO.

Sampson, G. (1980), *Schools of Linguistics: Competition and Evolution*, London: Hutchinson.

Sheila, I. (2018) 'Interview' [Personal communication. Interview with the author], 8 February.

Scupham, J. (1967), *Broadcasting and the Community*, London: C. A. Watts.

Selleck, R. J. W. (1972), *English Primary Education and the Progressives, 1914–1939* [Vol. 33], London: Routledge & Kegan Paul.

Simon, B. (1991), *Education and the Social Order: 1940–1990*, London: Lawrence & Wishart.

Sieg, G., and T. Stühmeier (2015), '"Fixing What Ain't Broke" through Public Service Broadcasting', *FinanzArchiv/Public Finance Analysis*, 71 (4): 440–59.

Thisislanguage (2020), 'Home page', *This Is Language Ltd*. Available online: https://www.thisislanguage.com/.

Broadcast series

Alles Klar (1982–5) [TV programme] BBC1
Appuntamento in Italia (1978–85) [TV programme] BBC1
Bitesize Daily (2020) [TV programme] CBBC
Celebrity Supply Teacher (2020) [TV programme] CBBC
Dès le Début (1979–88) [TV programme] BBC1
Descubra España (1981–7) [TV programme] BBC1
Dicho y Hecho (1981–8) [TV programme] BBC1
Kontakte (1974–8) [TV and Radio programme] BBC1, BBC Radio 4
La Chasse au Trésor (1968–70) [TV programme] BBC1
La Marée et Ses Secrets (1984–93) [TV programme] BBC1
Le Café des Rêves (1992–2007) [TV programme] BBC1
Parliamo Italiano (1963–7) [TV programme] BBC1
Russian Language and People (1980–9) [TV programme] BBC1, BBC2
Stories from World History (1940–66) [Radio programme] BBC Radio 4
Tout Compris (1973–7) [TV programme] BBC1
Travel Talks (1925–65) [Radio programme] BBC Radio 4
Treffpunkt Deutschland (1977–85) [TV programme] BBC1

Part Two

Interactive Screen Media: Informed Research and Practice

7

Designing an International Tourism Fair to Improve Students' Learning with Collaborative Work

M. Azahara Veroz-González and Soledad Díaz Alarcón

Introduction

The educational reform in HE proposed by the Bologna Process pursued the priority objective of creating a European Higher Education Area (EHEA) (see Benito and Cruz 2005; Rue 2007; Espacio Europeo de Educación Superior 2019). The main aim was to launch a complex and ambitious plan for education that would provide a common and quality basis and harmonization of HE systems that would favour the development of Europe as an open, democratic, egalitarian and advanced knowledge society, while respecting diversity within a complex modern society. Thus, for European universities, and in particular for Spanish universities, the implementation of the EHEA meant a significant change in terms of the educational offer, learning methods and teaching models because the educational programme had to prioritize the training of students in generic and transversal competences, including digital skills (see De Miguel 2005; Esteve and Gisbert 2011) – that is, in skills that would lead to the students' integration into society, not only nationally but also in any country in the European Union (EU). Hence, the prioritization and promotion of student mobility have become an important objective of this plan.

Given this context, active methodologies have a prominent place in this new educational framework. The acquisition of specific knowledge and competences requires students to play the leading role in the acquisition of knowledge. Some active methodologies that have been put into practice are problem-based learning, cooperative learning and case method, among others, in which the student works inside and outside the classroom to gain a set of skills in a participatory mode (communication, critical thinking, teamwork, etc.). This chapter presents an innovative educational project carried out during the 2017–18 academic year in the French Culture and Civilization Module, part of the Degree in Translation and Interpreting at the University of Córdoba. The project applied the student-centred learning model proposed by Jarauta Borrasca (2014), who informs much of the theoretical framework. The main aim of the study was to make students active agents of their own education, while also guaranteeing the quality of their learning under the guidance of the teaching team. The three main objectives of the project embedded in this unit were teaching French culture and civilization in an autonomous and collaborative way, motivating students to engage in a subject that had previously been reported as tedious, and offering an opportunity to celebrate publicly their learning success. To achieve the learning outcomes, the innovative proposal integrated collaborative project-based learning with the development of materials and resources by the students. A central point was to improve student engagement and motivation by making them aware of their own learning and engaging them in real-world experiences.

The theoretical foundations on which this project is based are described below, with a focus on the method of collaborative work, which is a form of interactive learning that is based on negotiation, acceptance of hierarchy, assumption of roles and responsibility for the individual, and collective tasks of the group members. The description of collaborative work also allows us to contrast it with the methodology of cooperative work, since these concepts have laid the foundations for the approach taken in this unit and the activities designed for it.

In the methodological section, we present the development of the creation of a simulated International Tourism Fair with the students of the module. This was an activity organized in teams, whose members had to prepare authentic materials, both written and audiovisual resources, about a French-speaking region. This chapter describes the steps, presents the results obtained from this project, and considers limitations and measures for improving it.

Theoretical framework

This project emerged from considerations around collaborative-work theory. This section aims to establish how it differs from cooperative work and project-based learning.

Collaborative learning and cooperative learning

Collaborative work and cooperative work have been defined in so many ways that some authors use them interchangeably (Maldonado Pérez 2007). However, some nuances differentiate them, especially when considering student–teacher and student–student interaction. For the project presented in this chapter, it is important to point out these differences because collaborative learning is the basis of the design of the methodology carried out in the French Culture and Civilization Module during the 2017–18 academic year.

While they share many similarities, cooperative work is often mediated by an educator, while collaborative work emerges from the decisions taken by the students. Cooperative work focuses on the procedural dimension of a teacher's competence through what they design, such as activities, sequences and products.[1] These are intentional actions aimed at the achievement of results. For example, the teacher proposes a problem and indicates what each member of the group should do, each one taking responsibility for the solution of a part of the problem. Yet, it is the teacher who designs and almost entirely maintains the structure of interactions and the results achieved (Panitz and Panitz 1998). In other words, the responsibility for learning lies with the teacher. According to Bruffee (1995), cooperative work focuses on basic or 'foundational knowledge', which is often perceived as valuable in society, serves as building blocks for other knowledge, and depends on memorization processes. This 'foundational knowledge' is usually identified with the concepts of grammar, timetables, spelling rules, calculations, mathematical processes, geography and history (e.g. facts, dates and places). Because of these characteristics, Bruffee (1995) also indicates that this type of learning can be quite useful in primary education.

Collaborative work, on the other hand, facilitates the learning process through group interactions (Dillenbourg et al. 1996). When interacting and discussing a topic, the members apply a type of knowledge considered by Bruffee (1995) as 'non-foundational'. This type of knowledge cannot be learnt by memorizing, but demands reasoning and discussion by the group members, and is better suited for the development of critical thinking. In other words, collaborative work gives the student the responsibility of learning and develops their reasoning. In this situation, the teacher's job is still relevant as the teacher must design and articulate the activities in advance so that the students learn to learn (see Niemi 2009).

Maldonado Pérez (2008) brings together a compilation of the most accepted definitions of collaborative work. She points out that for collaborative work to exist, reciprocity between a group of individuals is necessary. This aspect is particularly important in the proposal presented in this chapter since, thanks to this reciprocity between the members of the group, individuals can generate knowledge. However, it should be noted that working in collaboration implies sharing experiences and knowledge in pursuit of a clear common goal that enriches the group. Likewise, thanks to this methodology, the group decides what role each individual plays based on their capabilities, i.e. each member of the group contributes with their expertise. From a motivational point of view, this is a very important aspect; since the team members will work comfortably, they will invest more time in those aspects that interest them the most. They will also share this knowledge with their colleagues while learning from them at the same time. In other words, the fundamental purpose of collaborative work is the construction of consensual learning through the collaboration of the members of the group, where the authority role is shared and responsibility for the group's actions is accepted by all. It is also worth highlighting the role that the teacher plays here. Although the educator is the one who designs the activities to be carried out by the students, the teacher becomes also a collaborator who guides them in this task. To sum up, in collaborative learning activities, none of the members of a group would be able to achieve the objectives if they do not work both individually and as part of a group (Maldonado Pérez 2007). To work together, they must put into practice skills such as dialogue, negotiation and showing respect. The members of the group must assume that the group's effectiveness will not be possible if positive affective relationships are not sought within the group, as Maldonado Pérez affirms. Once the students have learned the methodology and their teachers have developed interpersonal links with them, the students can go on to achieve excellent results (Maldonado Pérez 2007; Pérez et al. 2007). The following table (Table 7.1) presents Maldonado Pérez's (2007: 273) overview of the differences between both types of work:[2]

The project discussed in this chapter was designed as collaborative learning, since collaborative work meets the aims of the EHEA and the project objectives: to involve students to make them active agents of their own learning and to guarantee the quality of learning, providing more broad and engaging training for the students. Furthermore, the cross-cutting nature of collaborative work should also be emphasized, as not only it is possible for students to learn and generate knowledge related to the discipline they are studying, but there is also learning taking place that relates to interacting with people. In order words, collaborative group activities develop reflective thinking and stimulate the formulation of judgements, the identification of values, and the development of respect and tolerance for the opinion of others as 'a legitimate other' (Maldonado Pérez 2007). All in all, it develops important lifelong learning skills.

Table 7.1 Differences between collaborative work and cooperative work

Feature	Collaborative work	Cooperative work
Teacher	The teachers offer guidance and are a mediator	The teachers structure the work to be done by each group
Task	Defined by the members of the group	Assigned by the teacher
Responsibility for tasks	Individual and group	Each member is responsible for one task
Work distribution	The students work together	Either the teacher or the group may distribute the work among the members of the group
Subtasks	Intertwined, requiring group work	Independent
Working process	All together: never the sum of the parts	Bringing together the parts made by each member
Responsibility for learning	Responsibility is shared by the members of the group, with the guidance of the teacher	The teacher is made responsible and structures the work in a way that they believe will make the group learn
Type of knowledge	Non-foundational: reasoning, discussion and questioning are required	Basic, foundational: memorization and sometimes reasoning

Project-based learning (PBL)

The university's teaching environment has changed since the implementation of the EHEA. Concepts, methods and tools have been adopted in an attempt to converge on a higher quality of learning in all EU member states. In this sense, it is not just the role of universities (as teaching centres) that has changed; the role of students has altered, too. Those very students who were once seen as passive recipients of knowledge are now considered to be active agents, who acquire knowledge inside and outside the classroom (Reitmeier 2002: 43). Students are critical thinkers or, at least, they are expected to be. Thus, universities are no longer limited to teaching specific subjects to students; they must also fulfil other social aspects and commitments, as stated by Rodríguez-Sandoval, Vargas-Solano and Luna-Cortés (2010: 15). Therefore, it is essential to consider preparation beyond mastery of content related to particular disciplines. Students should develop key skills (analysis, synthesis, modelling, design, optimization), attitudes (social responsibility, environmental awareness, entrepreneurial spirit), values (ethics, tolerance, appreciation for knowledge) and qualities (creativity, initiative, leadership, critical thinking) (Salinas 2000).

In this sense, project-based learning complements collaborative learning to fulfil one of the main objectives of this project: learning to learn, so they are able to progress, develop and even reskill independently throughout life. Given the dynamics of global markets and technological change in current and future jobs, HE students will have to keep learning in formal, non-formal and informal environments once they graduate in order to respond to changes and challenges arising in the future. As Jones Rasmussen and Moffitt (1997) state, project-based learning (PBL), as a pedagogical model, develops the necessary skills to tackle these difficulties because it includes a set of learning tasks based on answering questions or solving problems, it involves learners in designing and planning their learning, making decisions and doing research, it allows learners to work relatively autonomously most of the time, and it results in a real project. In PBL, the main goal is to develop students' skills, abilities, attitudes and values (Maldonado Pérez 2008). The project should encourage students to work in realistic scenarios to develop skills such as research, critical thinking, creativity and even interpersonal skills.

Furthermore, in PBL the roles of the teacher and the students are completely transformed. The teacher becomes a designer of real-life experiences and acts as a guide. As in collaborative learning, teachers facilitate student-centred learning and create a classroom environment that leads to this type of work, by offering students the tools they need to realize their potential. Rodríguez-Sandoval, Vargas-Solano and Luna-Cortés (2010) have established different functions for the teacher in this context, which have been applied to the design of the project presented in this chapter. First, tutors must encourage the use of metacognitive processes to empower students to think about their learning needs and strategies. Secondly, tutors must reinforce group and individual study efforts. Thirdly, tutors should diagnose problems, offer solutions and offer appropriate feedback individually, both to each student and to the group as a whole. Finally, tutors must conduct assessment and provide feedback. In addition, Alcober, Ruiz and Valero (2003) indicate that the PBL process should be carried out under the supervision of the teacher and, for this reason, they conclude that follow-up mentoring is important to help students to develop their skills. Furthermore, they emphasize that the teacher's main role is not to provide direct instruction focused on content (although they can teach part of it), but to articulate good projects, offer each group a learning plan and provide frequent feedback on the progress of their work (Alcober, Ruiz and Valero 2003).

Likewise, for the students to be involved in their own formative processes, they must each make decisions about their learning goals and carry out research. In this way, PBL instruction offers a variety of benefits for the students (Rojas 2005, cited in Maldonado Pérez 2008: 161). First, PBL prepares students for their professional lives, as students develop key skills such as collaboration, project planning, decision-making and time management. Secondly, it increases motivation, which favours content-knowledge acquisition. Thirdly, PBL makes a connection between learning at university and in real life, which enhances deep learning. Through projects, students make use of higher-order mental skills rather than memorizing data with no connection to when and where it can be used in the real world. The more the projects look like the ones they will be involved in during their professional life, the more they will be engaged and therefore learn. And last, but not least, PBL increases self-esteem, as students take pride in accomplishing something of value outside the classroom, allowing them to make use of their individual strengths. Moreover, PBL tends to rely on information and communications technology (ICT). This makes the work even more attractive to students and helps them develop cross-cutting skills that are crucial in the professional world, i.e. instrumental skills (computer science, documentation and research), analytical and synthetic skills, linguistic skills, self-assessment and meta-assessment, and interpersonal skills that contribute to their ability to work with a diverse group (commitment, tolerance and solidarity).

For all these reasons, collaborative learning and project-based learning were the basic pillars of the project discussed in this chapter. They provided the foundation for a solid methodology that would achieve the learning objectives of the revised module.

Project background

The unit project started when we were assigned the French Culture and Civilization Module for the 2017–18 academic year. In previous years, students' academic results had been lower than expected – especially when we assume that undergraduates studying a Translation and Interpreting degree should be interested in learning about a new culture. For this reason, we conducted a survey asking former students to give their opinion on how the module had been taught. We also examined the syllabus to view the course content and, above all, to understand how it had been taught (see Table 7.2).

Table 7.2 Syllabus for this unit, from 2016 to 2017

---

1. PHYSICAL AND POLITICAL GEOGRAPHY OF FRANCE
   1.1 Orography (mountain ranges), hydrography (bodies of water) and climate: the shaping elements of 'gentle France'.
   1.2. Historical regions, administrative regions and territorial organization: from the "Hexagon" to the overseas territories.
2. MAJOR PERIODS OF HISTORY
   2.1. From pre-Roman Gaul to the great invasions.
   2.2. Medieval France: from Charlemagne to the Hundred Years War.
   2.3. The Renaissance: from religious wars to absolutism.
   2.4. The Age of Enlightenment: from the *Ancien Régime* to the Revolution.
   2.5. From the Empire to the Restoration.
   2.6. From the Restoration to the Commune.
   2.7. From the Third Republic to May 1968.
   2.8. From the Fifth Republic to Postmodernity.
3. IDENTITY FEATURES OF FRENCH CULTURE
   3.1 France "Land of Literature": Paris and the artistic avant-garde.
   3.2. La Francophonie: diversity of French-speaking communities in Europe, Africa and America.
   3.4. The world of education in France. The major cultural institutions.
   3.5. The media.
   3.6. The cinema
   3.7. The "French song".
   3.8. Gastronomy, fashion and cosmetics.
   3.9. France is a tourist country.

To restructure the syllabus effectively, three fundamental aspects were analysed. First, the distribution of the content throughout the module, as we pondered whether the order in which they were taught could influence the interest of students. Secondly, we considered whether the weight (number of hours) given to each topic was appropriate; considering the professional future of the students, we must bear in mind that this module should help them to solve any problems encountered in their future as translators and interpreters of French, so we wanted to prioritize what would be useful in their professional future. And thirdly, the opinion of the students, as it is important to know what students' interests are to forge a real commitment to their learning.

From our analysis of the syllabus, content and structure, we drew conclusions that were vital for redesigning the module. First, the order of the content did not necessarily coincide with students' interests concerning their Degree in Translation and Interpreting. Although this order might not seem to influence the learning, we consider it to be important because it constitutes the starting point and it could work as a 'hook' for the whole subject. Therefore, if students discover early on the usefulness of the subject for their future professional life, they will want to continue studying it. Likewise, bearing in mind the students' professional future as translators, we estimated that the module needed to prioritize the country's current affairs over its history. This approach would help students identify real-life applications of their learning, as they would be more likely to have to translate a text on educational or environmental policy than on Roman Gaul or the French Revolution. In addition, learning about what is happening today could awaken students' curiosity about how this has been influenced by past events. Prioritizing current affairs would also reduce the volume of content that students would need to memorize (i.e. information related to historical data). Finally, the course syllabus was overloaded with content, which made it difficult to teach all the topics during the expected four-month semester.

The feedback from former students confirmed our perception that the course was imbalanced and almost exclusively focused on French history and geography. The subject was based on lectures and the students were passive subjects of their own learning, which led to a lack of interest and motivation. For this reason, they did not believe that the module was useful to their professional development. These findings suggested that students were missing the opportunity to learn about French culture, which is a much-needed component of the translation process. In addition, it is important to involve students in their learning as a dynamic and ongoing process, inside and outside the classroom, to prepare them for their professional future. Students had to 'learn to learn' to face their present and future challenges as translators.

We wanted to make our students the protagonists of their learning, so we decided to ask them to organize an international tourism fair that would be hosted by the university. This event would focus on the students' learning instead of acting as part of the assessment, and it would celebrate their learning success.

Methodology

As explained above, when designing our syllabus, we wanted to attract the students' attention so that they would learn in a dynamic, intuitive and collaborative way with the rest of their classmates, the final objective of which would not be the grade obtained in the activity but the skills they developed. For this reason, the content of the syllabus was changed to ensure the quality of the learning (an objective of the EHEA) and to increase students' motivation by adapting the content to the realities of working in professional translation. Therefore, we adapted the syllabus to meet the thematic axes of the professional reality of the translator, seeking to increase the students' motivation. In this sense, we simplified it, focusing to a large extent on geopolitics and culture and reducing the topics dedicated to history. Instead, when approaching history, we decided to focus on those historical events that have marked France to this day and, therefore, the current political, financial and cultural situation. Secondly, we restructured the work's methodology, including project-based collaborative work to achieve lifelong learning and commitment on the part of the students. We split the module into two methodological parts, both containing project-based collaborative learning. Part One was taught over sixteen weeks and focused on the topics proposed in the syllabus. Part Two was focused on the final project, the international tourism fair. The theoretical content, corresponding with the topics presented in Table 7.3, was developed over sixteen weeks. Bearing in mind that the EHEA advocates procedural rather than conceptual learning

Table 7.3 Syllabus for this unit, from 2018 to 2019

1. Geopolitics
    1) Geography and regions of France
    2) Politics in France
    3) The educational structure
    4) The environment in France
    5) The economy in France
2. Culture
    1) Francophonie
    2) Tourism
    3) French music
    4) French cinema
    5) Gastronomy
3. History
    1) Charlemagne
    2) Joan of Arc History or Myth
    3) The Kings of Versailles
    4) The French Revolution

(i.e. learning based on the development of tasks through which the student learns by working), it was necessary to balance the weight of theoretical training and combine it with the performance of collaborative tasks. In this way, we alternated lectures on the cultural content of France with collaborative work in class, which focused on the preparation for the fair.

Structurally, the class was divided into groups of between two and four people. Each of the groups chose a topic from those offered in the syllabus, for which they had to prepare by carrying out prior research work so that instrumental competence would also be reinforced. After preparing the content, they gave a presentation to the rest of the class for a maximum of five to six minutes. Depending on the topics, the presentation instructions changed, although they always had to deliver the slides and a script in French, covering what they were going to explain. In addition, we gave each group the freedom to determine the depth of the study of the chosen content, although we also designed several instructions depending on the topics addressed. For example, for the geopolitical topics, they had to compare the French system of what was being taught with that of their own country. For the cultural topics, they had to study one aspect of the topic taught, in depth – for example, a musical genre, a film director, the gastronomy of a particular region, the most important monuments and festivities of a region, etc. And finally, regarding the history topics, it was necessary to construct a comparison between what was happening in France at the time and what was happening in their own country.

This phase was of vital importance for the students' learning and motivation, given that the research work was comparative, making them learn not only about French culture but also the culture of their classmates' countries and their own, if different. It also allows them to delve into issues of the past, their relevance in the present, and potential correlation in the future so that the knowledge acquired went beyond what could be taught in a masterclass, while also allowing them to pursue knowledge according to their interests.

Once the objectives of the preparation and documentation phase (research) were achieved, we moved on to the dissertation phase (presentation), which consisted of the oral presentation of the topic worked on by the students. This phase, which was carried out in two class sessions, included two aspects: on the one hand, the discovery aspect, in which the students learned other points of view and interests that had not been revealed or had been ignored in the previous phase; and secondly, the presentation of their work, not only to the teacher but also to the rest of their classmates. Once the students had presented their work in turn, they created questions about the content of their work and offered answers. In this sense, they prepared study materials not only for themselves but also for the rest of their classmates, as these topics had to be revised because they were part of the assessment. The relevance of this activity is substantial, because students not only prepare the material but also determine the content according to their learning interests and what they consider more valuable for that topic, feeling that their work is of real use.

The second part also followed a series of stages related to the organization, planning and delivery of the project (international tourism fair). However, this work took place mostly outside the classroom. We chose tourism because it allowed us to put collaborative work into practice again and tourism is a subject that includes many aspects of French culture studied in Part One, such as geography, culture and history. As in the first part and given that the respective work teams had already been set up, the first phase consisted of developing the content. It was structured into three compulsory activities: the preparation of a tourist brochure on a monument or site of interest, chosen freely by the group; the production of a tourist guide on a French-speaking region or city, written first in Spanish and subsequently translated into French (it is important to highlight that the brochure had to belong to the same region); and finally, the students were allowed to produce audiovisual material by making a promotional video of the region or city chosen by the group.

After the preparation of all the resources, in the next stage, we would celebrate the international tourism fair. This involved, on the one hand, setting up stands and making available the material related to their area of work, whether it was brochures, guides, videos, posters, gastronomy or any other material of the group's choice. Finally, as in the previous stages, each group had to prepare ten questions for the exam on the topic they worked on.

The first part represented 30 per cent of the total mark and was evaluated through a rubric with a score ranging from one to four, one being unsatisfactory and four being excellent, considering indicators such as the compilation of content, the selection of content, written expression in the presentation, written expression in the script, and oral expression and clarity in the presentation.

The second part corresponded to 40 per cent of the final mark, and like the previous one, was evaluated through a rubric from one to four, with one being unsatisfactory and four being excellent. In this case, the indicators were the following: compilation and selection of contents; translation of the contents in the brochure, guide and video; written expression in French, both for the brochure and the guide; oral expression, both in the recording of the video and also during the tourism fair in their communicative exchanges at their stand.

Finally, the presentation of the contents was also assessed. It should be noted that the result derived from the evaluation by rubric is subsequently transferred to the Spanish evaluation system of one to ten.[3]

The remaining percentage of assessment, 30 per cent, was reserved for the final exam. As mentioned above, for each topic (fourteen), each group prepared ten multiple-choice questions from the presentations plus ten questions on the final project for a total of 750 questions. The exam included 100 random questions from those prepared by the students and was carried out through the Moodle platform.

Results and discussion

This section discusses the results and includes reflections on the students' attainment in both parts of the assessment. We present the results divided into the two parts explained in the previous section: the 'learning in class' (Part One) and 'learning at home' (Part Two). We also discuss the students' commitment to learning and the content learned because, for us, it was not only the grade classification that was important but also the degree to which students were engaged in their own learning.

Part One: Learning in class

The students demonstrated motivation and a commitment to learning as the course progressed. Although it was not evident at the beginning, as the course progressed, we observed greater interest and participation in the understanding of the topics covered in class. After the first two weeks of the course, attendance continued to be high, at 90–95 per cent. Furthermore, class participation was fluent, French was increasingly used as a vehicular language and, by the end of the course, it was the only language spoken in the classroom. This situation was enhanced thanks to the arrival of Erasmus students from Germany, Turkey and the United Kingdom because they did not speak fluent Spanish and all the students had to make an effort to communicate between them in French, which encouraged their participation. It is important to add that the quality of the students' projects increased steadily thanks to the implemented project-based learning, as they expanded their knowledge of various areas of French culture and society. This is objectively reflected in the assessment rubrics for each of the projects and dissertations presented. The steady increase in the quality of the students' work was beneficial for the whole class and evident in the development of their academic and interpersonal skills: the students reported to have learned to be more tolerant, improved their collaboration skills and developed their team spirit. Likewise, based on qualitative observation, the students' oral and written competence improved as a result of the projects, presentations and debates carried out in class. Concerning the objective assessment, the average score for each group was between nine and ten, although at the beginning the grades had been lower (seven to eight). As the course progressed and the students' motivation increased, their marks improved. However, a reported negative aspect was that the module covered too many topics. For this reason, we plan to adjust the syllabus design so that it is possible for students to learn about each topic in more depth.

Part Two: Learning at home

The students engaged positively in this activity, generating high-quality material. Thanks to the project-based collaborative work, which led them to investigate and cover more aspects than had been asked of them, they developed a strong team spirit. Thus, they produced brochures and tourist guides that looked professional and were more linguistically accurate than what had been expected in relation to the level required for this module. Of the five groups, two of them chose to record scenes in places in our city but pretending to be in the region of France that they had to promote, performing as tourist guides, and showing places of interest and customs. Two other groups decided to edit videos of the studied region taken from the internet. They wrote the script, voiced and edited the video, with one of these groups even subtitling it. The last group decided to combine both modalities. The group members recorded themselves presenting the places and mixed these videos with others they had found on the internet. The video editing was done to a professional standard. In terms of content, all the groups referred to the places of interest, customs and typical gastronomy of the studied regions. They used persuasive language, typical of tourist guides who might want to cajole a potential tourist. As far as oral expression is concerned, it should be noted that these were students whose first foreign language is English and not French. However, they took great care in their oral expression in French and, in all cases, exceeded the level required in this module. All the students and teaching staff in the Faculty of Arts were invited to the international tourism fair, at which the students presented their work in French, offered samples of food and drink from the region they had studied, screened their videos and answered any questions from the attendees in French. The activity celebrated the learning of the entire class. Concerning the students' grades, out of five groups (four or five students in each), three obtained a score between 9 and 10 (outstanding), while one obtained an 8 and the remaining one a 6. These results are good, but there is room for improvement. The results of the student satisfaction survey were positive (4.32 out of 5; the overall score for the University of Córdoba is 4 out of 5). However, the survey does not gather specific data on the methodology used, but rather on the teaching in general. It would have been of great interest to check students' satisfaction levels with the progress they made through the project.

The final exam

Out of the twenty-one students who took the exam,[4] 71.4 per cent scored between 9 and 10, 28.6 per cent scored between 8 and 7, and none scored less than a 7. In other words, the results for the final section of the assessment were highly satisfactory.

Conclusions

As we have seen throughout this chapter, we aimed to report on the application of a new method for the teaching of the French Culture and Civilization Module in the Degree of Translation and Interpreting at the University of Córdoba (Spain) during the academic year 2017–18.

As universities adapt their curricula and syllabi to the EHEA, they are implementing and consolidating new learning methodologies that centre on the competencies that university students must achieve by the time they have completed their degree. Students must learn to adapt to different work environments and professional situations, so tutors and lecturers must base their teaching on a transversal and non-linear model.

To achieve two of the main objectives of the EHEA – lifelong learning and quality assurance – a student-centred learning method was implemented for the French Culture and Civilization Module of the Degree in Translation and Interpreting. To this end, the key objectives were to increase students' motivation and develop a positive attitude towards collaborative learning. The international tourism fair project emphasized students' learning outcomes rather than their marks and celebrated their learning success.

To carry out these objectives successfully, we focused on the methodologies proposed by collaborative work and project-based learning. These two points laid the foundations for the development of this project, which focused on the premises established by the EHEA. We must ensure that the knowledge acquired by our students is lasting and enables them to develop new competences in the future, especially with a view to their professional future. To this end, a learning plan was designed from the outset, the theoretical and practical contents that had been taught to date were analysed and the students were involved in drawing up a guide, always under the supervision of the teaching staff. Moreover, learning was divided into two parts: on the one hand, the acquisition of knowledge in class, and on the other, the acquisition of knowledge at home. The first part took place in class with activities ranging from lectures, project development and project presentation. The second part focused on the preparation of materials for a tourism fair. The students were also involved in the preparation of some of the material for assessment, such as the preparation of the exam questions, for which they had to prepare the content as explained previously in the chapter. As we have seen in the previous sections, the results of this project were very positive, both qualitatively and quantitatively in terms of the grades obtained and the improvements in reading comprehension, and oral and written expression skills.

This has been demonstrated in the evaluations carried out and in the development of the classes themselves. On the one hand, as mentioned above, the results of the projects assessed using the rubric described above became increasingly high, and after two weeks of classes, attendance was almost 100 per cent and French became the vehicular language. In addition, students commented on several occasions that they felt very satisfied in class and that they were learning. During the fair, the students were able to communicate fluently in French with the audience, easily explaining all aspects of the area they had researched. Once the fair was over, in the last class, they commented on their impressions of the fair and all their evaluations were very positive. However, we set out the below measures for improvement which we intend to implement in future:

1) Simplification of the length of the material produced with a word-count limit to avoid the imbalance of textual content that was present in written material such as guides and brochures.

2) Improvements in the management of groups: a) establishment of well-defined guidelines for collaborative work through group mentoring, such as the assignment of roles to each group member, chosen according to the skills of the students (coordinator, documentalist, translator, reviewer, layout designer and

video editor); b) creation of a general forum on the Moodle platform for the resolution of generic and common doubts about the work, while the teacher will answer specific questions about specific cases; c) together with the textual material and the promotional video, the students will hand in a video in which they will explain the methodology carried out and the description of the phases that make up the project (group organization and meetings, with the specification of dates and objectives, justified distribution of tasks, process and phases of the project, problems encountered and ways or strategies of resolution implemented); and d) updating the survey for the participating students regarding their satisfaction with the project as a collaborative learning activity and with the procedural work in their team, emphasizing aspects such as respect, responsibility, meeting deadlines, communication and consensus in decision-making, etc.

As for future proposals, we consider it necessary to make methodological adaptations, given the recent reduction in attendance due to unforeseen circumstances, such as the COVID-19 pandemic. These adaptations will be implemented in subsequent academic years. The video conferencing tools that we currently use at the University of Córdoba (BlackBoard Collaborate, Microsoft Teams and Cisco-Webex) allow us to divide the class into groups, so it is possible to successfully develop collaborative work without in-class presence. Therefore, we propose that the next international tourism fair is carried out virtually through the Cisco-Webex platform. This will give the students the possibility to showcase their learning beyond the walls of the Faculty of Arts. To carry out this proposal, we consider it necessary to add a community manager to the groups for the tasks described above. Each group will have to promote their virtual stand before the fair. To do so, they will have to create a Twitter profile and disseminate content, either referring to their work or the promotion of the region chosen for their work, and always tag the teaching staff so that we can include it in the final assessment. We expect that the virtualization of the international fair and the inclusion of social media in the work could further encourage student motivation. However, despite any obstacles described above, we are convinced that collaborative experiences such as this one greatly enhance the motivation of students taking this module. This was conducive to an improvement in oral and written comprehension, as well as expression skills in the second language and, therefore, an improvement in the obtained grades and learning results.

Finally, the professional world requires people to be motivated by and committed to their work and their learning. Therefore, it is essential to tailor any learning plan to students' future professional needs. If students' professional needs are not considered, they will not value what they have learned. They will simply study to pass an exam, and they will lack training when carrying out their work in the professional world.

Notes

1 For cooperative work, see Ovejero 1990; Johnson et al. 1999; Morales 2008a, 2008b; Guitert and Jiménez 2000; García et al. 2001.
2 All translations in Table 1 have been made by the authors of the chapter.
3 The system corresponds approximately to the rubric published by Goldsmiths, University of London for Erasmus students, where they offer equivalences between the UK and participating European countries' grading systems. The grades are presented here in the format 'Spain (UK %, ECTS)': 10 (80%, A), 9 (70%, A), 8 (65%, B), 7 (57%, C), 6 (50%, C), 5 (43%, E), 4.9 and below (39% and below, F). Available online: https://www.gold.ac.uk/media/documents-by-section/staff-and-students/students/go-abroad/erasmus-conversion-tables.pdf.
4 Twenty-eight students were enrolled, twenty-one took the exam, the remaining seven followed the Erasmus programme in other countries.

References

Alcober, J., S. Ruiz and M. Valero (2003), 'Evaluación de la implantación del aprendizaje basado en proyectos en la EPSC (2001–2003)', in *XI Congreso Universitario de Innovación Educativa en las Enseñanzas Técnicas* (23), 23–5, Vilanova i la Geltrú, Barcelona: Escola Universitària Politècnica de Vilanova i la Geltrú.

Benito, A., and A. Cruz (2005). *Nuevas claves para la docencia universitaria en el Espacio Europeo de Educación Superior*, Madrid: Narcea.

Bruffee, K. (1995), 'Sharing Our Toys. Cooperative Learning versus Collaborative Learning', *Change*, 27 (1): 12–18.

De Miguel, M. (2005), *Modalidades de enseñanzas centradas en el desarrollo de competencias. Orientaciones para promover el cambio metodológico en el espacio europeo de educación superior*. Oviedo: Ministerio de Educación y Ciencia and Universidad de Oviedo.

Dillenbourg, P., M. Baker, M. Blaye and O. Malley (1996), 'The Evolution of Research on Collaborative Learning', in E. Spada and P. Reiman (eds), *Learning in Humans and Machine: Towards an Interdisciplinary Learning Science*, 189–211, Oxford: Elsevier.

Espacio Europeo de Educación Superior (2019), European Education Area: Higher Education, *European Commission*. Available online: https://education.ec.europa.eu/es/education-levels/higher-education.

Esteve, F., and M. Gisbert (2011), 'El nuevo paradigma de aprendizaje y las nuevas tecnologías', *Revista de Docencia Universitaria*, 9 (3): 55–73.
García, R., J. A. Traver and I. Candela (2001), *Aprendizaje cooperativo: Fundamentos, características y técnicas*. Madrid: CCS.
Guitert, M., and F. Jiménez (2000), 'Trabajo cooperativo en entornos virtuales de aprendizaje', in J. M. Duart Montoliu and A. Sangrá Morer (eds), *Aprender de la virtualidad*, 113–34, Barcelona: Gedisa.
Jarauta Borrasca, B. (2014), 'Collaborative Learning in the University: Models and Practice', *REDU: Revista de docencia universitaria*, 12 (4): 281–302.
Jones, N. F., C. M. Rasmussen and M. C. Moffitt (1997), *Real-life Problem Solving: A Collaborative Approach to Interdisciplinary Learning*, Washington DC: American Psychological Association.
Johnson, D. W., R. Johnson and E. Holubec (1999), *Nuevos círculos del aprendizaje* (Spanish ed.), Buenos Aires: Aique.
Maldonado Pérez, M. (2007), 'El trabajo colaborativo en el aula universitaria', *Laurus*, 13 (23): 263–78.
Maldonado Pérez, M. (2008), 'Aprendizaje basado en proyectos colaborativos. Una experiencia en educación superior', *Laurus*, 12 (14): 158–80.
Morales, P. (2008a), *El aprendizaje cooperativo*, Barcelona: Graó.
Morales, P. (2008b), 'Nuevos roles de profesores y alumnos, nuevas formas de enseñar y aprender', in L. Prieto Navarro (ed.), *La enseñanza universitaria centrada en el aprendizaje*, 17–29, Barcelona: Octaedro.
Niemi, H. (2009), 'Why from Teaching to Learning?', *European Journal of Education*, 8 (1): 1–17.
Ovejero, A. (1990). *El aprendizaje cooperativo: una alternativa eficaz a la enseñanza tradicional*, Barcelona: Promociones y Publicaciones Universitarias.
Panitz, T., and P. Panitz (1998), 'Encouraging the use of collaborative learning in higher education', in J. J. Forest (ed.), *Issues Facing International Education*, 161–202, New York: Garland Publishing.
Pérez, I., S. Bustamante and M. Maldonado (2007), 'Aprendizaje en equipo y coaching en educación. Una experiencia innovadora', Publicación en extenso en Memoria de VII Reunión Nacional de Currículo y I Congreso Internacional de Calidad e Innovación en Educación Superior. Caracas: Universidad Simón Bolívar.
Reitmeier, C. A. (2002), 'Active Learning in the Experimental Study of Food', *Journal of Food Science Education*, 1: 41–4.
Rodríguez-Sandoval, E., E. Vargas-Solano and J. Luna-Cortés (2010), 'Evaluación de la estrategia "aprendizaje basado en proyectos"', *Educación y Educadores*, 13 (1): 13–25.
Rué, J. (2007), *Enseñar en la universidad. El EEES como reto para la Educación Superior*, Madrid: Narcea.
Salinas, J. (2000), 'El aprendizaje colaborativo con los nuevos canales de comunicación', in J. Cabero (ed.), *Nuevas tecnologías aplicadas a la educación*, 199–277, Madrid: Síntesis.

8

Translating Film Reviews as a Means of Improving Students' Interlinguistic and Plurilingual Abilities

Mazal Oaknín

Introduction

Film reviews carry out an evaluation of a film's overall quality with the purpose of determining whether the film in question should or should not be recommended to the public. Unlike scholarly film articles, whose target readership is a specialized one, film reviews are intended for a wider readership that is mostly comprised of non-specialists. Both the formal techniques employed and the thematic content are analysed in an expert, yet accessible way. It is also common to observe a critic's subjective biases and individual perception of the film within their review (Corrigan 2001).

The important role that feature films and, in particular, film clips play in the foreign-language curriculum has been remarked upon by many scholars (Kaiser 2011; Kaiser and Shibahara 2014; Viebrock 2016; Thaler 2017; Herrero and Vanderschelden 2019; Herrero, Suarez and Sánchez-Requena's chapter in this volume). Tied in with the popular commercial appeal of motion pictures, film reviews have proven to be a valuable tool in the advanced levels of foreign-language education, particularly in the translation classroom (Edwards 1999; Holden 2000; Fluitt-Dupuy 2001). The textual characteristics of these relatively short pieces of writing encompass a mixture of registers, an abundance of adjectives, intensifiers, locutions and different tenses used in the description of the film's plot, technical words, idiomatic and colloquial expressions, and metaphors, among others. As Edwards (1999: 554) asserts, film reviews provide 'material to teach awareness toward the linguistic, textual, elements important within translation work'; furthermore, these authentic texts 'reveal attractive, innovative and dynamic use of language, frequent use of intertextuality, and, undeniably, reviews also reflect a society and its cultural values'.

While Edwards's article focuses on the use of film reviews to develop students' linguistic skills, the objective of this paper is to address the significant gap in the pedagogical use of film reviews in the translation classroom by examining how these versatile materials can also be used to improve students' plurilingual skills. Utilizing Calhourn's (2010) *Time Out* review of *Invictus* (Eastwood 2009) as a case study, this classroom-based study describes the design and implementation of the task-based activities in the English–Spanish translation module for HE students of Spanish. *Invictus* revolves around the events taking place in South Africa before and during the 1995 Rugby World Cup that followed the dismantling of apartheid, the system of institutionalized racial segregation that ruled in South Africa and South West Africa (present-day Namibia) from 1948 until the early 1990s. Therefore, besides encompassing the textual characteristics listed above, this particular review is rich in historical and social references to life under apartheid. The interactive assignment was conceived as a series of preliminary discussions to be carried out in small groups of students prior to the translation of the text. While some of the activities involve close textual analysis, others centre on the development of students' awareness and knowledge of other cultures. Thus, a case will be made for the use of film reviews in the translation class as a means of improving not only students' linguistic abilities, but their interlinguistic and intercultural abilities as well. Based on the Process in the Acquisition of Translation Competence and Evaluation (PACTE) group's identification of six translation sub-competences (2003) and on Carreres, Noriega-Sánchez and Calduch's (2018) recommended preparatory activities, the discussion-based approach will seek to fine-tune students' translation skills and to improve their command of Spanish. Likewise, by capitalizing on the film's historical background, and through the use of mediation (Trovato 2016; North and Piccardo 2017), my approach focuses on the development of their interlinguistic and plurilingual abilities. Finally, recommendations are given on how teachers might choose film reviews which are best suited for this purpose based on the film's main themes and on their potential for mediation in plurilingual groups.

Theoretical background

Film reviews as a genre

In *A Short Guide to Writing about Film*, Timothy Corrigan posits that 'the way we write about film and the critical position we choose vary on the audience we are writing for' (2001: 8), and this view is subsequently shared by Clayton and Klevan (2011), De Jong and Burgers (2013) and Davis (2019). In order to determine which type of film essays can be best exploited in the translation classroom, Corrigan's categorization is a very valuable starting point for textual analysis. He specifically distinguishes between four types of text: a screening report, a movie review, a theoretical essay and a critical essay. The screening report is an objective, descriptive assignment used to prepare for class discussions and examinations whose sole readership is the course's instructor. The theoretical essay is a highly specialized piece of work aimed at an academic and intellectual community possessing extensive knowledge of the film in question. The critical essay, typically written for film studies modules, assumes that its readership is familiar with the film in question and, rather than dwelling on the film's plot, tends to delineate the diegetic complexities and extra-diegetic context of the film. This chapter, however, focuses on film reviews, a journalistic genre which Corrigan defines as 'the type of film analysis with which most of us are chiefly familiar, since it appears in almost every newspaper' (2001: 9). As the aim of a film review is to introduce the said film, such texts presume the reader has not (yet) watched the film.

Film reviews encompass personal and idiosyncratic reactions to and evaluations of a film as well as objective analyses of the film's formal techniques and thematic content. While film reviews tend to have a relatively low word count (approximately 600 to 1,200 words), Corrigan (2001) warns that a great deal of preparation is needed prior to their writing. Authors are advised to watch previous films by the same director or writer or to familiarize themselves with the bodies of work by the actors and screenwriters involved in order to better contextualize the film in question. According to Corrigan (2001), at least two viewings of the film are recommended. The first viewing should focus on the overall cinematic experience. The second viewing should highlight the film's formal techniques and thematic elements. Some of the main aspects of filmmaking to be taken into account, which will be highlighted in the film review, are the following: cinematography, editing, mise-en-scène, lighting, diegetic and non-diegetic sound, genre, narratology, acting, themes and tone, production design, pace and dialogue. After combining the film's formal and thematic elements, authors will create a strong central claim that will act as the backbone of their film review.

In the twenty-first century, however, the distinctions between the different texts categorized by Corrigan (2001) are often blurred. This is due to the fact that a considerable proportion of what constitutes writing about film appears on the internet, where different intended audiences are merged. With the aim of developing students' interlinguistic and plurilingual abilities, we recommend focusing on film essays that prominently showcase main characteristics of film reviews. Hence, a great deal of the essay should be dedicated to summarizing the film's plot and/or contextualizing the film, considering that the intended readership should be the general public with no prior knowledge of the film and no expertise in film studies.

Developing students' interlinguistic capabilities

The PACTE research group was created in 1997 with the aim of investigating the acquisition of translation competence in inverse and direct translation. All its founding members are translators and translation teachers who train professional translators in the Facultat de Traducció i d'Interpretació of the Universitat Autònoma de Barcelona. The PACTE defines translation competence as 'the underlying system of knowledge and skills needed to be able to translate. This competence is actualized in different ways in different situations' (PACTE 2000: 100). However, there is a great deal of taxonomies regarding the sub-competences conforming the translation competence (PACTE 1998, 2000, 2001a, 2001b). We shall work with PACTE's revised translation competence (TC) model (2003) with the purpose of showing how appropriate film reviews can teach awareness towards the different elements (cultural, linguistic, textual) that are key in translation. The TC is defined as the underlying knowledge system of declarative and procedural knowledge needed to translate. According to PACTE, the translation competence is composed of a system of sub-competences that are defined as inter-related and hierarchical, and these relationships are open to variations. The sub-competences of translation competence include the following: 'a language sub-competence in two languages; an extra-linguistic sub-competence; an instrumental/professional sub-competence; a psychophysiological sub-competence; a transfer sub-competence; and a strategic sub-competence' (PACTE 2003: 3–4). As will be seen when considering these sub-competences, film reviews offer a more dynamic, rewarding source of authentic texts for affording materials with which students can develop their translation competence as per the above definition.

The language sub-competence is understood as the underlying system of knowledge and abilities that are needed in order to establish linguistic communication in both the source language and the target languages. Film reviews commonly combine formal and informal registers of the language.

While film reviews tend to include technical terms associated with film production, they also contain accessible, informal plot summaries. Students will be required to detect the different registers used in the source text, and to successfully produce a target text that reproduces these shifts in tone, style, nuance and lexical choice.

The extra-linguistic sub-competence mainly refers to the implicit or explicit bicultural, encyclopaedic and subject knowledge. Since film reviews are aimed at a non-specialist readership that does not have any prior knowledge of the film in question, students need to acquire the necessary knowledge to provide the potential readers of the target text with an appropriate background on the topic.

The instrumental/professional sub-competence comprises the knowledge and abilities related to the practice of professional translation. Students are required to use all kinds of documentation sources and new technologies that equip them with the necessary linguistic and contextual knowledge to successfully translate the film review. This entails using suitable specialized or technical terms in the target language, keeping in mind the intended readership, and adequately grasping all the figures of speech related to the film's plot that are so common in film reviews.

The psycho-physiological sub-competence is defined as the ability to use psychomotor, cognitive and attitudinal resources. This involves relying on one's memory, creativity, logical reasoning and reflexes. When translating film reviews, it should be anticipated that not all students are familiar with the film analysed in the text. Furthermore, not every student is able to fully grasp all the figures of speech and technical terms used. In their work as part of a group, this sub-competence needs to be used optimally in order to achieve a satisfactory result.

The transfer sub-competence is defined as the ability to complete the transfer process from the source text to the target text, and as such is considered to be the central competence that integrates all the others. Not only will students need to fully understand the film review in the source language and re-express it in the target language, but they should also keep in mind what the aim of the translation is and what type of readership they are writing for.

The strategic sub-competence comprises the series of individual procedures that are needed to solve the problems faced during the translation process. With the purpose of producing a high-quality translated text, students should be able to identify any challenges, brainstorm, make choices, and solve any problems and compensate for any weaknesses in the other sub-competencies.

While film reviews allow students to develop their translation competence by fostering the knowledge and acquisition of the sub-competences explained above, Edwards (1999: 553) highlights the potential for fostering the 'improvement' technique.[1] Due to the fact that reviews appear in different types of publications with varying 'quality' – and may include transferred words – one can often find examples of texts where students have to identify orthographic mistakes and erroneous film titles, and therefore produce an improved text.

Fostering plurilingual skills through the use of film reviews

As indicated previously, the case study text in this chapter is a review of *Invictus*, a 2009 American-South African biographical sports drama film directed by Clint Eastwood and starring highly acclaimed actors Morgan Freeman and Matt Damon. The film is based on John Carlin's book *Playing the Enemy: Nelson Mandela and the Game That Made a Nation* (2008), which details the events in South Africa before and during the 1995 Rugby World Cup. Having spent twenty-seven years in jail, Nelson Mandela is released from Victor Versten Prison on 11 February 1990. Four years later, in 1994, Mandela is elected the first black president of South Africa. His presidency faces significant challenges in the post-apartheid era, such as abject poverty and appalling crime rates. Mandela is particularly troubled about racial divisions between black and white South Africans, which could result in large-scale violence. Taking advantage of the fact that South Africa is set to host the 1995 Rugby World Cup in one year's time, Mandela convinces the newly black-dominated South African Sports Committee to support the traditionally all-white Springboks, the national rugby union team that had yet not competed in the first two World Cups due to international anti-apartheid sporting boycotts. He subsequently makes contact with the captain of the Springboks rugby team, François Pienaar (Matt Damon), and suggests that a Springboks victory in the World Cup will bring together and inspire the South African nation.

The original text of the *Invictus* review published in the *Time Out* online magazine was approximately 600 words long and goes on to examine the performances given by both lead actors and Eastwood. However, for the Advanced Translation class, only the opening three paragraphs were used. While the word count tallies up to 275, this selected excerpt abounds in collocations, compounding in English, metaphors, technical terms, idioms, colloquial language and false friends. This text is brief enough to be covered in a single lesson yet sufficiently rich in material for analysis and group discussion:

> He turns 80 this year and claims *Gran Torino* was his last outing as an actor. But, as a director, Clint Eastwood is keeping his nose to the grindstone. He spent the

end of 2009 filming a Peter Morgan-penned thriller, *Hereafter*, in Europe and the US, and earlier last year decamped to South Africa to film this respectful, rousing drama about Nelson Mandela's canny co-opting of the 1995 Rugby World Cup Finals as a tool to promote racial harmony across the social and political tinderbox that was the new, post-apartheid state.

Eastwood isn't a director to indulge in shades of grey and so the film's first shots of the historic, televised release of Mandela (lead actor Morgan Freeman) from prison in 1990 are preceded by a full shot of white boys playing rugby on one side of the road while their black equivalents kick a football on the other. Simple editing: a background of division established – job done.

A similar, no-nonsense efficiency colours the whole film, which jumps forward to Mandela's inauguration in 1994, again mixing reconstruction and news footage, before ditching this early documentary feel to jump cut into a behind-the-scenes walk-through of the early months of his presidency. This was a time when existing presidential staff wrongly expected to be booted out of their jobs; a black civil-rights group believed, also wrongly, that Mandela would support their desire to change the name and colours of the national rugby team; and somewhere in a white suburb the captain of that same team, François Pienaar (Matt Damon) and his family were shaking their heads at the assumption that their country was heading to the dogs.

Calhourn 2010

This adapted film review was used as part of the module SPAN0034 Translation into Spanish, a mandatory component of the BA Spanish and Latin American Studies which I teach at University College London's Department of Spanish, Portuguese and Latin American Studies. This is an advanced Spanish language module designed for finalists, consolidating level C1 and exploring level C2 of the CEFRL. SPAN0034 is a final-year module whose main objectives are the following: to improve students' linguistic and translation skills (from English into Spanish); to introduce students to a variety of text types and textual conventions; to foster collaborative learning and teamwork; to teach students to use reliable sources and to develop their dictionary and documentation skills; to prepare students for the 'translation from English into Spanish' section of the written exam in Term 3; and to use translation as a valuable communicative skill in order to develop students' interlinguistic and intercultural abilities. These objectives mirror the trend in recent years which has seen translation teachers and professionals acknowledge the role of translation as an irreplaceable pedagogical vehicle. In today's increasingly globalized world, translation plays a double role, not only as a useful tool for foreign-language learning, but also as a valuable communicative skill which is key in intercultural mediation. The approach when designing this module was very much informed by Carreres, Noriega-Sánchez and Calduch's *Mundos en Palabras. Learning Advanced Spanish Through Translation* (2018), a pioneering work which provides its readers with a current approach to the question of how to use translation in class thanks to an innovative bridge between Translation Studies and Additional Language Learning. As argued by these authors, the role of translation in language teaching is two-fold: as a means – in as much as it contributes to the improvement of the command of the language – and as an end – in as much as it constitutes a skill per se. It should be noted that this latter notion of translation as an end is not limited to the professional arena, for it is also intrinsically connected to the development of students' interlinguistic and intercultural capabilities. Moreover, the recent trend in language teaching is to consider translation as the fifth skill in foreign-language learning, and to integrate it into grammar lessons (Naimushin 2002; Baker 2006; Gaspar 2009; Leonardi 2010; Ayachia 2018). Recent studies have suggested different areas that should be highlighted when considering the use of translation in the language classroom. Jiménez-Crespo (2018) explores the role of translation technologies in Spanish-language learning; Naga and McGill (2018) and Schechter (2018) address cultural difference and interpretive diversity in the classroom; Calduch and Talaván (2018) focus on the use of audiodescription in teaching Spanish as a foreign language; and Cerezo (2018) and Sánchez Cuadrado (2018) have highlighted the value of collaborative translation in the context of language learning.

On average, the SPAN0034 groups are composed of twelve students. According to UCL Student Registry Services, in the academic year 2017/18 the university boasted a total of 18,271 undergraduate students.[2] At the time of making their applications, 52.9 per cent were UK residents, 15.7 per cent were domiciled in other countries within the European Union, and 31.4 per cent were domiciled in other overseas countries. Given these figures, it is only logical to expect that many of the students in the Department of Spanish, Portuguese and Latin American Studies speak English as a second language, and that for many of them Spanish is not the only foreign language they have studied. In fact, some of them choose to study Portuguese along with Spanish on this programme, and others opt for the various combinations on UCL's Modern Languages BA, which besides offering more traditional options, such as Portuguese and German, proposes over 300 possible modern language combinations. Not only do these students come from different countries, but normally they have just returned from their year abroad, as the third year is spent in a Spanish-speaking country – an experience which benefits students' linguistic and cultural understanding.

Moreover, those students combining Spanish with another language split their year abroad between two different countries. It is, therefore, safe to avow that these classes are plurilingual environments. In the manual *Mundos en Palabras*, Carreres, Noriega-Sánchez and Calduch (2018) propose that, prior to translating any given text, students start by reading the target text very carefully. In addition to fully grasping its general meaning, students should also carry out a detailed textual analysis. This will inform their decisions as translators and help to better define their translation strategy. Table 8.1, which shows issues and related questions to be discussed for the translation of the film review, is a condensed version of the exhaustive list of questions put forward by these authors (Carreres, Noriega-Sánchez and Calduch 2018: 24–5).

When attempting to answer these questions with regards to the film review of *Invictus*, it is evident that not all students will be able to answer all of them correctly and/or completely. Not all students have the same fluency in English since not all of them are native speakers. Similarly, not all students have the same command of Spanish grammar; their cultural knowledge and awareness of different registers differ, as does their familiarity with the film in question, with South African history, with rugby as a sport and as a symbol of the apartheid regime, and with film analysis. Prior to the group activity of translating the review, the students were asked to work together to answer the below questions, which they had to mediate with their peers.

Table 8.1 Guide to pre-translation textual analysis based on Carreres, Noriega-Sánchez and Calduch's (2018) model (source: the author of the chapter)

Subject, author and context	Who is the author and what is their aim?
	What is the overall message or theme of the text?
	What is the textual typology?
	What is the intended readership?
	Are there any extra-linguistic references?
Textual structure and cohesion	How is the text structured?
	What are the linking words and cohesive devices used?
Grammar and vocabulary	What is the lexical repertoire? Are there any technical terms?
	What kind of grammar and syntactic structures appear in the text?
	Are there any idiomatic expressions and colloquialisms?
Stylistic elements	What is the language variety used in the text?
	Does the text use a single register?
	Are there any figures of speech?

Mediation in translation

In May 2018, the Council of Europe published the *CEFR Companion Volume with New Descriptors* as an official extension of the CEFR(L). This volume introduces the concept of mediation as a mode of communication. In the United Kingdom, foreign-language departments and schools have different historical backgrounds and distinctive educational traditions, as do the rest of European institutions, so the integration of mediation as a newly introduced communication skill in the curriculum is still to be explored and investigated in further depth.[3] The topic prompts important questions such as: How can language learners and translators act as mediators in international communication? In which ways can language teachers train translators and students to mediate in multicultural settings? How can mediation be assessed as a new communicative competence in language and translation modules? It has been demonstrated that international exchanges such as the Year Abroad programme can support the development of mediation competences. Nonetheless, it is crucial to find new avenues for students to develop and improve complex communicative skills in the context of the language classroom. These complex communicative skills must comprehend not only the traditional language skills – reading, writing, listening and speaking – but also more advanced skills such as reformulating ideas, condensing information, providing definitions, explaining extra-linguistic and cultural references, shifting registers, etc. Indeed, the importance of these 'soft skills' cannot be underestimated, for much of our language students' future work will involve interpersonal interaction. Indeed, interaction is a crucial skill and one for which our language lessons should provide activities in order to develop it. Taking on board the need to incorporate mediation into Spanish as a foreign-language syllabus and emphasizing the link between translation and mediation,[4] Trovato (2016) avows that mediation is the result of the merging of two skills: communicative competence and translative competence. From a teacher's point of view, the objective should not be to train students to become professional mediators, but to encourage students to play an active role in the overall integration process. This can be achieved by formally or informally mediating for people who do not yet have proficiency in the language or a full understanding of the culture and norms of the host society.

Moreover, North and Piccardo (2017: 85) distinguish between four types of mediation: a) linguistic mediation, which includes both interlinguistic and intralinguistic elements, can take place in the target language, in the source language, and also when using multiples languages in a multilingual environment; b) cultural mediation seeks to facilitate cultural awareness and understanding;

c) social mediation is put into practice when an intermediary or 'mediator' helps people who are unable to understand each other to communicate (the reasons for this lack of understanding are not limited to language, for they comprise political and cultural reasons); and d) pedagogic mediation is key in the teacher–student relationship. Mediation is a tool that, among others, allows educators to promote critical thinking, organize work, and prevent and solve problems, among others. Showing a practical application of North and Piccardo's (2017) approach, the case study, based on film reviews, will illustrate how mediation can be successfully integrated into the translation class and make the teaching of Spanish more effective. The Council of Europe names cognitive gaps, disability, lack of relevant information and cultural differences among the main reasons for needing mediation. Therefore, the following step is to bolden a series of textual elements that belong to the different categories composing Carreres, Noriega-Sánchez and Calduch's (2018) guide to pre-translation textual analysis. Students are encouraged to carry out an in-depth preparatory textual analysis and to develop different types of mediation through group discussions (See Table 8.2 and Appendix). These exchanges seek to connect our wide variety of students: those who have grown up in the host community of the United Kingdom and/or who are English native speakers; and those who are in the process of settling in the United Kingdom and who speak English as a second language. Thus, integration is understood – both in the context of migration and in the context of higher education – as a two-way process. In this way, students are also made aware of the translation sub-competences that make up the translation competence.

Table 8.2 Application of the guide to pre-translation textual analysis based on Carreres, Noriega-Sánchez and Calduch (2018)'s model. See related film review in the Appendix

Textual element in the *Invictus* film review	Translation sub-competence actualized by students	Category of textual analysis that will help students define their translation strategy	Type of mediation fostered by students
Keeping his nose to the grindstone	Language Psycho-physiological Strategic	Grammar and vocabulary	Students were divided up in heterogeneously – assigned groups, which
Peter Morgan-penned thriller	Language Transfer		

(*continued*)

Table 8.2 Continued

Textual element in the *Invictus* film review	Translation sub-competence actualized by students	Category of textual analysis that will help students define their translation strategy	Type of mediation fostered by students
Decamped	Language Instrumental/professional	Stylistic elements	prompted them to exercise linguistic, cultural and social mediation when discussing each of the textual elements highlighted
Canny co-opting	Language Psycho-physiological Strategic Extra-linguistic Transfer	Grammar and vocabulary	
New, post-apartheid	Language Extra-linguistic Transfer	Grammar and vocabulary Subject, author and context	
Indulge in shades of grey	Language Psycho-physiological Strategic	Grammar and vocabulary Subject, author and context	
Historic, televised release	Language Transfer	Grammar and vocabulary	
Full shot	Language Extra-linguistic Instrumental/professional	Stylistic elements	
White boys playing rugby	Language Extra-linguistic	Textual structure and cohesion Subject, author and context	
Black equivalents kick a football on the other	Language Extra-linguistic	Textual structure and cohesion Subject, author and context	
No-nonsense efficiency	Language Transfer	Grammar and vocabulary	
Colours	Language Extra-linguistic Instrumental/professional	Stylistic elements	

Table 8.2 Continued

Jumps forward to	Language Extra-linguistic Instrumental/ professional	Stylistic elements
Jump cut	Language Extra-linguistic Instrumental/ professional	Stylistic elements
Behind-the-scenes walk-through	Language Extra-linguistic Psycho-physiological	Grammar and vocabulary
Booted out	Language Extra-linguistic Instrumental/ professional	Stylistic elements
Black civil-rights group	Language Psycho-physiological Strategic	Subject, author and context
Name and colours of the national rugby team	Language Extra-linguistic	Subject, author and context
Shaking their heads at the assumption	Language Extra-linguistic Strategic Instrumental/ professional	Grammar and vocabulary
Heading to the dogs	Language Psycho-physiological Strategic Extra-linguistic Instrumental/ professional	Grammar and vocabulary

Final recommendations for teachers and conclusions

This chapter has made a case for the use of film reviews in the translation class as a means of improving not only students' linguistic abilities, but their interlinguistic and intercultural abilities also, especially through the use of mediation in pre-translation group discussions. When considering how teachers might choose film reviews which are best suited for this purpose, the following recommendations must be kept in mind: a) suitability for teaching translation;

b) teaching objectives and students' proficiency level; c) the appeal for the learners; d) the heterogeneously assigned groups.

Edwards (1999: 556) highlights the suitability offered by film reviews for teaching different translation concepts and techniques. In particular, film reviews that are eye-catching, striking and dynamic, such as the review of *Invictus*, offer ample opportunity for students to practise a good range of classic techniques: reformulation (he is keeping his nose to the grindstone / *sigue al pie del cañón*; their country was heading to the dogs / *su país se iba a pique*), transposition (Nelson Mandela's canny co-opting of the 1995 Rugby World Cup Finals / *el uso tan astuto que Nelson Mandela hizo de la Final de la Copa Mundial de Rugby de 1995*), compensation (shaking their heads / *se llevaban las manos a la cabeza al pensar*), collocation (tinderbox / *caja de Pandora*) and borrowing (apartheid / *apartheid*).

Teaching objectives and student proficiency are also basic criteria when selecting film reviews (Edwards 1999). The linguistic and textual elements in the text must be in line with the module's syllabus. Therefore, factors such as the text's organizational patterns, lexical repertoire and syntax must be taken into account.

Students' potential interest and engagement play a pivotal role in successfully exploiting film reviews in the language classroom. The film must be appealing to students and prompt them to engage in animated discussion, maximizing their practice time and encouraging socialization. As an added value, it should contain enriching cultural elements and descriptive imagery that can elicit creativity and inventiveness. The review of Clint Eastwood's film revolves around a simple yet powerful plot – the power of sport to fight racism and promote unity in a fractured nation. Furthermore, it makes reference to Morgan Freeman and Matt Damon, two international stars and very likeable actors. Students found the story inspiring and rousing, and conversation flowed easily given the film's universal message.

In order to maximize the effectiveness of cooperative learning (Kagan 1994), a key teaching strategy in developing mediation skills, teachers should divide students up into heterogeneously assigned groups. That is, teachers should purposefully group students with different proficiency levels in Spanish and English, different backgrounds and dissimilar interests in one group. In this way, each student will bring unique strengths and knowledge to the group. Likewise, any cognitive and/or cultural gaps in the group, such as lack of knowledge of South African history or rugby, will have to be dealt with through mediation. Idioms, cultural references to life under apartheid and to South African history, cinematic terms, cultural differences in body language are among many other elements that might be improperly understood by some of our students in a plurilingual group and abound in the review of *Invictus*. These highly possible linguistic, cognitive and cultural gaps make this text a most productive source for students to mediate and further their plurilingual skills. The Liberating the Curriculum (LTC) project was founded by University College London in 2016 with the purpose of building a more inclusive, diverse curriculum. This initiative involves students and teachers who work together to complement traditional, male-dominated, Eurocentric curricula of different University College London degree programmes by ensuring a fairer representation of those authors, scientists and scholars who have been traditionally marginalized due to their gender, race, sexuality, religion or disability. Since the Council of Europe names cognitive gaps, disability, lack of relevant information and cultural differences among the main reasons for needing mediation, teachers can help liberate the curriculum by choosing film reviews that fulfil the LTC's objectives and make a positive impact in both their curricula and on minority students. Indeed, one of the reasons why I selected the *Invictus* review, in particular, is that it deals with apartheid, a system of institutionalized racial segregation that, in spite of remaining in power until the early 1990s, is a period of history that had not been widely studied by students. As part of a set of preparatory activities, teachers can supplement the published film review to be translated with other materials that will prompt students to further develop the four language skills (listening, speaking, reading and writing). Thus, through the use of film reviews that can be accompanied by stimulating, amusing film trailers and compelling film clips, interviews with authors and directors, or opposing film reviews, teachers can thereby maximize the use of instructional time and expose their students to a large amount of language in many different forms. In the case of the *Invictus* review, students were first exposed to a short scene of the film depicting a powerful conversation between Morgan Freeman, as President Nelson Mandela, and Matt Damon, as Captain François Pienaar, which prompted an ice-breaking initial discussion on leadership. Likewise, a short clip of the 1995 Rugby World Cup final match between South Africa and New Zealand ('Joost van der Westhuizen tackles Lomu in the 1995 RWC final') was used for an audiodescription exercise, which not only allowed students to practise their Spanish writing skills but helped them become familiar with the film's plot.

Linguistic and cultural forms of mediation have been a topic of interest since the CEFRL recognized them as technical skills involved in language learning. This chapter has highlighted how teachers are increasingly using mediation in the language and translation classroom as a means to deal with students' cognitive gaps, sensorial and mental disabilities, and cultural alienation. Using a case study, I have argued that film reviews also offer a most productive vehicle to further students' plurilingual skills. While the textual, linguistic and cultural elements inherent to film reviews make them most productive materials to be used in language and translation classrooms, their value is increased by their suitability as tools to develop students' mediation skills in plurilingual groups. This study has looked at a number of ways that reviews can be exploited in the translation classroom, devising exercises and questions for discussion that set students on a journey of linguistic, textual, cultural and cinematic discovery, in which both the tutor and the students are collaborative members of a learning community.

Appendix

Example of film review worked in class.

He turns 80 this year and claims 'Gran Torino' was his last outing as an actor. But, as a director, Clint Eastwood is **keeping his nose to the grindstone.** He spent the end of 2009 filming a **Peter Morgan-penned thriller,** 'Hereafter', in Europe and the US, and earlier last year **decamped** to South Africa to film this respectful, rousing drama about Nelson Mandela's **canny co-opting** of the 1995 Rugby World Cup Finals as a tool to promote racial harmony across the social and political tinderbox that was the **new, post-apartheid** state.

Eastwood isn't a director to **indulge in shades of grey** and so the film's first shots of the **historic, televised** release of Mandela (lead actor Morgan Freeman) from prison in 1990 are preceded by a **full shot** of **white boys playing rugby** on one side of the road while their **black equivalents kick a football on the other**. Simple editing: a background of division established – job done.

A similar, **no-nonsense efficiency colours** the whole film, which **jumps forward** to Mandela's inauguration in 1994, again mixing reconstruction and news footage, before ditching this early documentary feel to **jump cut** into a **behind-the-scenes walk-through** of the early months of his presidency. This was a time when existing presidential staff wrongly expected to be **booted out** of their jobs; a **black civil-rights group** believed, also wrongly, that Mandela would support their desire to change the **name and colours of the national rugby team**; and somewhere in a white suburb the captain of that same team, François Pienaar (Matt Damon) and his family were **shaking their heads** at the assumption that their country was **heading to the dogs.**

Calhourn 2010: online

Notes

1 Edwards's proposal is based on Newmark's (1988) identification of twelve basic translation techniques: transference, naturalization, calque, transposition, modulation, functional and descriptive equivalence, recognised translation, compensation, componential analysis, reduction and expansion, reorganization and rearrangements, and improvements. Although Newmark (1988) also includes the technique of adaptation, Edwards (1999: 53) does not consider it necessary when working with English and Spanish, given how close these languages and cultures are.
2 Further information can be found on: https://www.ucl.ac.uk/about/what/key-statistics#student-numbers.
3 See North and Piccardo (2016).
4 Trovato (2016) understands mediation as a type of interaction that takes place among people that due to various reasons are unable to communicate with each other.

References

Ayachia, H. (2018), 'The Revival of Translation as a Fifth Skill in the Foreign Language Classroom: A Review of Literature', *AWEJ for Translation & Literary Studies*, 2 (2): 187–98.

Baker, P. (2006), 'Jumping the Language Barrier: The "Fifth Skill"', *English Teaching Matters*, 7 (1): 22–4.

Calduch, C., and N. Talaván (2018), 'Traducción audiovisual y aprendizaje de español como L2: el uso de la audiodescripción', *Journal of Spanish Language Teaching*, 4 (2): 168–80.

Calhourn, D. (2010), 'Invictus 2010. Review', *Time Out*, February. Available online: https://www.timeout.com/movies/invictus.

Carlin, J. (2008), *Playing the Enemy: Nelson Mandela and the Game that Made a Nation*, New York: Penguin.

Carreres, Á., M. Noriega-Sánchez and C. Calduch (2018), *Mundos en Palabras: Learning Advanced Spanish Through Translation*, London: Routledge.

Cerezo, L. (2018), 'Always Together or Alone First? Effects of Type of Collaborative Translation on Spanish L2 Development', *Journal of Spanish Language Teaching*, 4 (2): 152–67.

Clayton, A., and A. Klevan, eds (2011), 'Introduction', in *The Language and Style of Film Criticism*, 1–26, New York: Routledge.

Corrigan, T. (2001), *A Short Guide to Writing About Film*, New York: Longman.

Council of Europe (2018), *Common European Framework of Reference for Languages: Learning, Teaching, Assessment. Companion Volume with New Descriptors*, Strasbourg: Council of Europe.

Davis, N. (2019), 'Bridging the Gaps between Scholarly Essays and Mass-market Film Writing', in L. Patti (ed.), *Writing About Screen Media*, 238–42, London: Routledge.

De Jong, I. K. E., and C. Burgers (2013), 'Do Consumer Critics Write Differently from Professional Critics? A Genre Analysis of Online Film Reviews', *Discourse, Context & Media*, 2 (2): 75–83.

Edwards, M. (1999), 'Exploiting Published Film Reviews in the Translation Class', in F. Sierra Martínez and C. Hernández González (eds), *Las lenguas en la Europa comunitaria. Volumen III*, 549–58, Amsterdam: Rodopi.

Fluitt-Dupuy, J. (2001), 'Teaching Argumentative Writing through Film', *TESOL Journal*, 10 (4): 10–15.

Fox Sports (n.d.), 'Joost van der Westhuizen Tackles Lomu in the 1995 RWC Final'. Available online: https://www.youtube.com/watch?v=NSFSBwITH_s.

Gaspar, N. F. (2009), 'Translation as a Fifth Skill in EFL Classes at Secondary School Level', in A. Witte, T. Harden and A. Ramos de Oliveira Harden (eds), *Translation in Second Language Learning and Teaching*, 173–80, Bern: Peter Lang.

Herrero, C., and I. Vanderschelden, eds (2019), *Using Film and Media in the Language Classroom: Reflections on Research-led Teaching*, Bristol: Multilingual Matters.

Holden, W. R. (2000), 'Making the Most of Movies: Keeping Film Response Journals. Classroom Ideas', *Modern English Teacher*, 9 (2): 40–5.

Jiménez-Crespo, M. Á. (2018), 'The Role of Translation Technologies in Spanish Language Learning', *Journal of Spanish Language Teaching*, 4 (2): 181–93.

Kagan, S. (1994), *Cooperative Learning*, San Clemente, CA: Kagan Publishing.

Kaiser, M. (2011), 'New Approaches to Exploiting Film in the Foreign Language Classroom', *L2 Journal*, 3 (2): 232–49.

Kaiser, M., and C. Shibahara (2014), 'Film as Source Material in Advanced Foreign Language Classes', *L2 Journal*, 6: 1–13.

Leonardi, V. (2010), *The Role of Pedagogical Translation in Second Language Acquisition: From Theory to Practice*, Bern: Peter Lang.

Naimushin, B. (2002), 'Translation in Foreign Language Teaching: The Fifth Skill', *Modern English Teacher*, 11 (4): 46–9.

Naga, N., and R. McGill (2018), 'Negotiating Cultural Difference in Creative Writing Workshops, Close Reading Translations and Interpretive Diversity', *Pedagogy. Critical Approaches to Teaching Literature, Language, Composition, and Culture*, 18 (1): 69–86.

Newmark, P. (1988), *A Textbook of Translation*, London: Prentice Hall International.

North, B., and E. Piccardo (2016), 'Developing Illustrative Descriptors of Aspects of Mediation for the Common European Framework of Reference (CEFR), A Council of Europe Project', *Language Teaching*, 49 (3): 1–5.

North, B., and E. Piccardo (2017), 'Mediation and the Social and Linguistic Integration of Migrants: Updating the CEFR Descriptors', in J. C. Beacco, H. J. Krumm, D. G. Little and P. Thalgott (eds), *The Linguistic Integration of Adult Migrants: Some Lessons from Research / L'intégration linguistique des migrants adultes: Les enseignements de la recherche*, 83–90, Berlin: de Gruyter.

PACTE (1998) [Beeby, A., M. Fernández, O. Fox, A. Hurtado Albir, I. Kozlova, A. Kuznik, W. Neunzig, P. Rodríguez-Inés and L. Romero], 'La competencia traductora y su aprendizaje: Objetivos, hipótesis y metodología de un proyecto de investigación'. Poster presented in the *IV Congrés Internacional sobre Traducció*, Bellatera: Universitat Autònoma de Barcelona.

PACTE (2000) [Beeby, A., L. Berenguer, D. Ensinger, O. Fox, A. Hurtado Albir, N. Martínez Melis, W. Neunzig, M. Orozco, M. Presas and F. M. Vega], 'Acquiring Translation Competence: Hypotheses and Methodological Problems of a Research Project'. In A. Beeby, D. Ensinger and M. Presas (eds), *Investigating Translation*, 99–106, Amsterdam: John Benjamins.

PACTE (2001a) [Beeby, A., L. Berenguer, D. Ensinger, O. Fox, A. Hurtado Albir, N. Martínez Melis, W. Neunzig, M. Orozco, and M. Presas], 'La competencia traductora y su adquisición', *Quaderns. Revista de Traducció*, 6: 39–45.

PACTE (2001b) [Beeby, A., I. Berenguer, D. Ensinger, O. Fox, A. Hurtado Albir, N. Martínez Melis, W. Neunzig, M. Orozco and M. Presas], 'La investigación empírica y experimental en traductología. Dossier especial.' *Quaderns. Revista de Traducció*, 6: 9–10.

PACTE (2003) [Beeby, A., M. Fernández, O. Fox, A. Hurtado Albir, W. Neunzig, M. Presas, P. Rodríguez Inés and L. Romero], 'Building a Translation Competence Model', in F. Alves (ed.), *Triangulating Translation: Perspectives in process oriented research*, 43–66, Amsterdam: John Benjamins.

Sánchez Cuadrado, A. (2018), 'Validación empírica del potencial pedagógico de la traducción: la atención a la forma en actividades colaborativas de traducción', *Journal of Spanish Language Teaching*, 4 (2): 136–51.

Schechter, L. (2018), '"On the Outside Facing the Wooded Ridge": Close Reading Translations and Interpretive Diversity', *Pedagogy. Critical Approaches to Teaching Literature, Language, Composition, and Culture*, 18 (1): 51–68.

Thaler, E., ed. (2017), *Short Films in Language Teaching*, Tübingen: Narr Francke Attempto.

Trovato, G. (2016), *Mediación lingüística y enseñanza de español/LE. Cuadernos de didáctica del español/LE*, Madrid: Arco/Libros.

Viebrock, B., ed. (2016), *Feature Films in English Language Teaching*, Tübingen: Narr Studienbücher.

Benefits and Drawbacks of Using Social Networking Sites in Higher Education: The Case of Facebook as a Transmedia English-Language Teaching Tool

Jelena Bobkina and Elena Domínguez Romero

Introduction

Facebook is the biggest social networking service worldwide, with 2.38 billion monthly active users in the first quarter of 2019 (Facebook Newsroom n.d.). Mark Zuckerberg founded the company in 2004 'to give people the power to build community and bring the world closer together. People use Facebook to stay connected with friends and family, to discover what's going on in the world, and to share and express what matters to them' (Facebook Newsroom n.d.). They do so by sharing text, photographs, audio and video.

The Facebook–Cambridge Analytica data scandal in early 2018, when it was revealed that Cambridge Analytica had harvested the personal data of millions of people's profiles without their consent and used it for political advertising, precipitated a massive fall in the stock price of Facebook and calls for tighter regulation of tech companies' use of data (Cotton 2019). Nevertheless, the wide range of Facebook-related apps ensures that the company continues to be one of the most popular app publishers in the world, based on downloads. As stated in the fourth reported quarter 2020, 3.14 billion people were using at least one of the company's core products (Facebook, WhatsApp, Instagram or Messenger) each month (Tankovska 2021). According to the Facebook full-year 2020 report, there were 1.84 billion daily active users on average in December 2020 and 2.80 billion monthly active users as of 31 December 2020, an increase of 11 per cent year on year and 12 per cent, respectively (Facebook 2021).

Web 2.0 technologies and social networking sites serve as ideal learner-centred environments where students can engage in collaborative and constructive learning processes. Digital natives do not just use social media for accessing content and information; they also use it for connecting information from various sources and generating new information that can be shared with others, resulting in an interactive cycle of knowledge creation and consumption (Maloney 2007). The social publishing features that support the creation and dissemination of user-generated content act as powerful drivers in converting social media sites into informal, networked and constructive virtual learning environments (Chugh and Ruhi 2018). High levels of flexibility, user-friendly interfaces and varied dynamic functionalities make social media attractive in instructional contexts, turning passive media consumer learners into active media *prosumer* learners, a concept which refers to learners who are consumers, co-producers and distributors of content (Bermejo Berros 2008), increasing their levels of satisfaction and promoting their deep acquisition of knowledge (Aydin 2012; Manca and Ranieri 2013; Gamble and Wilkins 2014; Forbush and Foucault-Welles 2016; Kitchakarn 2016; Mnkandla and Minnaar 2017).

Regarding language teaching, the use of social networking sites has evolved over the last few years. To give but a few examples, wikis, forums and blogs have been used to facilitate the writing process in language teaching (Chao and Lo 2011; Turmo and Fisher 2011; Hadjerrouit 2012; Li 2014). Instagram, Twitter and Facebook have been shown to encourage group communication and teacher–student interaction (Hamid et al. 2011; Yeboah and Ewur 2014; Ricoy and Feliz 2016; Aloraini 2018; Madge et al. 2019), and YouTube has enabled students' creation and dissemination of videos (Johnson et al. 2011; Fleck et al. 2014). Social media platforms also improve students' general interest in language learning (Liou and Peng 2009; Jones and Shao 2011; Shih 2011; Buzzetto-More 2012; Wang and Vasquez 2012).

Language teachers are exploring new ways to use social media platforms like Facebook to improve their teaching methods and foster active forms of language learning (Lockyer and Patterson 2008; Nakatsukasa 2009; Aydin 2012; Wang et al. 2012; Manca and Ranieri 2013; Fleck et al. 2014; Chugh and Ruhi 2018). Nevertheless, the growth of social media usage for pedagogical purposes is still in its infancy (Vivakaran and Neelamalar 2018).[1] Empirical research in this field continues to be rather limited, especially in the use of Facebook as a transmedia teaching tool that makes it possible to adapt traditional teaching practices to the new socio-technical needs of today's students (Hamid et al. 2015; Tananuraksakul 2015; Delgado García et al. 2018).

The study that this chapter focuses on contributes to filling this significant gap by drawing on the claim that HE students of English for Specific Purposes (ESP) need to be approached as active *prosumers*. Our aim was to explore the potential of controversial social networking sites like Facebook as transmedia language teaching tools for enhancing collaboration, reflection and autonomous learning practices among *prosumer* ESP university learners. More specifically, our intention was to carry out a classroom-based study to gather information about our students' opinions on the uses, usefulness and drawbacks of Facebook as a transmedia teaching tool in the ESP classroom.

To fulfil the purpose of the study, the following research questions were raised:

1. What are the main ways in which Facebook is used as a transmedia teaching tool in the HE ESP classroom?
2. What are HE students' opinions on the usefulness of Facebook as a transmedia teaching tool in the ESP classroom?
3. What are HE students' opinions on the drawbacks of using Facebook as a transmedia teaching tool in the ESP classroom?

Theoretical background

Today's social relationships are built on social networking sites such as Facebook, Instagram, Twitter, YouTube and Vimeo (Meyers et al. 2013; Scolari 2013, 2018; Sleeman et al. 2016). Media consumers have thus become active agents of user-generated content, creating and editing content to be shared (Martinez et al. 2018) and taking on communication strategies both as consumers and *prosumers*.

The rapid development of social networking platforms has led to the evolution of innovative pedagogical practices – social and dynamic – whose educational benefits have been documented in the specialized literature (Avci and Askar 2012; Manca and Ranieri 2013; Njoku 2019). Much research has explored students' opinions about the use of social networking sites as teaching tools, with positive results (Kabilan et al. 2010; Tashir et al. 2011; Wang et al. 2012; Luo et al. 2013; Manca and Ranieri 2013; Tess 2013; Gupta 2014; Kitchakarn 2016; Li 2017). Findings have revealed that the use of social media tools in educational contexts motivates students to take part in constructive learning through online interactions and collaborations (Liburd and Christensen 2013). As an example, Sugimoto et al. (2015) claimed that learning experiences based on social media increase students' engagement in the classroom. Al-Rahmi et al. (2015) reported that social technologies enhance collaborative learning environments, increasing the overall academic performance of the students. In the same vein, Sobaih et al. (2016) supported the use of social tools for academic purposes in HE, claiming that these students are already active in online networks.

Facebook is one of the most popular social media tools for pedagogical purposes, because it provides learners with great opportunities and space for expression through the exchange of texts, photographs, audio recordings and videos, which can be shared free of charge (Mazman and Usluel 2010). It has been claimed that interaction – or 'academic socializing' (Niu 2019) – is the core value offered by Facebook in academic settings (Manasijević et al. 2016). Students can give and receive feedback and comments while being engaged in learning activities (Alm 2006). Facebook supports open communication between teachers and learners, enabling the flow of information (Mena et al. 2012; Bowman and Akcaoglu 2014; Sánchez et al. 2014). Building communities and promoting a sense of belonging in a group are also among its positive effects (Razak et al. 2013; Rasiah 2014; Hamid et al. 2015).

Alongside social networking sites, course management systems, such as Blackboard and Moodle, have become essential tools in university teaching because of the growing interest among educators in adapting their traditional teaching methods to the new demands of today's students (Meléndez Tamayo 2013; Becerra and Martín 2015). Most researchers agree that course management systems are more centred on the class. Nevertheless, these systems lack the personal touch and networking capacity offered by social networking sites, which are more user-centred, extend learning beyond the boundaries of the classroom and encourage online community building (Brady et al. 2010; Petrovic et al. 2013; Delgado García et al. 2018).

Method

Participants

This classroom-based study involved seventy-nine Industrial Engineering undergraduates from the Universidad Politécnica de Madrid, Spain. All of them, aged between 21 and 25, were taking a compulsory course on English for specific and academic communication in the 2017–18 academic year. At the time of the study, their level of English ranged from B2 to C1, as classified by the CEFRL (Council of Europe 2001). As a prerequisite for the course, we asked our students to complete a questionnaire to identify their experiences and give their opinions about using social networking platforms (see Appendix).

The vast majority of our participants were frequent users of social media: 77 per cent (n=61) reported daily use. Facebook was identified as their preferred social platform (50.6 per cent, n=40) followed by Instagram (16.5 per cent, n=13) and Twitter (15.2 per cent, n=12). However, only 19 per cent (n=15) had used social media as an educational tool.

Instruments

A mixed-method approach was followed to explore the potential of Facebook as a transmedia tool for English-language learning and teaching by this group of Spanish undergraduate Engineering students. This involved the development and administration of a 19-item questionnaire, which comprised three sections with both statement and open question items. Section 1 (8 items) aimed to explore students' uses of Facebook as a transmedia language learning and teaching tool in the ESP university classroom. Section 2 (8 items) analysed students' opinions about the usefulness of Facebook as a transmedia teaching tool. Section 3 included three open questions regarding our students' opinions on the main drawbacks of using Facebook as a transmedia teaching tool in the language classroom.

The initial design of the questionnaire observed Fowler's (2002) principles of reliability: use of English lexicon; clarity of wording; absence of biased words and phrases; item formatting; standardized response expectations; and clarity of instruction. The questionnaire was piloted for clarity by a volunteer group of ten university students. Modifications were then introduced to ensure reliability, which increased to 0.75 (Cronbach's alpha), showing an acceptable level of consistency among the items in the questionnaire.

Procedures

The study was carried out over fifteen weeks of classes. The group met twice a week for 110 minutes from February to May 2018. At the beginning, students were told that 10 per cent of their final grade would be allocated to their participation in the Facebook group of the course that had been opened by the instructors. They were asked to open a Facebook account and join our Facebook group.

The Facebook-based tasks included the following: creating video content; sharing videos, links and text related to the topics discussed in the classroom; posting content and reacting to posts submitted by classmates and teachers;

asking questions and resolving doubts; and interacting with the instructors. A paper-based version of the questionnaire was administered for completion at the end of the course.

Data analysis

A descriptive analysis of the quantitative data obtained about our students' opinions on the uses and usefulness of Facebook as a transmedia teaching tool in the ESP university classroom was conducted using SPSS version 25.0 (SPSS 2017). To analyse the qualitative data gathered with a view to exploring our students' opinions on the drawbacks of the platform, we used a content-based approach. The data were first sorted between positive and negative answers so that the positive answers were classified into broad categories. As with most content-based analyses, a small portion of the content remained uncategorized and was therefore classified as 'other'.

Results

To answer the first research question – on students' opinions on the use of Facebook as a transmedia teaching and learning tool in the ESP classroom – a descriptive analysis of the data retrieved from Section 1 of the questionnaire was carried out.

First, the raw data from items 1–11 of Section 1 of the questionnaire were condensed and recoded in new variables with verbal descriptors: 'Quite unfavourable', 'Unfavourable', 'Favourable' and 'Quite favourable'. This enabled us to assess our students' overall attitude towards using Facebook as a transmedia teaching tool in the ESP classroom.

Table 9.1 shows that 60.8 per cent of the respondents had either a positive or a very positive attitude towards using Facebook, while 39.2 per cent had either a negative or a strongly negative attitude.

As shown in Table 9.2, the data analysis revealed that our students had a positive attitude towards using Facebook to watch videos created by their classmates (74.7 per cent), watch video files shared by their classmates (62.1 per cent) and share information (60.8 per cent). They were also very positive about using Facebook as a tool to practise English outside the classroom (62.1 per cent). Almost half of them (49.4 per cent) reported that they would have taken part in the Facebook group of the course even if it had been optional.

Table 9.1 Overall results: students' attitude towards the use of Facebook as a teaching tool

		Frequency	Valid percentage
Valid	Quite unfavourable	8	10.1
	Unfavourable	23	29.1
	Favourable	39	49.4
	Quite favourable	9	11.4
	Total	79	100.0
Total		79	100.0

Table 9.2 Uses of Facebook as a learning and teaching tool

	Using Facebook as an educational tool	Strongly disagree (%)	Disagree (%)	Agree (%)	Strongly agree (%)
Q1	I was an active member of the Facebook group.	10.1	38.0	35.4	15.2
Q2	I enjoyed the opportunity to communicate with my classmates outside the classroom.	15.2	26.6	43.0	17.7
Q3	I enjoyed sharing information with my classmates.	13.9	25.3	39.2	21.5
Q4	I enjoyed watching the video files shared by my classmates.	10.1	27.8	44.3	13.9
Q5	I enjoyed watching videos created by my classmates.	10.1	15.2	25.3	48.1
Q6	I enjoyed posting comments.	7.6	35.4	48.1	6.3
Q7	I appreciated the opportunity to practise English outside the classroom.	10.1	27.8	41.7	16.4
Q8	I would have taken part in the Facebook group even as an optional task.	21.5	29.1	27.8	17.7

To address the second research question – on our students' opinions on the usefulness of Facebook as a transmedia learning and teaching tool in the ESP classroom – the data retrieved from Section 2 of the questionnaire were analysed.

First, a descriptive analysis was carried out to assess our students' overall attitude towards the usefulness of Facebook for this purpose. The raw data from items 1–8 were condensed and recoded as new variables with verbal descriptors: 'Completely useless', 'Useless', 'Partly useful', 'Useful' and 'Very useful'.

Table 9.3 shows that almost 66 per cent of the respondents highlighted the usefulness of Facebook for active learning, while just 10.3 per cent reported that the platform was completely useless or useless.

Table 9.4 reveals our students' specific opinions about the usefulness of Facebook. The highest-rated items were those pointing to the usefulness of Facebook for sharing information (76.3 per cent), posting files, polls and videos (73.7 per cent) and learning from shared video talks (75.2 per cent).

To address the third research question, concerning our students' opinions about the major drawbacks of using Facebook as a transmedia learning and teaching in the ESP classroom, the qualitative data retrieved from Section 3 of the questionnaire were processed qualitatively. We combined and themed their answers following an inductive approach.

Table 9.5 reveals the themed categories, the frequency of responses and some selected relevant comments from our students.

Students' major concerns were privacy (15.4 per cent) and either not having an account or being unwilling to use social networking sites (10.1 per cent). In addition, a considerable number of participants complained about being easily distracted when entering the Facebook group of the course (10.1 per cent). This explains why some of them would have opted for a more traditional education platform, such as Moodle (7.6 per cent). They also reported that the information was organized in a chronological rather than a thematic order, hampering their access to important files (3.8 per cent). Finally, some students felt that the amount of information they received was excessive (2.5 per cent).

Table 9.3 Students' attitude towards the usefulness of Facebook as a learning and teaching tool

		Frequency	Percentage	Valid percentage
Valid	Completely useless	1	1.3	1.3
	Useless	7	9.0	9.2
	Partly useful	18	23.1	23.7
	Useful	38	48.7	50.0
	Very useful	12	15.4	15.8
	Total	76	97.4	100.0
Total		78	100.0	

Table 9.4 Usefulness of Facebook as a learning and teaching tool

	Usefulness of Facebook as an educational tool	Strongly disagree (%)	Disagree (%)	Agree (%)	Strongly agree (%)
Q1	Facebook is a good tool for sharing information with teachers and students.	5.3	18.4	43.4	32.9
Q2	Facebook is a good tool for resolving students' doubts.	15.8	23.7	35.5	25.0
Q3	Facebook is a good tool for exchanging files, polls and videos.	7.9	18.4	28.9	44.7
Q4	Facebook is a good tool for practising English outside the classroom.	15.8	32.9	36.8	14.5
Q5	Facebook is a good tool for learning from shared video talks.	7.9	17.1	48.7	26.3
Q6	Facebook is a good tool for motivating students to learn English.	19.7	25.0	42.1	13.2
Q7	Facebook is a good tool for having fun learning English.	13.2	34.2	32.9	19.7
Q8	Facebook is a good tool for overcoming the fear of public speaking.	13.2	30.3	40.8	15.8

Despite these concerns, Table 9.6 reveals that 64.9 per cent of our students supported the use of Facebook as a transmedia teaching tool in the ESP university classroom. Meanwhile, 10.8 per cent would not recommend its use and 24.3 per cent were indecisive.

Table 9.5 Drawbacks of Facebook as a learning and teaching tool

Inductive categories	Frequency of responses	Typical participant responses
Threat to privacy	15.4%	Some students do not use social networks or dislike uploading their recordings because of privacy reasons.
		Some people do not feel like uploading their video recordings, as they find it a threat to their privacy.
Lack of use / no account	10.1%	Some students do not have a Facebook account.
		I do not use Facebook regularly, so it was difficult for me to follow the group.
		I do not usually check my Facebook account.
Distraction from studies	10.1%	Logging on to Facebook to check the teachers' posts distracted me, because I wanted to check my friends' posts.
		It makes you tired and distracts you a bit.
		The Facebook group was great, but sometimes I wasted my time checking my Facebook stuff when entering the English for Professional and Academic Communication (EPAC) group.
		It is difficult for us to avoid being distracted when using Facebook.
Facebook is not an educational platform	7.6%	It is a commercial platform that does not belong in the university setting. It forces you to mix your private life and your studies.
		Other platforms are specifically designed for educational uses.
Compulsory use	6.3%	Some students do not feel like using social networks.
		Using Facebook should not be compulsory.
Lack of organization	3.8%	Documents and files are not organized, so it is difficult to find the right document when necessary.
		It is difficult for students to find the important files that the teacher uploads.
		Teachers' posts often get lost among the students' posts.
Addiction to social networks	2.5%	Some people are addicted to social networks. There is no way to disconnect if you have to use one as a part of the course.
		The use of social networks can be abusive and stressful.

An excessive amount of information	2.5%	Too much information from a large number of students uploaded every day.	
		Too many people posting makes me feel dizzy.	
Other	2.5%	Uploading videos from different networks was a painstaking task.	

Table 9.6 Students' views on Facebook use in future versions of the English for Professional and Academic Communication (EPAC) course

		Frequency	Percentage	Valid percentage
Valid	Supportive	48	60.8	64.9
	Not supportive	8	10.1	10.8
	Not sure	18	22.8	24.3
	Total	74	93.7	100.0
Missing	Did not answer	5	6.3	
Total		79	100.0	

Finally, when asked about the possibility of using other social platforms as part of the EPAC course, only 26.5 per cent claimed that they would have opted for other platforms, while the rest reported that they would have rather continued with Facebook. Of those who would have preferred an alternative platform, 64.3 per cent opted for Moodle and 7.2 per cent chose WhatsApp.

Discussion and conclusions

This classroom-based study explored the potential of Facebook as a transmedia learning and teaching tool, with a focus on our ESP university students' opinions about its uses, usefulness and drawbacks. The findings revealed positive opinions about using Facebook to share information, communicate with classmates and practise English outside the classroom. This supports previous research showing that students tend to have a positive attitude towards learning through Facebook (Aydin 2012; Tananuraksakul 2015; Kitchakarn 2016) and conversing on Facebook (Omar et al. 2012; Suthiwartnarueput and Wasanasomsithi 2012), and that they prefer online communication to traditional settings for practising second languages outside the classroom (Kitchakarn 2016; Akbari et al. 2017).

The results also revealed the usefulness of Facebook for sharing information, posting files, polls and videos, and learning from shared videos. Here, too, these results are in line with previous research (Maloney 2007; Bosch 2009; Gamble and Wilkins 2014; McCarthy 2012) indicating that sharing information and enabling interaction are the most beneficial aspects of using social networking sites (Maloney 2007; Bosch 2009; Gamble and Wilkins 2014; McCarthy 2012; Datko 2019). In agreement with previous findings, the 'affordance of opportunities for students to collaborate and share knowledge and its capacity to promote greater interactive learning opportunities through genuine communication' (Gamble and Wilkins 2014: 67) were also highlighted among the benefits of Facebook.

The major drawback for our students was privacy, as they considered Facebook to be a private platform that should not be used for academic purposes. This comes as no surprise, given that research has proven that students have become more concerned about the privacy of their personal data since the Facebook–Cambridge Analytica scandal (Al-Dheleai and Tasir 2015; Marek and Skrabut 2017; Njoku 2019). It is clear that exploiting the potential of Facebook in the ESP university classroom requires following Madge et al.'s (2019: 152) advice to 'caution about moving into a social networking space that students feel is theirs for social rather than academic purposes'. Some other common concerns included distractions associated with the use of the platform, the non-chronological order of uploaded files, difficult access to information, information overload and the risk of addiction.

Despite the limitations of the study presented in this chapter, it can be concluded that social networking sites should be seen as complementary transmedia teaching tools that must be used alongside other course management systems because their main function is to enable student communication and build on a participatory culture. HE needs to acknowledge this potential and extend its pedagogical implementation.

More research on ways of developing and implementing Facebook-based activities in the ESP university classroom is needed. Further research should involve widespread, larger-scale studies with university students from different parts of the world, who are learning languages other than English for either specific or non-specific purposes. More social networking sites, such as Instagram, Twitter, YouTube and Vimeo, should be studied. Further research about the value of social networking sites as opposed to course management systems (such as Blackboard or Moodle) is needed. Attention needs to be paid to more variables that affect the function and usefulness of Facebook and other social networking sites. Finally, more university teachers should break down the barriers of prejudice and fear, and observe the pedagogical implications of previous research examining students' uses of and views on social networking sites.

References

Akbari, E., P. R. J. Simons, A. Pilot and A. Naderi (2017), 'Peer Feedback in Learning a Foreign Language in Facebook', *Global Journal of Human-Social Science*, 17 (2): 31–44.

Al-Dheleai, Y. M., and Z. Tasir (2015), 'Facebook and Education: Students' Privacy Concerns', *International Education Studies*, 8 (13): 22–6.

Alm, A. (2006), 'CALL for Autonomy, Competency, and Relatedness: Motivating Language Learning Environments in Web 2.0', *JALT CALL Journal*, 2 (3): 29–38.

Aloraini, N. (2018), 'Investigating Instagram as an EFL Learning Tool', *Arab World English Journal*, 4: 174–84.

Al-Rahmi, W., M. S. Othman and L. M. Yusuf (2015), 'Social Media for Collaborative Learning and Engagement: Adoption Framework in Higher Education Institutions in Malaysia', *Mediterranean Journal of Social Sciences*, 6 (3 S1): 246–52.

Avci, U., and P. Askar (2012), 'The Comparison of the Opinions of the University Students on the Usage of Blog and Wiki for their Courses', *Educational Technology and Society*, 15 (2): 194–205.

Aydin, S. (2012), 'A Review of Research on Facebook as an Educational Environment', *Educational Technology Research and Development*, 60: 1093–106.

Becerra, M. T., and F. Martín (2015), 'Visión de las plataformas virtuales de enseñanza y las redes sociales por los usuarios estudiantes universitarios. Un estudio descriptivo', *PixelBit. Revista de Medios y Educación*, 47: 223–30.

Bermejo Berros, J. (2008), 'El receptor publicitario del siglo XXI en el marco de la interactividad: Entre el consumer y el prosumer', in M. Pacheco Rueda (ed.), *La publicidad en el contexto digital*, 49–78, Sevilla: Comunicación Social.

Bosch, T. E. (2009), 'Using Online Social Networking for Teaching and Learning: Facebook Use at the University of Cape Town', *Communication: South African Journal for Communication Theory and Research*, 35 (2): 185–200.

Bowman, N. D., and M. Akcaoglu (2014), '"I See Smart People!": Using Facebook to Supplement Cognitive and Affective Learning in the University Mass Lecture', *Internet and Higher Education*, 23: 1–8.

Brady, K. P., L. B. Holcomb and B. V. Smith (2010), 'The Use of Alternative Social Networking Sites in Higher Educational Settings: A Case Study of the E-Learning Benefits of Ning in Education', *Journal of Interactive Online Learning*, 9 (2): 151–70.

Buzzetto-More, N. A. (2012), 'Social Networking in Undergraduate Education', *Interdisciplinary Journal of Information, Knowledge, and Management*, 7: 63–90.

Chao, Y. J., and H. C. Lo (2011), 'Students' Perceptions of Wiki-Based Collaborative Writing for Learners of English as a Foreign Language', *Interactive Learning Environments*, 19 (4): 395–411.

Chugh, R., and U. Ruhi (2018), 'Social Media in Higher Education: A Literature Review of Facebook', *Education and Information Technologies*, 23 (2): 605–16.

Cotton, B. (2019), 'Could Facebook Be about to Receive a Record Data Breach Fine of £4bn?' 15 July. Available online: https://www.businessleader.co.uk/could-facebook-be-about-to-receive-a-record-data-breach-fine-of-4bn/70619/.

Council of Europe (2001). *Common European Framework of Reference for Languages: Learning, Teaching, Assessment*, Cambridge: Press Syndicate of the University of Cambridge.

Datko, J. (2019), 'The Nature of the Facebook Group Learning Environment: Insights from University Students', *International Journal of Information and Communication Technologies in Education*, 8 (1): 20–9.

Delgado García, M., F. García Prieto and I. Gómez Hurtado (2018), 'Moodle y Facebook como herramientas virtuales didácticas de mediación de aprendizajes: Opinión de profesores y alumnos universitarios', *Revista Complutense de Educación*, 29 (3): 807–27.

Facebook (2021), 'Facebook Reports Fourth Quarter and Full Year 2020 Results'. *PRNweswire*, 27 January. Available online: https://www.prnewswire.com/news-releases/facebook-reports-fourth-quarter-and-full-year-2020-results-301216628.html.

Facebook Newsroom (n.d.), 'Company info', *Facebook*. Available online: https://newsroom.fb.com/company-info/.

Fleck, B. K., L. M. Sterns and H. D. Hussey (2014), 'YouTube in the Classroom: Helpful Tips and Student Perceptions', *Journal of Effective Teaching*, 14: 21–37.

Forbush, E., and B. Foucault-Welles (2016), 'Social Media Use and Adaptation among Chinese Students Beginning to Study in the United States', *International Journal of Intercultural Relations*, 50: 1–12.

Fowler, F. J. (2002), *Survey Research Methods*, 3rd ed., Thousand Oaks, CA: Sage.

Gamble, C., and M. Wilkins (2014), 'Student Attitudes and Perceptions of Using Facebook for Language Learning', *Dimension*, 50: 49–72.

Gupta, A. (2014), 'Scope and Implications of Social Media in the Context of Higher Education: Review of Researches', *MIER Journal of Educational Studies, Trends and Practices*, 4 (2): 231–53.

Hadjerrouit, S. (2012), 'Using Wikis to Foster Collaborative Writing: Exploring Influencing Factors to Successful Implementation', in D. G. Sampson, J. M. Spector,

D. Ifenthaler and P. Isaias (eds), *Proceedings of the International Association for Development of the Information Society (IADIS) International Conference on Cognition and Exploratory Learning in Digital Age (CELDA)*, 131–8, Madrid: IADIS Press. Available online: https://www.learntechlib.org/p/132366.

Hamid, S., J. Waycott, S. Chang and S. Kurnia (2011), 'Appropriating Online Social Networking (OSN) Activities for Higher Education: Two Malaysian Cases', in G. Williams, P. Statham, N. Brown and B. Cleland (eds), *Proceedings of ASCILITE – Australian Society for Computers in Learning in Tertiary Education Annual Conference*, 526–38, Melbourne: Australasian Society for Computers in Learning in Tertiary Education. Available online: https://www.learntechlib.org/p/43593/.

Hamid, S., J. Waycott, S. Kurnia and S. Chang (2015), 'Understanding Students' Perceptions of the Benefits of Online Social Networking Use for Teaching and Learning', *The Internet and Higher Education*, 26: 1–9.

Hew, K. F. (2011), 'Students' and Teachers' Use of Facebook', *Computers in Human Behavior*, 27 (2): 662–76.

Johnson, L., R. Smith, H. Willis, A. Levine and K. Haywood (2011), *The 2011 Horizon Report*, Austin, TX: The New Media Consortium. Available online: http://www.nmc.org/pdf/2005_Horizon_Report.pdf.

Jones, C., and B. Shao (2011), *The Net Generation and Digital Natives: Implications for Higher Education*, York: Higher Education Academy.

Kabilan, M., N. Almad and M. Zainol (2010), 'Facebook: An Online Environment for Learning of English in Institutions of Higher Education', *Internet and Higher Education*, 13 (4): 179–87.

Kitchakarn, O. (2016), 'How Students Perceived Social Media as a Learning Tool in Enhancing their Language Learning Performance', *Turkish Online Journal of Educational Technology*, 15 (4): 53–60.

Li, V., (2014), 'Collaborative Learning: Implication of Online Forum in English Academic Writing for Engineering Students', in *Proceedings 9th International Conference on Computer Science & Education August (ICCSE 2014)*, 443–8, UBC, Vancouver: IEEE.

Li, V. (2017), 'Social Media in English Language Teaching and Learning', *International Journal of Learning and Teaching*, 3 (2): 148–53.

Liburd, J., and I. M. Christensen (2013), 'Using Web 2.0 in Higher Tourism Education', *Journal of Hospitality Leisure Sport and Tourism*, 12 (1): 99–108.

Liou, H. C., and Z. Y. Peng (2009), 'Training Effects on Computer-Mediated Peer Review', *System: An International Journal of Educational Technology and Applied Linguistics*, 37 (3): 514–25.

Lockyer, L., and J. Patterson (2008), 'Integrating Social Networking Technologies in Education: A Case Study of a Formal Learning Environment', in P. Díaz, I. Kinshuk Aedo and E. Mora (eds), *2008 Eighth IEEE International Conference on Advanced Learning Technologies*, 529–33, Santander: IEEE.

Luo, X., J. Zhang and W. Duan (2013), 'Social Media and Firm Equity Value', *Information Systems Research*, 24 (1): 146–63.

Madge, C., M. R. Breines, M. T. B. Dalu, A. Gunter, J. Mittelmeier, P. Prinsloo and P. Raghuram (2019), 'WhatsApp Use among African International Distance Education (IDE) Students: Transferring, Translating and Transforming Educational Experiences', *Learning, Media and Technology*, 44 (3): 267–82.

Maloney, E. (2007), 'What Web 2.0 Can Teach Us about Learning', *Chronicle of Higher Education*, 53 (18): B26.

Manasijević, D., D. Živković, S. Arsić and I. Milošević (2016), 'Exploring Students' Purposes of Usage and Educational Usage of Facebook', *Computers in Human Behavior*, 60: 441–50.

Manca, S., and M. Ranieri (2013), 'Is it a Toll Suitable for Learning? A Critical Review of the Literature on Facebook as a Technology-Enhanced Learning Environment', *Computer Assisted Learning*, 29: 487–504.

Marek, M. W., and S. Skrabut (2017), 'Privacy in Educational Use of Social Media in the US', *International Journal on E-Learning*, 16 (3): 265–86.

Martínez-Sala, A. M., J. Segarra-Saavedra and J. Monserrat-Gauchi (2018), 'Los millennials como prosumers y adprosumers en las redes sociales corporativas', *Cuadernos.info*, 43: 137–59.

Mazman, S. G., and Y. K. Usluel (2010), 'Modelling Educational Usage of Facebook', *Computers and Education*, 55 (2): 444–53.

McCarthy, J. (2012), 'International Design Collaboration and Mentoring for Tertiary Students through Facebook', *Australasian Journal of Educational Technology*, 28 (5): 755–75.

Meléndez Tamayo, C. F. (2013), 'Plataformas virtuales como recurso para la enseñanza en la universidad: Análisis, evaluación y propuesta de integración de Moodle con herramientas de la Web 2.0', PhD thesis, Universidad Complutense de Madrid. Available online: http://eprints.sim.ucm.es/20466/.

Mena, G., A. Llupià, A. L. García-Basteiro, M. Aldea, V. G. Sequera and A. Trilla (2012), 'The Willingness of Medical Students to Use Facebook as a Training Channel for Professional Habits: The Case of Influenza Vaccination', *Cyberpsychology, Behavior and Social Networking*, 15 (6): 328–31.

Meyers, E., I. Erickson and R. Small (2013), 'Digital Literacy and Informal Learning Environments: An Introduction', *Learning, Media and Technology*, 38 (4): 355–67.

Mnkandla, E., and A. Minnaar (2017), 'The Use of Social Media in E-Learning: A Metasynthesis', *International Review of Research in Open and Distributed Learning*, 18 (5): 227–48.

Nakatsukasa, K. (2009), 'The Efficacy and Students' Perceptions of Collaborative Blogging in an ESL classroom', in C. A. Chapelle, H. G. Jun and I. Katz (eds), *Developing and Evaluating Language Learning Materials*, 69–84, Ames, IA: Iowa State University Press.

Niu, L. (2019), 'Using Facebook for Academic Purposes: Current Literature and Directions for Future Research', *Journal of Educational Computing Research*, 56 (8): 1384–406.

Njoku, C. P. (2019), 'Strengths in Using Social Media: Facebook as an Educational Technology', *International Journal of Computers in Education*, 2 (1): 1–17.

Omar, H., M. A. Embi and M. M. Yunus (2012), 'ESL Learners' Interaction in an Online Discussion via Facebook', *Asian Social Science*, 8: 67–74.

Petrovic, N., V. Jeremic and M. Cirovic (2013), 'Facebook vs. Moodle: What Do Students Really Think?', in L. Morris and C. Tsolakdis (eds), *International Conference on Information Communication Technologies in Education (ICICTE 2013)*, 413–21, Rhodes: Southampton Solent University and University of the Aegean. Available online: https://www.researchgate.net/publication/258338422.

Rasiah, R. R. V. (2014), 'Transformative Higher Education Teaching and Learning: Using Social Media in a Team-Based Learning Environment', *Procedia – Social and Behavioral Sciences*, 123: 369–79.

Razak, N. A., M. Saeed and Z. Ahmad. (2013), 'Adopting Social Networking Sites (SNSs) as Interactive Communities among English Foreign Language (EFL) Learners in Writing: Opportunities and Challenges', *English Language Teaching*, 6 (11):187–98.

Ricoy, M. C., and T. Feliz (2016), 'Twitter as a Learning Community in Higher Education', *Journal of Educational Technology and Society*, 19 (1): 237–48.

Sánchez, R. A., V. Cortijo and U. Javed (2014), 'Students' Perceptions of Facebook for Academic Purposes', *Computers and Education*, 70: 138–49.

Scolari, C. A. (2013), 'Media Evolution: Emergence, Dominance, Survival and Extinction in the Media Ecology', *International Journal of Communication*, 7: 1418–41.

Scolari, C. A. (2018), *Adolescentes, medios de comunicación y culturas colaborativas. Aprovechando las competencias transmedia de los jóvenes en el aula*, Barcelona: Universitat Pompeu Fabra. Available online: https://repositori.upf.edu/handle/10230/34245.

Shih, R. (2011), 'Can Web 2.0 Technology Assist College Students in Learning English Writing? Integrating Facebook and Peer Assessment with Blended Learning', *Australasian Journal of Educational Technology*, 27: 829–45.

Sleeman, J., C. Lang and N. Lemon (2016), 'Social Media Challenges and Affordances for International Students: Bridges, Boundaries, and Hybrid Spaces', *Journal of Studies in International Education*, 20 (5): 391–415.

Sobaih, A. E. E., M. A. Moustafa, P. Ghandforoush and M. Khan (2016), 'To Use or Not to Use? Social Media in Higher Education in Developing Countries', *Computers in Human Behavior*, 58: 296–305.

SPSS (2017), *Statistical Packages for the Social Sciences 25.0 for Macintosh*. Armonk, NY: IBM Corp.

Sugimoto, C., C. Hank, T. Bowman and J. Pomerantz (2015), 'Friend or Faculty: Social Networking Sites, Dual Relationships, and Context Collapse in Higher Education', *First Monday*, 20 (3). Available online: http://dx.doi.org/10.5210/fm.v20i3.5387.

Suthiwartnarueput, T., and P. Wasanasomsithi. (2012), 'Effects of Using Facebook as a Medium for Discussions of English Grammar and Writing of Low-Intermediate EFL Students', *Electronic Journal of Foreign Language Teaching*, 9 (2): 194–214.

Tananuraksakul, N. (2015), 'An Investigation into the Impact of Facebook Group Usage on Students' Effect in Language Learning in a Thai Context', *International Journal of Teaching and Learning in Higher Education*, 2: 235–46.

Tankovska, H. (2021), 'Number of Monthly Active Facebook Users Worldwide as of 4th Quarter 2020 (in millions)', 2 February. Available online: https://www.statista.com/statistics/264810/number-of-monthly-active-facebook-users-worldwide/.

Tashir, Z., Y. M. H. Al-Dheleai, J. Harun and N. A. Shukor (2011), 'Students' Perception towards the Use of Social Networking as an E-Learning Platform', in A. Zaharim, K. Sopian, N. Mastorakis and V. Mladenov (eds), *Proceedings of the 10th WSEAS International Conference on Education and Educational Technology (EDU'11)*, 70–6, Penang: SEAS Press.

Tess, P. A. (2013), 'The Role of Social Media in Higher Education Classes (Real and Virtual) – A Literature Review', *Computers in Human Behavior*, 29 (5): 60–8.

Turmo, M. P., and R. Fisher (2011), 'Breaking Up the Writing Process: How Wikis Can Support Understanding the Composition and Revision Strategies of Young Writers', *Language and Education*, 25: 451–66.

Vivakaran, M. V., and M. Neelamalar (2018), 'Utilization of Social Media Platforms for Educational Purposes among the Faculty of Higher Education with Special Reference to Tamil Nadu', *Higher Education for the Future*, 5 (1): 4–19.

Wang, Q., H. L. Woo, C. L. Quek, Y. Yang and M. Liu (2012), 'Using the Facebook Group as a Learning Management System: An Exploratory Study', *British Journal of Educational Technology*, 43 (3): 428–38.

Wang, S., and C. Vasquez (2012), 'Web 2.0 and Second Language Learning: What Does the Research Tell Us?', *CALICO Journal*, 29 (3): 412–30.

Yeboah, J., and G. Ewur (2014), 'The Impact of WhatsApp Messenger Usage on Students' Performance in Tertiary Institutions in Ghana', *Journal of Education and Practice*, 5 (6): 157–64.

Appendix

Facebook Questionnaire

Section 1. Uses of Facebook as a learning and teaching tool.

Please choose the answer that best reflects your view for each item. Answer each item as truthfully as possible using the following rating scale.

Strongly Disagree	Disagree	Agree	Strongly Agree
1	2	3	4

1. I was an active member of the Facebook group.

2. I enjoyed the opportunity to communicate with my classmates outside the classroom.
3. I enjoyed sharing information with my classmates.
4. I enjoyed watching the video files shared by my classmates.
5. I enjoyed watching videos created by my classmates.
6. I enjoyed posting comments.
7. I appreciated the opportunity to practise English outside the classroom.
8. I would have taken part in the Facebook group even as an optional task.

Section 2. Usefulness of Facebook as a learning and teaching tool.

This next set of questions asks for your opinion on the usefulness of Facebook as a learning and teaching tool. Please choose the answer that best reflects your view for each item. Answer each item as truthfully as possible using the rating scale from above.

9. Facebook is a good tool for sharing information with teachers and students.
10. Facebook is a good tool for resolving students' doubts.
11. Facebook is a good tool for exchanging files, polls and videos.
12. Facebook is a good tool for practising English outside the classroom.
13. Facebook is a good tool for learning from shared video talks,
14. Facebook is a good tool for motivating students to learn English.
15. Facebook is a good tool for having fun learning English.
16. Facebook is a good tool for overcoming the fear of public speaking.

Section 3. Major drawbacks of using Facebook as a transmedia learning and teaching tool.

The next set of questions asks your opinion on the use of Facebook as a transmedia learning and teaching tool in the ESP classroom. Provide a brief answer on each of the following questions.

17. What do you consider the main pitfalls of the use of Facebook in university educational settings?
18. Do you think it might be a good idea to keep using Facebook as part of the *English for Professional and Academic Communication* course?
19. Would you prefer to use any alternative tool to Facebook? If yes, mention which one.

Section 4. Personal Information.

20. Age:
21. Language level: A1   A2   B1   B2   C1   C2
22. Indicate if you are using social media platforms on regular basis: Yes   No
23. Indicate the social platforms you use more frequently:

    Facebook   Twitter   Instagram   Pinterest   LinkedIn   Other (specify which one)

24. Indicate if you have been using any social platform as an educational tool before this course:

   Yes   No

Note

1 As Vivakaran and Neelamalar (2018: 5) state, '[T]hough most faculty members hold a positive attitude towards the pedagogical application of social media tools, only a very few implement them.' In line with Hew (2011), the authors see as barriers 'their stereotypic view of social media being a source for social and entertainment activities', privacy issues and 'lack of control or monitoring features and the credibility of content' (Vivakaran and Neelamalar 2018: 5).

10

The Kinaesthetics of Gamification: Exploring the Theory Behind Exergaming as a Potential Aid to Language Learning

Chris McGuirk

Introduction

Gamification research – in this case, the use of video games as a way of promoting learner engagement, has been growing in popularity for a few years, but it is important to note that this term is not solely used to refer to gaming in education. Prominent researchers in the field (Deterding et al. 2011; Werbach 2014; Bogost 2015) have stated on a number of occasions that they define gamification to be, essentially, the use of video games for any purpose other than entertainment or recreation. Such a broad definition arguably accounts for why substantial pockets of research exist in the fields of health, sports science and psychology, as opposed to research specifically in the field of education. If the explanation of the term simply posits any non-recreational use of video games, then the term theoretically has the advantage of being both applicable as a solution to multiple challenges and impactful in a wide range of research contexts.

Exergaming, which can generally be defined as a specific form of gamification combining some kind of physical activity, often a competitive physical activity, with a video gaming platform – for instance, games such as the *Just Dance* series from Ubisoft, the exercise-based role-playing game *Ring-Fit Adventure*, or *Mario and Sonic at the Olympic Games* – has already been shown in the field of gaming and health (Peng, Crouse and Lin 2013; Höchsmann, Schüpbach and Schmidt-Trucksäss 2016) to correlate to positive impacts on general physical health and reductions in obesity among children with relatively sedentary lifestyles. Laato et al. (2020) observe that, in recent years, the term 'exergame' has also applied to smartphone-based geocaching games, to use Baranowski's (2017) term, such as

Pokemon GO and *Harry Potter: Wizards Unite*. Within these games, key items are superimposed on the camera view of a player's local area. The goal is to walk around and collect these items within their local vicinity, so there is clearly a need for significant physical activity if players want to succeed within them. In essence, all the research mentioned in this paragraph was intended to look at how relatively non-active child gamers could be encouraged to exercise by aligning fitness goals to goals within the game. However, the fact that the research was openly directed towards encouraging physical activity arguably also limits the scope of what exergaming research could investigate. For example, this research did not discuss the scope for exergaming to enhance the learning process.

Unfortunately, though research into the benefits of exergaming is extensive, specific research into exergaming as a tool to aid the language-learning process has so far yet to be conducted. Having said that, research exploring how varied forms of digital technologies can enhance the language-learning process can be confidently described as an approach still operating in relative infancy. This is largely based on an influential observation made by Philip Hubbard (2008) that while language-learning-technology research is quick to celebrate technology, it is often slow to discuss the theoretical underpinnings of the technology or practical applications in a classroom, which many practitioners would cite as the main reason for their interest in the research. Interestingly, other areas of learning-technology research appear to support Hubbard's view strongly. Gee (2013) has rallied against the perception of games in education being a 'silver bullet' – a magic solution to what many practitioners consider the more complex problem of reforming education. Bogost (2013) has perhaps been more vocal in his criticism of certain facets of gamification research, coining the concept of 'exploitationware' – in other words, research that is broad-spectrum, and conducted purely on the assumption that the researcher will likely find something, as opposed to focusing on a specific use of a game, that might be beneficial. Generally speaking, there appears to be a transdisciplinary perception that the majority of research into language-learning technologies is panacean in tone, i.e. arguing that it serves as a potential cure for all of a teacher's problems in the language classroom. The reality presented by researchers like Hubbard, Gee and Bogost is this: common sense would tell practitioners that the practice of viewing any approach as a magic cure for any anticipated problem in class is unrealistic, so research needs to focus on the exact ways in which learning technology could be employed in a manner that learners perceive as worthwhile.

There is other research to support Bogost's impressions (2013, 2015) that a lot of gamification studies may have more hype than substance, as shown by

McGonigal's (2011) call to focus on game-like qualities that could enhance the learning process as opposed to looking at ways to dramatically revolutionize the learning process using video games. This is a thought process that she describes as 'gamefulness' or 'gameful thinking', which Chou (2019) supports by arguing that gamification is essentially a branch of human-focused design. It is therefore difficult to utilize video games meaningfully in a language classroom without first understanding what motivates humans to interact with video games in the first place. There is also evidence that academics in recent years have heeded these concerns and attempted to design various frameworks for assessing digital content and technologies. For example, Burden and Atkinson's (2010) Digital Artefacts for Learner Engagement (DiAL-e) framework and Kukulska-Hulme's (2012) framework for Mobile-Assisted Language Learning both seek to assess the usefulness of learning technologies in relation to the learner experience itself, and, therefore, affordances of a form of technology that the learner might find directly beneficial.

In any case, there is a demonstrable lack of research on exergaming as a tool for facilitating language learning, but as with any change in technology use, the case needs to be argued for looking at exergames from this perspective. On that basis, this chapter will discuss the theory of change, i.e. the theoretical grounds for why we might repurpose exergames as a tool for language learning, and the case for research into exergaming employed in this manner. This discussion will be framed in terms of how exergames have been utilized in the past for learning, but also discuss the key tenets within existing research that may put forward exergames as a way of facilitating or enhancing the learning process.

What is exergaming?

Exergaming has more than one explanation depending on the research area; in this article, it is being used to mean a video game that encourages purposeful physical activity. In this case, the purpose is developing skills that a learner would ordinarily need to acquire a language successfully. However, for many researchers, simply encouraging physical activity, purposeful or otherwise, is the ultimate goal of an exergame, and the key variable is whether the researcher is based in the field of healthcare research or not. Take, for instance, Adams et al. (2009), whose realization of exergaming is the incorporation of any kind of physical activity into a video game, a working premise that other gaming-for-health researchers (Noah et al. 2011; Peng, Crouse and Lin 2013; Höchsmann,

Schüpbach and Schmidt-Trucksäss 2016) tend to support. Such clarification is important because it correlates with what seems to be the prevailing aim in gaming-for-health research into exergaming: games such as *Just Dance* or *Superhot VR* on the Sony Playstation 4 promote rigorous physical activity, so their benefits are often viewed from the lens of efforts to combat obesity in young people.

However, the term 'exergaming', in other areas – for instance, gamification (Klein and Simmers 2009; Best 2013) – is much more specific, directly citing a combination of exercise with video games, e.g. games such as *Wii Fit*, *Just Dance* and *Sparc VR* – a virtual reality exergame that combines racquet-based sports like tennis and squash with classic brick-breaking games such as *Breakout* on early Atari game consoles. This distinction is perhaps more relevant to language acquisition, however, as it focuses more on exergaming as a skills development tool, as opposed to a means of improving health. Such a shift in focus lends credence to the possible usefulness of exergaming in the field of education, and especially to using exergaming for learning a language which, as a process, requires the development of myriad productive and receptive skills.

Furthermore, there are established grounds for the implication that exergames may have a wider scope to impact on learner development, more specifically, in the development of soft skills that a regular language classroom may not always offer opportunities to practise, e.g. cooperative competition (Rüth and Kaspar 2020), interactional competence (Finco et al. 2015) and the lusory attitude described by Suits (2014), i.e. the sense of a video game being recognized as a form of purposeful play, usually to develop qualities that the players need to be successful in other aspects of their lives, such as work or school.

The notion of fostering a lusory attitude among learners is not new. Kim and Gupta (2017), for instance, explored using this attitude among learners to develop a goal-driven discourse, getting students to design their own game with a set of rules as a way of practising project management skills. Hjorth and Richardson (2014) expound upon the notion further, describing this lusory attitude as a form of 'playful sociality': an understanding on the part of learners that play, rather than simply being an action they partake in for recreation, is actually deeply integrated into their everyday lives.

Assuming the playful sociality that Hjorth and Richardson describe is something learners experience, then essentially, the key advantage that an exergame could offer over a language classroom environment is the fact that an exergame is ostensibly seen as a form of play, and therefore an informal setting separated from the classroom, where students could develop skills applicable to formal, real-world contexts. The question I would pose there, however, is what learning style may take place, which will be explored in the next section.

Multiple Intelligences and kinaesthetic learning

One area of theory that I would offer as possible grounds to suggest that exergaming could be used for educational purposes is learning styles and learner preferences. The theory of Multiple Intelligences (MI) was put forward initially by Howard Gardner ([1983] 2011). MI posits that people each have a distinct 'intelligence' indicating a kind of skill or style of learning that enables them to learn best. In general, MI theory is categorized into eight intelligences, as detailed in Figure 10.1. However, Gardner has since commented (2000) that people may not fall into one strictly defined type of intelligence. It is more likely someone would have a combination of intelligences, which implies that each learner has a unique set of preferences in terms of their individual learning needs.

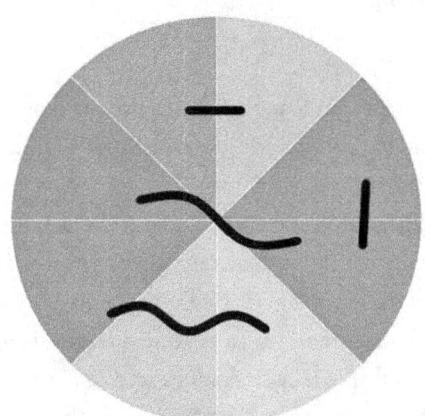

- Logical (numbers) • Linguistic (words)
- Kinaesthetic (body/movement/trial and error)
- Interpersonal (social skills)
- Intrapersonal (reflection) • Musical
- Visual/Spatial (Pictures)
- Naturalistic (awareness of nature and the World)

Figure 10.1 MI theory. Visual representation. Lines indicate a direct link (straight lines) or a loose link (wavy lines) in the potential to combine various intelligences to form an individual learning experience. Source: Author.

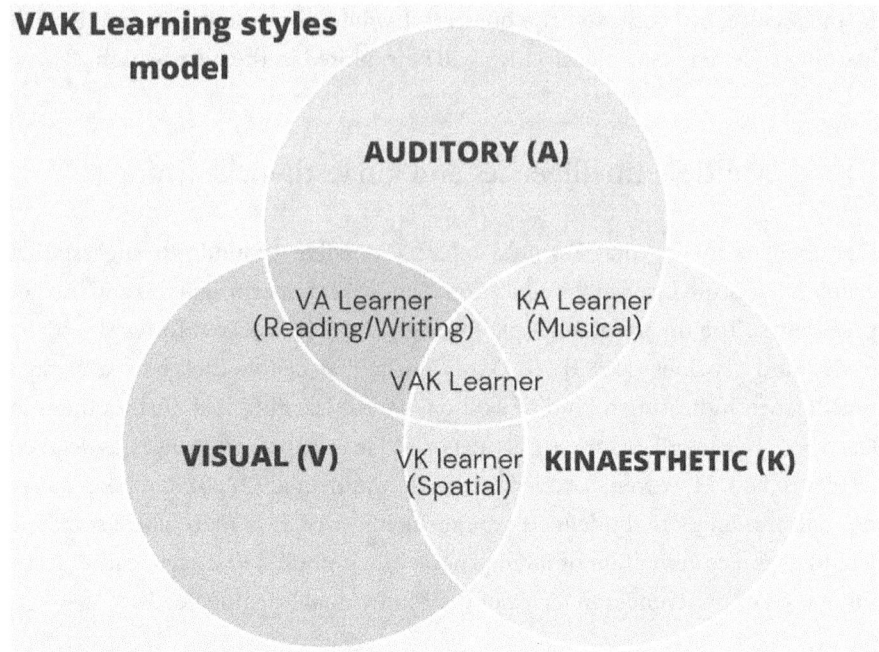

Figure 10.2 VAK learning styles model. Source: Author.

Secondly, there is a popular learning styles theory detailed in Figure 10.2 that was described by Oxford (2003) and Franklin (2006) as essentially three distinct categories of learner: visual, auditory and kinaesthetic (VAK). As the names of the categories suggest, visual learning is essentially learning through sight and visual aids, auditory learning is learning through sound and listening, and kinaesthetic learning is learning through the body, tactile experimentation, exploratory movement or attempting a practical task. It is important to note that Cassidy (2004) cites multiple learning styles and learning strategy theories that came before the VAK model, but I have chosen this model because there is considerable published research suggesting that VAK remains a commonly accepted learning style model in the field of language learning (Willis 2017; Khodabakhshzadeh, Hosseinnia and Rahimian 2017; Bakri, Rahman and Jabu 2019).

A crucial distinction between VAK and MI theory is that VAK is less rigidly defined. As shown in Figure 10.2, there is scope for the three learning styles to intersect, thus acknowledging that learners may not be so easily delineated in terms of one, all-encompassing learner style. Concerning exergaming, this potential for intersection is particularly useful. As I alluded to earlier, Gardner (2011) initially postulated that people tended to exhibit one of the eight intelligences he described, but in recent years his conceptualization has evolved to suggest that people may in fact exhibit a combination of intelligences. This evolution is arguably due in part to various criticisms of learning styles theory. For example, Waterhouse (2006) made the observation that although the learning styles theory had been cited widely in education research, the concept suffered from a lack of concrete empirical evidence. Elsewhere, Howard-Jones (2014) describes both VAK and MI theory as 'neuromyths': incorrect assumptions based on misunderstandings of how the brain works. Put simply, he declares outright that the complexity with which the brain processes information, and the interconnectivity of different processes, make it impossible for a learner's preferences to be defined within even the expanded MI model that Gardner offered in 2000. It is simply too finite as a set of categories, and to be fair, exergaming also challenges MI theory. Depending on the kind of game, at a given time, participants could be demonstrating up to four of the MI simultaneously, which directly contradicts Gardner's updated model.

It should also be noted that research into differentiation in schools (Noble 2004; Furnham and Fukamoto 2008) appears to question both theories, largely due to what differentiation is: the process of catering to students who, individually, have a wide range of learning styles and needs. Referring back to Waterhouse (2006), who openly challenged academics to empirically prove the applicability of MI and VAK theories, it could be argued that the need for differentiation in schools renders Waterhouse's challenge axiomatic. Students who require differentiated support are generally there because they have a diverse range of learning styles, ergo the way in which students learn cannot be broken down into a model as simplistic as those offered by MI and VAK. Interestingly, there is research arguing the opposite (Green and Tanner 2005; Jing 2013), that the ability to aid differentiation could serve as proof that MI exists and is effective. It is worth noting, of course, that these examples do not situate themselves in the traditional language classroom – one study links the MI model to online learning and the other compares MI theory against the China National English Curriculum, but this stark contrast in perceptions of MI theory serves more as to evidence why this, along with VAK theory, is contentious.

Although there appears to be a considerable bank of research discrediting both VAK and MI theory, research continues to be published suggesting that the VAK and MI models can be applied helpfully to exergames used in an educational context (Hwang et al. 2013; Orense, Decena and Feria 2013; Erenli 2016; Luo and Tang 2021). All of the studies mentioned here relate back to

Hjorth and Richardson's (2014) concept of playful sociality in the sense that they all appear to be using exergaming as a means of developing various real-world skills, thereby creating a case for VAK and MI to potentially still fit as theoretical bases for gauging the usefulness of exergaming.

Theories of cognitive development

As I mentioned in the Introduction, outside the gaming and health field much of the research surrounding the benefits of exergaming discusses the potential for cognitive development. Indeed, kinaesthetic learning, which could be seen as the main type of learning that students undergo within an exergaming space, appears to be regarded by several researchers as strongly linked to enhanced cognitive control (see Staiano and Calvert 2011). For instance, Pei-Shi (2012) makes the claim that a learner's 'intelligence', as defined by Gardner's ([1983] 2011) theory in the previous section, links to the learning style and that the combination of both help to develop cognitive control. The implication of this is that kinaesthetic learning from an exergame may enable a learner to develop a more useful approach to learning as a whole which, in turn, may either enhance or augment the cognitive and/or metacognitive skills the learner needs in order to make significant progress.

Moreover, assuming the premise that exergaming is a kind of kinaesthetic learning, in line with the VAK model, then research into neurodivergent students – or as Durkin et al. (2015) describe it, specific learning disabilities (SpLD) – and Alzheimer's Disease (Ben-Sadoun et al. 2016) suggests that exergaming may increase cognitive control and possibly rectify cognitive impairment. Anderson-Hanley, Tureck and Schneiderman (2011) develop the suggestion further, claiming that in their study among students on the autism spectrum, exergaming helped with repetitive behaviour and executive function (a term used to include behaviours such as task focus, concentration and other behaviours that enable people to perform tasks effectively or meet goals). These assertions are apparently supported by studies conducted among students who did not have SpLD (Best 2012; Gao and Mandryk 2012), both of which reported similar gains in cognitive awareness and executive function. That said, it is worth including a caveat here that the difficulty with a significant portion of educational psychology research on the subject (Winne and Perry 2000; Appleton et al. 2006; Mathewson et al. 2012) is that proving a causal link between enhanced cognitive control and improved aptitude for learning is almost impossible to definitively achieve. This is presumably for a similar reason to the one Howard-Jones (2014) outlined when talking about VAK and MI: the brain is simply too complex and has too many interconnected processes to confidently say that the two factors mentioned above correlate.

Considering the benefits and limitations apparent in the established literature, researchers working within exergaming could ponder the impact of increased cognitive control as a result that they may be unable to test directly. While the assumption does explain the impact of augmented cognitive control on learning in general, it does not necessarily explain how increased cognitive function may improve language learning.

At this stage, however, it is relevant to point out that the research into exergaming as a tool for cognitive development is controversial but not disproven. Interestingly, there do appear to be some links between learning a language and learning a form of physical activity, such as a dance or a sport, so what I would propose is a study employing a commercial off-the-shelf exergame, such as a title from Ubisoft's *Just Dance* series (2009), as an intervention that students could use in schools to develop soft skills, as part of a holistic learning process. What follows is a rationale for why an intervention of this kind may be beneficial.

Parallels found between learning dance and learning a language

It is apparent from research in the fields of both dance education and language education that there are a number of similarities to be perceived between the two disciplines. Giguere (2006), for example, indicates that the learning experience is very similar – typically, a process of trial and error, recursive (much like Tomlinson's (2012) observations about learning a language), and, although there is scope for creativity, there are distinct rules that must be mastered, which a language teacher could interpret as similar to mastering the grammar of a language. Opacic, Stevens and Tillman (2009) expound upon this notion, declaring outright that they believe dance to be a kind of language, and that learning a dance may, by proxy, enable learners to develop strategies for mastering other languages.

It is significant here to note Moerman's (2014) view that exergaming could be a platform for multimodal learning – i.e. it is designed to address all three of the VAK styles. Typically, samples of dance research (Golomer, Gravenhorst and

Toussaint 2009; Alaoui et al. 2012) mention this multimodal learning in the form of 'whole body interaction', which is, at heart, a complex process of acquiring and mastering steps, moves and routines. This requires the learner to develop a high level of cognitive and metacognitive functioning, in the sense that they often have to acquire the steps of a dance, which would arguably be a cognitive process, but then reflect on how they carried out those steps and consider ways in which they can improve the steps for future dances. As Silver (2013) points out, reflection is generally viewed as a metacognitive process. Additionally, Hanna (2001, 2008) describes dance as a platform on which to foster a plethora of skills unrelated to dance, including task focus, concentration, teamwork, problem solving and attention to detail. Almost all of these skills link to goal-orientated behaviour. Hanna's research implies a correlation between learning a dance and the increase of what Anderson-Hanley, Tureck and Schneiderman (2011) define as executive function (see above).

The other point to consider is the type of motivation on display when students take part in a dance-based exergame, like *Just Dance* or *Dance Dance Revolution*. Essentially, participants are motivated by direct feedback (comments within the game ranging from 'Ok' to 'YEAH' depending on the accuracy of the move), levelling up, and rewards that the game offers for good performances. It is arguably operant conditioning in action, based on Skinner's (1971) definition of the term: specific cues are being utilized to modify the participant's reactions within the game. Concerning exergames, the cues, termed 'reinforcers' by Skinner (1965), offer either positive praise or negative reinforcement designed to either encourage or discourage certain behaviours – in this case, to encourage success within the game or discourage failure. What is especially significant about a gaming experience is how an earlier behaviourist hypothesis – namely Thorndike's (Thorndike and Bruce 2017) 'Law of Effect' – also applies. This theory postulates that any animal, when presented with a positive feeling of success, will likely seek to find new, more efficient ways to repeat that feeling. There is no doubt that gamers experience this phenomenon; it is common for players to repeat a particular challenge or section of the game to achieve a higher score or boost their ranking.

Learner engagement in exergaming

As highlighted in the Introduction, influential criticisms of language-learning technologies and gamification (Hubbard 2008; Gee 2013; Bogost 2015) conjecture that a substantial body of learning-technology research moves directly to why the technology is interesting, often omitting the fundamental message for practitioners: how that technology may be meaningfully implemented into a classroom.

In relation to gamification, efforts have been made to increase engagement in learning technology, most notably the DiAL-e framework (Atkinson 2009; Burden and Atkinson 2010). The framework is designed to assess forms of learning technology in terms of the likelihood that students might engage with them, appreciate the relevance for their learning and find them useful (see Table 10.1). There is an established precedent for creating a framework for engagement such as DiAL-e. Chapelle and Jamieson (1983) make the point that learning technology tends to only be effective with student input and investment in the learning process. This assertion was demonstrated in action by Greenhow, Robelia and Hughes (2009), who observed in their own learning-technology study that students who did not perceive the immediate relevance of their chosen educational technology quickly disengaged.

The main emphasis of DiAL-e is on fostering a combination of personalization and self-regulation, in line with Steffens and Underwood's (2008) description of the two concepts. Essentially, personalization is the act of tailoring learning to individual needs in order to promote engagement, whereas self-regulation is the learner engaging with, and taking control of, their learning process. Personalization is ideally initiated by the teacher in order to encourage self-regulation among students.

Exergaming could be viewed as conforming to the DiAL-e framework in a number of distinct ways. To begin with, the multiplayer nature of certain exergames – in particular, dance-based exergames like the examples cited earlier – may potentially help to foster collaboration, tying in not only with the DiAL-e framework, but also with Ryan and Deci's (2000) dimension of relatedness. I would argue that the collaborative nature of exergaming may help students to develop their interpersonal skills and encourage teamwork, which Atkinson's (2009) framework cites as a crucial affordance of an engaging technological solution. In addition, exergaming promotes the two elements of authoring and inquiry, thus stimulating creativity (Johnston and Whitehead 2011). Although there is a degree of accuracy required to traverse levels within the game, scores and feedback are determined largely by the readings from a controller with a movement sensor. On that basis, provided the student's hand is in the correct position when the controller takes a reading, the rest of the move is irrelevant, and the student has the freedom to both invent elements of the routine and

Table 10.1 The DiAL-e Framework

	Environment	Mobile	Virtual	Independent	Practical	Small	Large
Stimulation							
Narrative							
Collaboration							
Conceptualization							
Inquiry							
Authoring							
Empathizing							
Research							
Representations							
Figurative							

Source: S. Atkinson and K. J. Burden, *The Dial-e Framework* (New Zealand: Sijen, 2009).

explore different options for achieving the same score using methods that diverge from what is immediately visible onscreen. This aspect of the exergame demonstrates Burden and Atkinson's (2010) arguments surrounding the need for self-regulation. Furthermore, it recalls the SLA research (Brown 2000; Hurd and Lewis 2008) in a manner which suggests a parallel between promoting risk-taking as a language-learning strategy and developing creativity within an exergame.

Finally, several SLA practitioners (e.g. Stoller 2004; Colpaert 2018) make the observation that a lot of learning-technology solutions tend to be content-driven. As a result, they may focus more on the target knowledge to impart than the student experience, and indeed, successful measures of whether students had acquired the target knowledge. Atkinson and Burden's research (Burden and Atkinson 2008; Burden and Maher 2014; Burden and Kearney 2016) suggests that the DiAL-e model might offer a student-driven, learner-oriented solution to the reflections. The implication is that a piece of technology that conformed to DiAL-e – for instance, exergaming – may be more aligned with more student-driven approaches, such as Dogme (Thornbury and Meddings 2001) or post-method approaches (Kumaravadivelu 2006). One of the key distinctions between these approaches – where the teacher is simply there to provide the right conditions for learning and the focus is on working with emergent language during the class – and the ones traditionally used in language classrooms, such as communicative language teaching or grammar translation, is that they place the onus on the learner to decide what they want to study and take steps to tailor the learning process to their own specific learning goals.

In consideration of the above arguments, there remains a need to clarify an important distinction in the context of learning technologies, that between enhancement and augmentation. Bogost (2015: 67) makes the point that gamification, in his eyes, offers people 'a pique in an otherwise noisy environment' of possible solutions on offer. Granted, Bogost's research focuses mainly on gamification for business, but the idea may resonate with many practitioners thinking back to times when learning technology was implemented in their school mainly because it 'looked interesting.' Hubbard's (2008) research would seem to support this view, as he extends a challenge to practitioners to really consider the pedagogical merits of using certain learning technologies. This challenge, of course, was based on his general feeling that the majority of learning-technology research described the chosen technology solution as something to augment as opposed to enhance the learning process, i.e. much of the research talks about learning technology in terms of simply a potential addition to the classroom, in line with Harasim's (2017) definition of augmentation.

There is, however, a counterargument to the potentially problematic picture painted by researchers who argue that a lot of learning technologies seek to augment learning as opposed to enhance it. Young, Klemz and Murphy (2003) point out that some learning technologies enhance the learning process simply by their inclusion within it. They argue that learning technologies by nature can improve the student experience and produce more well-rounded learners with a greater understanding of the world around them.

In my view, the scope for exergaming to be beneficial in a language-learning environment is along the lines that Young, Klemz and Murphy (2003) describe. This conceptualization of exergaming owes to the fact that it is a type of kinaesthetic learning designed to potentially help students to increase cognitive control and executive function, which the students could then transfer into their language learning. Based on this understanding of how exergames could benefit learners, they are not necessarily intended for direct implementation in the classroom, but rather as a support session nurturing specific learning skills. Examples of transferable skills here may include time management, which could be directly applied to success in language proficiency exams; project management skills, which may apply to portfolio work on English-language courses but could also apply to assignments on degree programmes where English is the medium of instruction; and goal-oriented behaviour, which is important for learners working towards language-level targets for HE or finding work.

Where exergaming may benefit

The growing body of research into games for education – what a growing body of research describes as 'serious games' (Breuer and Bente 2010; Crookall 2010; Giessen 2015) establishes certain understandings of the subject which resonate with SLA researchers' perceptions of how distinct learners prefer to learn. This encompasses such aspects of the learning process as high levels of extrinsic motivation (Dörnyei 2003; Ushioda 2010; Glover 2013), goal-oriented behaviour (Anderson-Hanley, Tureck and Schneiderman 2011; Dörnyei, Ibrahim and Muir 2015) and a need to foster autonomy and learner creativity (Hurd and Lewis 2008; Reinders 2010; Johnston and Whitehead 2011). That said, not every language-learning environment would theoretically benefit from exergaming as an intervention. Therefore, I would like to break down the key potential impacts into three areas: high-stakes learning environments, teaching neurodivergent students, and contexts where communicative language teaching is not used.

The first area is high-stakes learning environments. These are environments where successful achievement of learning outcomes has consequences for the learner's future study or career (Ryan 2002; Zimmerman and Dibenedetto 2008). Basturkmen (2014) makes the point that learners who join high-stakes courses tend to do so with a specific goal orientation towards some form of professional development. As a result, the teacher often has to tailor target language and skills to apply to the learner's chosen degree programme and beyond. Because the indication of success in a high-stakes programme is usually obtaining a strong starting position after graduation, securing a promotion or gaining acceptance into a higher-level postgraduate programme, students often join with what Banks and Smyth (2015) describe as considerable pressure to achieve. This may impact the overall quality of the individual learning process, both in terms of addressing skills gaps that high-stakes learners may have and empowering high-stakes learners to achieve the standards that they have set. There is research available to suggest that dance-based exergaming could potentially help with this pressure. Indeed, research into dance-based learning (Viana et al. 2017) clearly implies that dance may lead to empowerment and reduced anxiety among learners, as well as increased feelings of competence (Song, Kim and Lee 2014).

The second area focuses on neurodivergent students. Durkin et al. (2015) and Anderson-Hanley, Tureck and Schneiderman (2011) observed exergaming leading to a noticeable improvement in cognitive control and executive function among students with Autism Spectrum Disorder (ASD). Although ASD is a broad area, it should also be noted that Anderson-Hanley et al. have observed similar success with people living with Alzheimer's Disease (2012a) and diabetes (2012b), with Ben-Sadoun et al. (2016) and Van Santen et al. (2018) coming to the same conclusions in their own independent research on patients who have dementia. These are not just benefits for health; they could also be viewed as impacts on retention of learning.

The third area concentrates on learners from contexts that may not ordinarily use communicative teaching approaches. A good example of this is China, where Liu and Jackson (2008, 2009) point out that many English-language students who speak Chinese as their mother tongue are seldom required to speak in class. Instead, they are expected to listen to the teacher and translate predetermined sentences, a mode which Chang (2011) describes as the 'grammar-translation method'. The complication with this non-communicative approach, as Liu and Jackson (2008, 2009) demonstrate, is that students may be largely reticent to speak, for fear of making errors. Exergaming can assist in this context in terms of reducing learner anxiety and increasing self-efficacy. This naturally relates to the two factors of self-efficacy that Peng (2008: 649) helpfully categorizes as 'enactive experience' and 'observational experience'. To clarify what Peng is implying by these two categories, allowing students to experiment with exergames – to make mistakes by themselves (enactive) and watch other classmates undergo the same experience (observational) – creates a space for the students to become less reticent and be more likely to speak in their language-learning classes.

Conclusions

On the subject of exergaming as a tool to aid language, there is evidence from research in other disciplines to suggest that utilizing exergames as a form of experience-based learning may lead to increased cognitive control and executive function, which could contribute to higher levels of motivation and increased feelings of competence within a language-learning setting. The working assumption here is that there may be a correlation between the increased cognitive control and executive function provided by kinaesthetic learning through exergaming and learners experiencing greater self-efficacy and reduced anxiety when they enter the language classroom.

This correlation has, to a certain extent, already been demonstrated in research conducted with neurodivergent students, so on that basis I would argue that there is merit in taking the assumption of augmented cognitive control as a given and studying exergaming anyway under that premise. Given existing research discussing the potential impacts of experimental inquiry into exergaming as an intervention, much of which mentions development of goal-oriented behaviour and soft skills as I have alluded to in this chapter, I would assert that exergaming as a tool for nurturing a proactive language-learning environment could be the next important direction for language-learning-technology research.

Time to consider installing a game console in language schools and asking learners to download the *Just Dance* app, perhaps?

References

Adams, M. A., S. J. Marshall, L. Dillon, S. Caparosa, E. Ramirez, J. Phillips and
    G. J. Norman (2009), 'A Theory-based Framework for Evaluating Exergames as

Persuasive Technology', in *Proceedings of the 4th International Conference on Persuasive Technology*, April (45): 1–8.

Alaoui, S. F., B. Caramiaux, M. Serrano and F. Bevilacqua (2012), 'Movement Qualities as Interaction Modality', in *Proceedings of the Designing Interactive Systems Conference*, June: 761–9.

Anderson-Hanley, C., K. Tureck and R. L. Schneiderman (2011), 'Autism and Exergaming: Effects on Repetitive Behaviors and Cognition', *Psychology Research and Behavior Management*, 4: 129–37.

Anderson-Hanley, C., P. J. Arciero, A. M. Brickman, J. P. Nimon, N. Okuma, S. C. Westen, M. E. Merz, B. D. Pence, J. A. Woods, A. F. Kramer and E. A. Zimmerman (2012a), 'Exergaming and Older Adult Cognition: A Cluster Randomized Clinical Trial', *American Journal of Preventive Medicine*, 42: 109–19.

Anderson-Hanley, C., P. J. Arciero, S. C. Westen, J. P. Nimon and E. A. Zimmerman (2012b), 'Serious Games for Diabetes, Obesity, and Healthy Lifestyle: Neuropsychological Benefits of Stationary Bike Exercise and a Cybercycle Exergame for Older Adults with Diabetes: An Exploratory Analysis', *Journal of Diabetes Science and Technology*, 6: 849–57.

Appleton, J. J., S. L. Christenson, D. Kim and A. L. Reschly (2006), 'Measuring Cognitive and Psychological Engagement: Validation of the Student Engagement Instrument', *Journal of School Psychology*, 44 (5): 427–45.

Atkinson, S. P., and K. J. Burden (2009), 'The DiAL-e Framework', *Sijen Project*. Available online: https://sijen.com/research-interests/dial-e-project/.

Bakri, R. A., M. A. Rahman and B. Jabu (2019), 'Exploring the Impact of VAK Learning Style on Teenager Level Language Learners in Indonesia', *Journal of Language Teaching and Research*, 10: 807–14.

Banks, J., and E. Smyth. (2015), '"Your Whole Life Depends on It": Academic Stress and High-Stakes Testing in Ireland', *Journal of Youth Studies*, 18: 598–616.

Baranowski, T. (2017), 'Exergaming: Hope for Future Physical Activity? Or Blight on Mankind?', *Journal of Sport and Health Science*, 6: 44–6.

Basturkmen, H. (2014), *Ideas and Options in English for Specific Purposes*, Abingdon: Routledge.

Ben-Sadoun, G., G. Sacco, V. Manera, J. Bourgeois, A. König, P. Foulon, B. Fosty, F. Bremond, F. d'Arripe-Longueville and P. Robert (2016), 'Physical and Cognitive Stimulation Using an Exergame in Subjects with Normal Aging, Mild and Moderate Cognitive Impairment', *Journal of Alzheimer's Disease*, 53 (4): 1299–314.

Best, J. R. (2012), 'Exergaming Immediately Enhances Children's Executive Function', *Developmental Psychology*, 48 (5): 1501–10.

Best, J. R. (2013), 'Exergaming in Youth', *Zeitschrift für Psychologie*, 221 (2): 72–8.

Bogost, I. (2013), 'Exploitationware', in R. Colby, M. S. S. Johnson and R. Shultz Colby (eds), *Rhetoric/Composition/Play through Video Games*, 139–47, New York: Palgrave Macmillan.

Bogost, I. (2015), 'Why Gamification Is Bullshit', in S. P. Walz and S. Deterding (eds), *The Gameful World: Approaches, Issues, Applications*, 65–79, Boston, MA: MIT Press.

Breuer, J., and G. Bente. (2010), 'Why So Serious? On the Relation of Serious Games and Learning', *Eludamos. Journal for Computer Game Culture*, 4: 7–24.

Brown, H. D. (2000), *Principles of Language Learning and Teaching*, New York: Longman.

Burden, K., and S. Atkinson (2008), 'Evaluating Pedagogical Affordances of Media Sharing Web 2.0 Technologies: A Case Study', *Proceedings ascilite Melbourne*, 121–5.

Burden, K., and S. Atkinson (2010), 'Personalizing Teaching and Learning with Digital Resources: DiAL-e Framework Case Studies', in J. O'Donoghue (ed.), *Technology-Supported Environments for Personalized Learning: Methods and Case Studies*, 91–108, Philadelphia: IGI Global.

Burden, K., and M. Kearney (2016), 'Conceptualizing Authentic Mobile Learning', in D. Churchill et al. (eds), *Mobile Learning Design*, 27–42, Singapore: Springer.

Burden, K., and D. Maher (2014), 'Mobile Technologies and Authentic Learning in the Primary School Classroom', in S. Younie, M. Leask and K. Burden (eds), *Teaching and Learning with ICT in the Primary School* (2nd ed.), 171–82, Abingdon: Routledge.

Cassidy, S. (2004), 'Learning Styles: An Overview of Theories, Models, and Measures', *Educational Psychology*, 24 (4): 419–44.

Chang, S. (2011), 'A Contrastive Study of Grammar Translation Method and Communicative Approach in Teaching English Grammar', *English Language Teaching*, 4 (2): 13–24.

Chapelle, C., and J. Jamieson (1983), 'Recognition of Student Input in Computer-Assisted Language Learning', *Calico Journal*, 1 (3): 7–10.

Chou, Y. (2019), *Actionable Gamification: Beyond Points, Badges, and Leaderboards*, Birmingham: Packt Publishing.

Colpaert, J. (2018), 'Exploration of Affordances of Open Data for Language Learning and Teaching', *Journal of Technology and Chinese Language Teaching*, 9 (1): 1–14.

Crookall, D. (2010), 'Serious Games, Debriefing, and Simulation/Gaming as a Discipline', *Simulation and Gaming*, 41 (6): 898–920.

Deterding, S., M. Sicart, L. Nacke, K. O'Hara and D. Dixon (2011), 'Gamification. Using Game-Design Elements in Non-Gaming Contexts', *Conference Proceedings CHI'11. CHI Conference on Human Factors in Computing Systems 2011*, 2425–8, New York: ACM.

Dörnyei, Z. (2003), 'Attitudes, Orientations, and Motivations in Language Learning: Advances in Theory, Research, and Applications', *Language Learning*, 53 (1): 3–32.

Dörnyei, Z., Z. Ibrahim and C. Muir (2015), 'Directed Motivational Currents: Regulating Complex Dynamic Systems Through Motivational Surges' in Z. Dörnyei, P. MacIntyre and A. Henry (eds), *Motivational Dynamics in Language Learning*, 95–105, Bristol: Multilingual Matters.

Durkin, K., J. Boyle, S. Hunter and G. Conti-Ramsden (2015), 'Video Games for Children and Adolescents with Special Educational Needs', *Zeitschrift für Psychologie*, 221 (2): 79–89.

Erenli, K. (2016), 'Generation I(mmersion)– How to Meet Learner Expectations of Tomorrow', *International Journal of Advanced Corporate Learning*, 9 (1): 19–25.

Finco, M. D, E. Reategui, M. A. Zaro, D. D. Sheehan and L. Katz (2015), 'Exergaming as an Alternative for Students Unmotivated to Participate in Regular Physical Education Classes', *International Journal of Game-Based Learning*, 5 (3): 1–10.

Franklin, S. (2006), 'VAKing out Learning Styles—Why the Notion of "Learning Styles" Is Unhelpful to Teachers', *Education 3–13*, 34 (1): 81–7.

Furnham, A., and S. Fukumoto (2008), 'Japanese Parents' Estimates of Their Own and Their Children's Multiple Intelligences: Cultural Modesty and Moderate Differentiation', *Japanese Psychological Research*, 50 (2): 63–76.

Gao, Y., and R. Mandryk (2012), 'The Acute Cognitive Benefits of Casual Exergame Play', *Conference Proceedings CHI'12. SIGCHI Conference on Human Factors in Computing Systems 2012*, May: 1863–72.

Gardner, H. E. (2000), *Intelligence Reframed: Multiple Intelligences for the 21st Century*, New York: Basic Books.

Gardner, H. E. (2011), *Frames of Mind: The Theory of Multiple Intelligences*, New York: Basic Books.

Gee, J. P. (2013), 'Games for Learning', *Educational Horizons*, 91 (4): 16–20.

Giessen, H. W. (2015), 'Serious Games Effects: An Overview', *Procedia – Social and Behavioral Sciences*, 174: 2240–4.

Giguere, M. (2006), 'Thinking as They Create: Do Children Have Similar Experiences in Dance and in Language Arts?' *Journal of Dance Education*, 6 (2): 41–7.

Glover, I. (2013), 'Play as You Learn: Gamification as a Technique for Motivating Learners', in J. Herrington, A. Couros and V. Irvine (eds), *Proceedings of World Conference on Educational Multimedia, Hypermedia and Telecommunications*, 1999–2008, Chesapeake: Association for the Advancement of Computing in Education (AACE).

Golomer, E. M., R. M. Gravenhorst and Y. Toussaint (2009), 'Influence of Vision and Motor Imagery Styles on Equilibrium Control during Whole-Body Rotations', *Somatosensory & Motor Research*, 26 (4): 105–10.

Green, C., and R. Tanner (2005), 'Multiple Intelligences and Online Teacher Education', *ELT Journal*, 59 (4): 312–21.

Greenhow, C., B. Robelia and J. E. Hughes (2009), 'Learning, Teaching, and Scholarship in a Digital Age: Web 2.0 and Classroom Research: What Path Should We Take Now?', *Educational Researcher*, 38 (4): 246–59.

Guichon, N., and M. Hauck (2011), 'Teacher Education Research in CALL and CMC: More in Demand than Ever', *ReCALL*, 23 (3): 187–99.

Hanna, J. L. (2001), 'The Language of Dance', *Journal of Physical Education, Recreation and Dance*, 72 (4): 40–5.

Hanna, J. L. (2008), 'A Nonverbal Language for Imagining and Learning: Dance Education in K–12 Curriculum', *Educational Researcher*, 37 (8): 491–506.

Harasim, L. (2017), *Learning Theory and Online Technologies*, Abingdon: Routledge.

Hjorth, L., and I. Richardson (2014), *Games and Cultural Play*, London: Palgrave Macmillan.

Höchsman, C., M. Schüpbach and A. Schmidt-Trucksäss (2016), 'Effects of Exergaming on Physical Activity in Overweight Individuals', *Sports Medicine*, 46 (6): 845–60.

Howard-Jones, P. A. (2014), 'Neuroscience and Education: Myths and Messages', *Nature Reviews Neuroscience*, 15 (12): 817–24.

Hubbard, P. (2008), 'CALL and the Future of Language Teacher Education', *CALICO Journal*, 25 (2): 175–88.

Hurd, S., and T. Lewis. (2008), *Language Learning Strategies in Independent Settings*, Bristol: Multilingual Matters.

Hwang, W., K. Wattanachote, T. K. Shih, S. C. Yeh and S. Y. Zhan (2013), 'Preliminary Investigation of Interactive Behaviors in Distant Collaborative Exergame', *International Conference on Web-Based Learning*, 213–22, Berlin: Springer.

Jing, J. (2013), 'Teaching English Reading through MI Theory in Primary Schools', *English Language Teaching*, 6 (1): 132–40.

Johnston, H., and A. Whitehead (2011), 'Pose Presentation for a Dance-Based Massively Multiplayer Online Exergame', *Entertainment Computing*, 2 (2): 89–96.

Khodabakhshzadeh, H., M. Hosseinnia and S. Rahimian. (2017), 'Learning Style, Metacognition and Creativity as Predictors of the Foreign Language Achievement: A Structural Equation Modeling Approach', *Psychological Studies*, 62 (4): 377–85.

Kim, B., and D. Gupta. (2017), 'The Game Design "Game": Engaging in Gameful Learning through Goal-Driven Design Discourse', *Brain, Digital, and Learning*, 7 (3): 131–41.

Klein, M. J., and C. S. Simmers (2009), 'Exergaming: Virtual Inspiration, Real Perspiration', *Young Consumers*, 10 (1): 35–45.

Kukulska-Hulme, A. (2012), 'Chapter One: Language Learning Defined by Time and Place: A Framework for Next Generation Designs', in J. Díaz-Verada (ed.), *Left to My Own Devices: Learner Autonomy and Mobile-Assisted Language Learning*, 1–20, Bingley: Emerald.

Kumaravadivelu, B. (2006), *Understanding Language Teaching: From Method to Postmethod*, Abingdon: Routledge.

Laato, S., S. Hyrynsalmi, S. Rauti, A. N. Islam and T. H. Laine (2020), 'Location-Based Games as Exergames – From Pokémon to the Wizarding World', *International Journal of Serious Games*, 7 (1): 79–95.

Liu, M., and J. Jackson (2008), 'An Exploration of Chinese EFL Learners' Unwillingness to Communicate and Foreign Language Anxiety', *The Modern Language Journal*, 92 (1): 71–86.

Liu, M., and J. Jackson (2009), 'Reticence in Chinese EFL Students at Varied Proficiency Levels', *TESL Canada Journal*, 26 (2): 65–81.

Luo, L., and H. Tang (2021), 'Applying Exergames in Classroom for Learning Chinese', *Language and Technology*, 3 (1): 1–12.

Mathewson, K. E., C. Basak, E. L. Maclin, K. A. Low, W. R. Boot, A. F. Kramer, M. Fabiani and G. Gratton (2012), 'Different Slopes for Different Folks: Alpha and Delta

EEG Power Predict Subsequent Video Game Learning Rate and Improvements in Cognitive Control Tasks', *Psychophysiology*, 49 (12): 1558–70.
McGonigal, J. (2011), *Reality is Broken: Why Games Make Us Better and How They Can Change the World*, London: Penguin.
Moerman, P. (2014), 'Dance and Learn! Why Dancing Is Fun and Fruitful in Learning', *International Journal of Pedagogy and Curriculum*, 19 (4): 1–20.
Noah, J. A., D. K. Spierer, A. Tachibana and S. Bronner (2011), 'Vigorous Energy Expenditure with a Dance Exer-Game', *Journal of Exercise Physiology Online*, 14 (4): 13–28.
Noble, T. (2004), 'Integrating the Revised Bloom's Taxonomy with Multiple Intelligences: A Planning Tool for Curriculum Differentiation', *Teachers College Record*, 106 (1): 193–211.
Opacic, T., C. Stevens and B. Tillmann (2009), 'Unspoken Knowledge: Implicit Learning of Structured Human Dance Movement', *Journal of Experimental Psychology: Learning, Memory, and Cognition*, 35 (6): 1570–7.
Orense, A., B. A. Decena and R. Feria (2013), 'Salapiggy: Usability Test of the Sifteo Cubes as a Game Interface for the Money Counting Game for Preschoolers', *International Conference on Educational Technologies (ICEduTech 2013)*, Malaysia: IADIS.
Oxford, R. L. (2003), 'Language Learning Styles and Strategies: Concepts and Relationships', *International Review of Applied Linguistics in Language Teaching*, 41: 271–8.
Pei-Shi, W. (2012), 'The Effect of Learning Styles on Learning Strategy Use by EFL Learners', *Journal of Social Sciences*, 8 (2): 230–4.
Peng, W. (2008), 'The Mediational Role of Identification in the Relationship between Experience Mode and Self-Efficacy: Enactive Role-Playing versus Passive Observation', *CyberPsychology and Behavior*, 11 (6): 649–52.
Peng, W., J. C. Crouse and J. Lin (2013), 'Using Active Video Games for Physical Activity Promotion: A Systematic Review of the Current State of Research', *Health Education and Behavior*, 40 (2): 171–92.
Reinders, H. (2010), 'Towards a Classroom Pedagogy for Learner Autonomy: A Framework of Independent Language Learning Skills', *Australian Journal of Teacher Education*, 35 (5): 40–55.
Rüth, M., and K. Kaspar (2020), 'Exergames in Formal School Teaching: A Pre-Post Longitudinal Field Study on the Effects of a Dance Game on Motor Learning, Physical Enjoyment, and Learning Motivation', *Entertainment Computing*, 35 (100372): 1–11.
Ryan, K. (2002), 'Assessment Validation in the Context of High-Stakes Assessment', *Educational Measurement: Issues and Practice*, 21 (1): 7–15.
Ryan, R. M., and E. L. Deci (2000), 'Intrinsic and Extrinsic Motivations: Classic Definitions and New Directions', *Contemporary Educational Psychology*, 25 (1): 54–67.

Silver, N. (2013), 'Reflective Pedagogies and the Metacognitive Turn in College Teaching', in M. Kaplan, N. Silver, D. Lavaque-Manty and D. Meizlish (eds), *Using Reflection and Metacognition to Improve Student Learning: Across the Disciplines, Across the Academy*, 1–17, Sterling, VA: Stylus Publishing.

Skinner, B. F. (1965), 'Review Lecture – The Technology of Teaching', *Proceedings of the Royal Society of London. Series B. Biological Sciences*, 162 (989): 427–43.

Skinner, B. F. (1971), 'Operant Conditioning', *The Encyclopedia of Education*, 7: 29–33.

Song, H., J. Kim and K. M. Lee (2014), 'Virtual vs. Real Body in Exergames: Reducing Social Physique Anxiety in Exercise Experiences', *Computers in Human Behaviour*, 36 (July): 282–5.

Staiano, A. E., and S. L. Calvert (2011), 'Exergames for Physical Education Courses: Physical, Social, and Cognitive Benefits', *Child Development Perspectives*, 5 (2): 93–8.

Steffens, K., and J. Underwood (2008), 'Self-Regulated Learning in a Digital World', *Technology, Pedagogy and Education*, 17 (3): 167–70.

Stoller, F. L. (2004), 'Content-Based Instruction: Perspectives on Curriculum Planning', *Annual Review of Applied Linguistics*, 24: 261–83.

Suits, B. (2014), *The Grasshopper: Games, Life and Utopia*, Peterborough: Broadview Press.

Thornbury, S., and L. Meddings (2001), 'Using the Raw Materials. A Dogme Approach to Teaching Language', *Modern English Teacher*, 10 (4): 40–3.

Thorndike, L., and D. Bruce (2017), *Animal Intelligence: Experimental Studies*, New York: Routledge.

Tomlinson, B. (2012), 'Materials Development for Language Learning and Teaching', *Language Teaching*, 45 (2): 143–79.

Ushioda, E. (2010), 'Motivation and SLA: Bridging the Gap', *Eurosla Yearbook*, 10 (1): 5–20.

Van Santen, J., R. Dröes, M. Holstege, O. B. Henkemans, A. Van Rijn, R. De Vries, A. Van Straten and F. Meiland (2018), 'Effects of Exergaming in People with Dementia: Results of a Systematic Literature Review', *Journal of Alzheimer's Disease*, 63 (2): 741–60.

Viana, R. B., C. L. Alves, C. A. Vieira, R. L. Vancini, M. Hebling Campos, P. Gentil, M. Santos Andrade and C. A. Barbosa de Lira (2017), 'Anxiolytic Effects of a Single Session of the Exergame Zumba® Fitness on Healthy Young Women', *Games for Health Journal*, 6 (6): 365–70.

Waterhouse, L. (2006), 'Inadequate Evidence for Multiple Intelligences, Mozart Effect, and Emotional Intelligence Theories', *Educational Psychologist*, 41 (4): 247–55.

Werbach, K. (2014), '(Re)defining Gamification: A Process Approach', in A. Spagnolli, L. Chittaro and L. Gamberini (eds), *Persuasive Technology. Lecture Notes in Computer Science Vol 8462*, 266–72, Berlin: Springer.

Willis, S. (2017), 'Literature Review on the Use of VAK Learning Strategies', *The STeP Journal*, 4 (2): 90–4.

Winne, P. H., and N. E. Perry (2000), 'Measuring Self-regulated Learning', in M. Boekaerts, P. R. Pintrich and M. Zeidner (eds), *Handbook of Self-Regulation*, 531–66, Amsterdam: Elsevier.

Young, M. R., B. R. Klemz and J. W. Murphy (2003), 'Enhancing Learning Outcomes: The Effects of Instructional Technology, Learning Styles, Instructional Methods, and Student Behavior', *Journal of Marketing Education*, 25 (2): 130–42.

Zimmerman, B. J., and M. K. Dibenedetto (2008), 'Mastery Learning and Assessment: Implications for Students and Teachers in an Era of High‐Stakes Testing', *Psychology in the Schools*, 45 (3): 206–16.

Games

Breakout (1976), Atari, Inc. [Game], US: Atari, Inc.

Dance Dance Revolution (1998), Arcade [Game], Japan: Konami.

Harry Potter: Wizards Unite (2019), iOS and Android [Game], San Francisco: Niantic and Warner Bros Interactive Entertainment.

Just Dance (2009), Wii, Nintendo [Game], Global Release: Ubisoft.

Mario and Sonic at the Olympic Games (2007), Wii, Nintendo [Game], Japan: Sega and Nintendo.

Pokémon Go (2016), iOS and Android [Game], Kyoto: Nintendo and The Pokémon Company.

Ring Fit Adventure (2019), Nintendo Switch [Game], Kyoto: Nintendo.

Sparc VR, Standard Edition (2017), Playstation 4, Sony [Game], Reykjavík: CCP Games.

Superhot VR (2017), Playstation 4, Sony [Game], Poland: SUPERHOT Team.

Wii Fit (2007), Wii, Nintendo [Game], Kyoto: Nintendo.

11

Video-Based Approaches to Foreign-Language Pedagogy: Two Case Studies on Techno-CLIL in the Secondary School Classroom in Italy and the Netherlands

Michael Thomas and Valentina Morgana

Introduction

The use of video-based instruction in the language classroom is not new but it has undergone several developments over the last three decades due to the emergence of the internet, social media, virtual reality and digital games in the lives of students and teachers (Alrehaili and Al Osman 2019; Peterson, Thomas and Yamazaki 2021). Video and other forms of digital media have increasingly appealed to language teachers due to their potential for providing the type of learning materials required by contemporary theories of SLA, especially those that stress the importance of meaningful interaction and context-based instruction rather than a primary focus on linguistic form (Dash and Kuddus 2020). Video technologies such as mobile phones and tablets have been a valuable source of learning materials as they allow classrooms faced with limited access to digital technologies to overcome these technical challenges through the use of portable devices which in turn have become increasingly normalized in and outside the language classroom (Makoe and Shandu 2018). Video-based materials have broadened the language curriculum from narrow linguistic approaches to those that engage with culture and society, even making it possible for learners to immerse themselves in virtual representations of English-speaking countries (Chatterjee and Kuddus 2015; Kuddus 2018). In order to bolster this potential, more research is needed on the role of video-based activities and Content and Language Integrated Learning (CLIL). CLIL is a pedagogical approach in which 'a foreign language is used as a tool in the learning of a non-language subject' in such a way that both the 'language and the subject have a joint role' (Marsh 2002: 58). CLIL derives from a tradition of bilingual language education in which content and language are integrated along a continuum ranging from a focus on the subject matter (content) to a focus on the L2 (communication) and it has been trialled in particular in school contexts in which subjects from history to science are taught (Pinner 2013, 2019). While CLIL raises questions about its applicability to classrooms in which learners have low foreign-language proficiency (Ball, Kelly and Clegg 2015), it is recognized that it may lead to hybridized approaches. The CLIL approach may employ a combination of L1 and L2 that is adaptable to diverse classroom situations and tasks (Goris, Denessen and Verhoeven 2019). CLIL also works in tandem with digital technologies to promote greater opportunities for project-based language learning that has been increasingly of interest to researchers (Thomas and Schneider 2020). In this context more research is also needed on the types of language materials that teachers can develop to better support learners in CLIL contexts (McDougald and Pissarello 2020; Mahan 2020).

This chapter addresses these established gaps in existing CLIL research by examining the findings from two case studies on techno-CLIL. The studies in question utilized digital video in two secondary schools in Italy and the Netherlands in which English was the medium of instruction. In the first case study CLIL is used to examine how multimodal types of input can improve L2 language learning for Italian students of English. Deploying captioned authentic videos the project examines the implications for students' subject-specific vocabulary and motivation. In the second case study short digital videos (called 'machinima') were recorded by the teacher in a 3D virtual world where objects and simulations had been created to help explain complex mathematics concepts for secondary students. Both studies examine the potential of techno-CLIL and the comparative approach applied in this chapter is valuable in enabling teachers and researchers to compare the opportunities and challenges this teaching technique presents in the secondary English classroom in non-English-speaking countries.

Case study 1: Multimodal input in a CLIL science project in Italy

Research suggests that teenagers and young adults (aged 13–21) intentionally use multimodal screen videos to autonomously increase their English exposure thus encouraging an informal language-learning experience. It must be noted, however, that the use of entertainment-oriented language materials cannot universally be transformed into meaningful pedagogical activities, owing to the fact that learners' attention often requires guidance towards specific language items or discourse patterns (Pavesi and Ghia 2020). This case study suggests that the use of CLIL language practices supported by multimodal input can enhance L2 language learning. The study specifically reports on ongoing research that focuses on the use of screen-captioned authentic videos for task-based English teaching in CLIL classrooms at the secondary education level in Italy. The project aims to improve students' competence and enhance their motivation. In particular it examines the potential of CLIL to foster the acquisition of English subject-specific vocabulary and describes the advantages of using technology and streaming videos in these situations as a way to engage foreign-language learners.

Review of the research

In recent years, multimedia learning settings have become increasingly popular, supported by easier access to TV series, video documentaries and films on online platforms. These screen media resources hold L2 learning potential as they boost students' motivation and active engagement. This type of L2 multimodal input is complex and rapid in nature. To that end, captions (L2–L2) or subtitles (L2–L1) are used to help learners understand the content. In this respect, two main areas of research informed this study. The first involves multimodal input in second-language learning, while the second is related to the teaching and acquisition of subject-specific vocabulary in EFL settings.

Since the study of Price (1983), the use of captioned video to develop listening and vocabulary skills in SLA contexts has been investigated widely (Vanderplank 2010). Stemming from such research, the idea that the simple use of video materials in language classrooms has not been effective, over the last three decades, captions and subtitles have been used to enrich and improve the use of language input in video-based learning to support SLA (Chapelle 2003). Research findings have demonstrated that the use of captioned video increases students' attention and motivation, improves listening comprehension and triggers vocabulary acquisition. However, the findings from these studies must not fall victim to excessive generalization as such research typically focuses on a variety of proficiency levels and contexts while investigating various aspects of listening and vocabulary acquisition (Montero-Perez, Van Den Noortgate and

Desmet 2013). Captioned videos typically use bimodal subtitling (e.g. L2 video with L2 subtitles) and have proven effective in vocabulary expansion (Winke, Gass and Sydorenko 2010; Pujadas and Muñoz 2019). This supports the idea that with the aid of multimedia input, learners tend to focus on the language presented in the video (Vanderplank 1990). Although research in this field has shown positive results, some issues related to multimedia input and captioned video remain. In particular, researchers have been concerned about the efficacy with respect to elementary-level learners (see, for example, Taylor 2005). Despite the complexities inherent in the technique, established research indicates that video materials in English-language learning have numerous advantages. As Vanderplank (2010) observes, authentic videos with captions require learners to read quickly in their L2 and access complex speech patterns and lexical variations. Certain videos have been indicated as less challenging for elementary and pre-intermediate learners as they offer a limited or specific range of vocabulary. This was certainly observed in the short science-based videos used in the project described in this case study. These videos were of similar lengths, followed the same structure, and presented a recurring, specialized vocabulary relating to astronomy.

In the last twenty years, a large body of research has investigated the impact of CLIL on learners' general language proficiency. Results have been increasingly positive, thus confirming the critical contribution of using a foreign language to teach non-language subjects (Mayo and Lázaro Ibarrola 2015; Nikula 2015; Ortega 2015). Based on research findings, EFL CLIL learners usually report higher general language proficiency than other language learners (Pérez-Vidal and Roquet 2015). Despite the potential of CLIL in this area, only a few studies in the literature report on the use of subject-specific vocabulary.

Gablasova (2014), for example, compares the learning and retention of twelve subject-specific words of two groups of EFL high-school students under L1 and L2 conditions. The study follows a pre- and post-test procedure, and the twelve lexical items selected were all new to the students involved. Findings illustrate how students receiving the input in L1 were able to recall more words than their L2 counterparts. In particular, it appeared that students from the L2 group could not retain the meaning of subject-specific words in the delayed post-test. A crucial aspect of this study is the selection of subject-specific vocabulary for CLIL. More recently, Rieder-Bünemann, Hüttner and Smit (2019) investigated the issues involved in selecting subject-specific vocabulary items in CLIL and proposed a holistic model for identifying them using quantitative corpus data and qualitative analysis.

Phase one of Gablasova's study included a quantitative analysis of subject-specific vocabulary from corpus data. Phase two was a qualitative pre-selection of subject-specific vocabulary made by the research team, and phase three consisted of a final qualitative selection of subject-specific vocabulary made by subject experts. While the model provided significant support in identifying subject-specific vocabulary in the reported study, it is not simple to implement as it requires a large amount of data.

Although research on acquiring specific vocabulary through CLIL remains scarce, the dual focus on content and language makes CLIL an ideal approach to teach specialized lexis. This study aims to investigate EFL learners' specific lexical competence through the use of multimodal science videos.

Methods

Case study 1 presents selected lexical data from an ongoing larger study on the impact of a CLIL science programme on EFL learners' specific language competence using multimodal input. The part of the study discussed here presents the use of authentic multimodal input and its impact on subject-specific vocabulary learning by comparing statistical analysis of pre- and post-tests. Additionally, the study used qualitative data from interviews with the science teachers (N=3) and students (N=4) to explore student and teacher perceptions of the CLIL project.

Seventy students aged 13–14 and three science teachers from a lower-secondary school in Italy participated in the study. Students were part of a CLIL school programme that included teaching a ten-week science module in English. Learners in Italy have three one-hour lessons of general English per week. In addition, students from the programme received one CLIL lesson per week over a period of ten weeks. Most of the participants were Italian L1 speakers (N=58), nine students were Chinese L1 and three Spanish.

Four captioned videos (L2–L2) from the National Geographic series *Science 101* were used in the study. The videos were retrieved from the National Geographic video library on Earth Science and Astronomy and focused on the Solar System, Mars, Mercury and the Sun. Each video was approximately 4 minutes in duration (about six hundred narrated words) and included an audio description, music, video images, and other visuals such as tables and text. Twenty-seven target items were selected for the study following the guidance in Rieder-Bünemann, Hüttner and Smit (2019) and according to the following criteria: (a) they were subject-specific words (Astronomy) including semi-technical terms (words with a general and a specific meaning related to the topic) and collocations; (b) they were recurring terms in the videos; and (c) they included different words classes (nouns, verbs and adjectives). All subject-specific vocabulary items were selected by two researchers (phase two of Rieder-Bünemann, Hüttner and Smit 2019) and two subject experts (phase three of Rieder-Bünemann, Hüttner and Smit 2019).

The project used a blended-learning mode of delivery. Students had a one-hour face-to-face lesson every week and then completed individual and group tasks in the Google classroom and all materials used in class were stored and shared in the virtual classroom.

An identical pre- and post-test was administered at the beginning and end of the project. The pre-test took place one week prior to the first lesson to reduce pre-test effects and measure learners' prior knowledge of the words selected for the study. The vocabulary test included twenty-seven questions designed around twenty-seven subject-specific words (see Table 11.1). It required students to answer multiple-choice and true/false questions and match words with the correct definitions.

All tasks performed during the study were unfocused (i.e. without any vocabulary pre-focus on form or content); therefore, the teacher did not plan any pre-viewing task activities to draw attention to the target vocabulary. Each of the ten CLIL science lessons followed the same procedures. Students watched a video about a planet in the Solar System with captions twice, and completed two immediate post-input tasks: a content comprehension task and a subject-specific vocabulary task to focus learners' attention on content, form and specific vocabulary (Pujadas and Muñoz 2019). After each lesson, students had one week to complete an individual technology-mediated task and submit it online. The online task required learners to manipulate the input and use appropriate vocabulary by screen-capturing part of the video and creating a short video summary or a voiceover presentation on the topic.

Findings

In the pre- and post-test, each correct response was worth one point. Words that learners scored correctly at both the pre- and the post-test were considered *known items*, while words unknown or incorrect at the pre-test and correctly scored at the post-test were considered *learned items* (Pujadas and Muñoz 2019). The pre- and post-project test scores were compared and analysed to understand which lexical items were most easily recalled. These results were triangulated with data from teachers and students' interviews.

Table 11.1 List of the twenty-seven subject-specific words selected from the science videos

Subject-specific word	Word class (as used in the video)
collapse	Verb
result in	Verb
run out of	Verb
massive	Adjective
debris	Noun
nebula	Noun
gravity	Noun
lava flow	Noun
surface	Noun
atmosphere	Noun
orbit	Verb
asteroid	Noun
galaxy	Noun
swirling object	Noun
core	Noun
matter	Noun
layer	Noun
greenhouse effect	Noun
revolve	Verb
rocky	Adjective
magnetic field	Noun
fuse	Verb
moist atmosphere	Noun
force	Noun
dust	Noun
axis	Noun
mantle	Noun

Table 11.2 indicates the comparison between the vocabulary pre- and post-tests. Scores at the post-test increased considerably and show that students were aware of almost 80 per cent of the target words. These data show a relevant increase in the minimum score from pre- to post-test, thus demonstrating that learners at the end of the project were generally able to recognize and/or recall the meaning of about 52 per cent of the subject-specific words considered.

Table 11.2 Students' scores in the vocabulary pre- and post-test

	Scores at PRE-TEST	Scores at POST-TEST
Valid	70	70
Missing	0	0
Mean	14.357	21.571
Std. Deviation	3.510	2.991
Shapiro-Wilk	0.942	0.954
P-value of Shapiro-Wilk	0.003	0.012
Minimum	5.000	14.000
Maximum	21.000	27.000

Furthermore, based on the analysis of incorrect responses, the nouns 'debris' and 'edge' and the verbs 'to run out' and 'to revolve' were scored correctly by only 15 per cent of the students in the pre-test and 35 per cent in the post-test. By contrast, students easily recognized four words in the pre-test ('collapse', 'gravity', 'orbit' and 'mass'), and the post-test reflected the same results. This suggests that subject-specific cognate words tended to be correctly defined and identified by learners.

Data from the student interviews confirmed that learners relied on their L1 to recall the specific meaning of certain words. Interestingly, the most common way that the majority of students identified the correct meaning of a word in the pre-test was to read it silently several times because pronunciation helped them to put the specific word in context, as shown in the following extract: 'I repeated the word in my mind because probably I heard that in Italian sometimes and I was right. Also, the pronunciation I think was similar' (Student 5, class 1). Learners reported difficulties in identifying the specific meaning of a word without having seen it before. The majority of students found it particularly challenging to attribute a particular meaning to a word they were convinced they knew already. The teachers experienced a similar frustration: 'The pre-test looked very hard for some of them ... I think because they couldn't recognize the meaning they were expecting to find' (Science teacher, class 1). Following the post-test, learners were generally enthusiastic, reporting a perceived improvement in subject-specific vocabulary and their English proficiency. In relation to this perceived improvement, students highlighted their ability to watch and listen to the video as many times as possible, and the use of captions helped to associate words with specific images or graphics in the science video. Moreover, the correspondence between sign and sound, word and pronunciation, was recurrently mentioned both by teachers and students as a fundamental strategy to learn a vocabulary item: 'Students felt more comfortable after the pre-test when we started using videos and interactive tasks' (Science teacher, class 1). This suggests that students may need an extended timeframe in order to select their best personal strategy to learn and easily recall a word in the future.

Discussion

This study explored the use of screen-captioned videos in a CLIL science EFL classroom and the opportunities it provided to learn subject-specific vocabulary. As mentioned, particular attention was paid to a list of twenty-seven subject-specific vocabulary items that learners repeatedly found in the science lesson videos.

The results confirm previous studies on the efficacy of using captioned videos to improve listening comprehension and vocabulary learning (Winke, Gass and Sydorenko 2010; Montero-Perez, Van Den Noortgate and Desmet 2013; Pujadas and Muñoz 2019). It appeared that learners felt particularly engaged in the tasks because they could learn through multimedia input and they had time to understand and even manipulate the input during the tasks. One of the concerns raised by the use of bimodal subtitles at elementary level is that they require learners to be fast readers and understand complex language simultaneously (Vanderplank 2010). Thus, the findings suggest that using tasks that require learners to understand and manipulate the input at their own pace can complement the difficulties of accessing authentic captioned videos and subject-specific language resources. The teachers supported learners by facilitating comprehension activities and providing real-time feedback during personalized tasks (such as creating a presentation using screenshots from video).

In some CLIL practices, the main focus is on content, and tasks are often designed around content learning (see Dalton-Puffer 2011). Other CLIL classrooms place the central focus on explicitly language-based tasks, as observed in the area of subject-specific vocabulary learning. In this respect, this study also sought to measure the number of subject-specific vocabulary items students were able to recall after the CLIL science project based on a list of twenty-seven selected words related to astronomy. The findings indicated that students already knew or retained most of the words in the list, particularly cognate words (i.e. words that are similar in spelling, pronunciation and meaning to their L1). One possible explanation for this is that elementary L2 learners tend to focus on cognates as an effective vocabulary development strategy (Hall 2002). Furthermore, the multimodal input and captions helped make the initial connection between sound and sign (pronunciation and word), adding a visual representation of the subject-specific concept.

Although no language-focused pre-tasks were designed to scaffold learners' performance in the study, a series of multimodal vocabulary-focused tasks were provided immediately after each video task. Particularly in the post-task phase, teachers invited learners to use subject-specific vocabulary to plan and deliver their language product (e.g. videos, oral presentations, etc.). These activities provided opportunities for learners' engagement with content and a focus on specific language items (Nikula 2015).

Summary

Among the findings that the study has identified, one particular conclusion stands out as particularly valuable to multimodal EFL teaching. The integration of subject-specific vocabulary and CLIL has excellent potential, but it also poses a series of challenges, especially with elementary and pre-intermediate learners. On the one hand, selecting discipline-specific vocabulary is crucial for second-language learning. However, it should follow accepted procedures (e.g. Rieder-Bünemann, Hüttner and Smit 2019) to ensure the reliability of analysis and findings. On the other hand, the use of captioned videos and multimodal input has proven to be effective in exposing learners to L2 authentic input and exploiting subject-specific vocabulary practices. Learners feel engaged while exposed to authentic and language-specific content. At the same time, technology-mediated tasks allow learners to adjust and modify the input mediating and guiding effective vocabulary-learning strategies such as noticing, recycling and meaning recall (e.g. Winke, Gass and Sydorenk 2010).

Case study 2: Teaching mathematics with CLIL and machinima in the Netherlands

Previous research (Thomas and Schneider 2020) indicates that the use of simulations and 3D objects such as those used in digital games and immersive worlds like *Second Life* and *OpenSim* can be valuable in (a) giving teachers opportunities to be creative and take ownership of the resources they use in class, and (b) providing students with authentic and highly engaging environments for experiential learning. While learners may be used to interacting with 3D digital environments in their out-of-class social lives, there is always the danger that they will lose interest in them when driven by more formal learning content, outcomes and assessments. This case study explores the use of CLIL and digital video content in the form of 'machinima', which is a neologism of the words 'machine' and 'cinema', to teach Pythagoras' theorem and to challenge learners' traditional conceptions of how such concepts can be taught in the Netherlands. The project aimed to identify the benefits and challenges associated with this approach with respect to learner engagement with mathematics in the medium of English.

A review of the research

Over the last three decades CLIL has steadily developed as a type of bilingual education alongside several different approaches such as immersion, especially in the European context. This review briefly explores the rationale for using CLIL before turning to consider how it might be integrated with authentic digital video content in 3D virtual worlds to teach foreign languages.

In CLIL content areas such as science or geography are taught via a foreign language and the approach has become popular across the school sector as well as in post-compulsory education. CLIL-based approaches are defined by their use of content from actual subject areas rather than the typical content found in language courses (Dalton-Puffer, Nikula and Smit 2010). Indeed, it is best seen as a fusion of two approaches called 'dual-focused education' (Marsh 2005), rather than one that privileges content or language exclusively, and instead of using language teachers, the subject-specific content is delivered by content specialists. There are 'hard' and 'soft' varieties of CLIL in which the content or the communicative aspects of the approach are uppermost but typically the emphasis is on mastering content in such a way that the foreign language is learned in a less obtrusive fashion.

In an earlier study, Navés (2009) outlined ten key principles for effective CLIL integration which are still valuable today: respect and support for learners' L1 and home culture; the use of multilingual and bilingual teachers; it functions as an integrated dual language optional programme rather than one that is imposed; it benefits from having long-term stable teaching staff to provide continuity of content and language instruction; the importance of parental involvement is key for supporting students in what can be a challenging environment, particularly during the initial stages; the joint effort of all parties involved such as the educational authorities, parents and teachers is important; the teachers' profile, training and knowledge of second language acquisition is as important as content knowledge; high expectations and clear assessment goals are required throughout CLIL instruction; the selection of appropriate materials for the CLIL classroom should be carefully planned; and an effective CLIL methodology is one that enables language-learning and content input to develop in harmony rather to be seen as in conflict with one another.

When these points receive less attention the use of CLIL may encounter several challenges. Of these, research suggests that the main challenge is how to effectively integrate content and language focus to the same level of expertise that is consistent (Marsh 1994). This is also evident in the challenges facing teachers. One such challenge is choosing the most appropriate learning materials for students, as the market for commercial products typically lacks expertise in language and content. This can be a barrier to some students in group contexts depending on their abilities, language proficiency and motivation. Consequently, effectively assessing students in CLIL classrooms can present challenges unless content and language are integrated effectively in learning outcomes related to clear exercises, tasks and projects (Goris, Denessen and Verhoeven 2019).

Interactionist and sociocultural approaches to SLA emphasize the importance of linguistic input that is comprehensible, rich, varied and engaging (Mayo and Lázaro Ibarrola 2015). As we have seen, CLIL and related task- and project-based approaches to language learning build on these assumptions to require authentic and meaningful opportunities for learners to interact in the target language, building a diverse skill-set which includes pragmatic and intercultural competence alongside a knowledge of traditional linguistic form (Thomas and Schneider 2020). Research on computer-mediated communication (CMC) in 3D virtual and immersive worlds suggests that opportunities are provided for learners to increase their exposure to authentic content and cultures (Dalgarno and Lee 2010); produce 3D visualizations and realistic contextualization for engaging learner input; extend opportunities for rich interaction, play and social presence; enable learners to experience immersion in the target culture and language-rich environments to improve motivation; and to take advantage of the technology's affordances to design and create their own content (Warburton 2009).

Machinima is the creation of recorded videos within 3D immersive environments such as *Second Life*, *OpenSim* or related game-worlds such as *Minecraft* or *World of Warcraft* (Middleton and Maher 2008). As Morozov (2008:

5899) indicates, machinima enables teachers and students to 'record and edit unique visual experiences incorporating 3D character models and objects, set designs, graphical textures, camera angles, special effects, weather filters, custom lighting ... with unlimited variations on plot, settings, and characters'. Highly polished machinima productions may involve a team of expert filmmakers or an individual teacher working alone. While many productions are highly technical and polished, others are valuable for the opportunities they provide for interaction and less for the quality of their production (Dalgarno and Lee 2010). Machinima can develop the blend of authentic content-based input and language-learning interaction required of CLIL approaches (Middleton and Mather 2008). Moreover, machinima productions combine techniques from the arts and sciences to create complex digital films which combine an appreciation of 'the visual attention of the viewer, the appearance, facial expression and gestures of the characters when they are talking, the duration and placement of each scene in the overall composition, the camera angle and focus, lighting, the mood of the surroundings, the soundtrack and ambient noise' (Morozov 2008: 5906).

In pedagogical contexts, machinima can be adapted to include projects or exercises that contain 'procedural language, problem solving, discussion, social pragmatics, storytelling, and code-switching between different genres of writing' (Lansiquot and Rosalia 2008: 2661). 3D virtual and immersive worlds stimulate the use of creative pedagogies through 'a range of functionality' to enable 'collaborative group and role-play' activities (Lansiquot and Rosalia 2008: 2661). Within immersive environments, these types of activities give rise to different learning models, in which ownership, coaching and mentoring, apprenticeship learning and collaborative social learning can be developed (Dieterle and Clarke 2007).

The use of machinima offers teachers the opportunity to develop resources that can fuse content with language use in often highly original and creative simulations. It can be used with a range of learning strategies that transcend form-focused and behaviourist types of instruction based on memorization in relation to vocabulary. As Herrington and Oliver (2000: 23) indicate, the use of video-based machinima can be useful in addressing the challenge that 'the abstract knowledge taught in schools and university is not retrievable in real-life situations because traditional approaches (lectures and tutorials) ignore *interdependence of situation and cognition*'. In an attempt to bridge this divide, research on machinima suggests that it can be used effectively to improve more active types of learning (Herrington, Oliver and Reeves 2002; Middleton and

Mather 2008) and help learners who feel marginalized by traditional forms of classroom interaction and are demotivated by content-based instruction to be less inhibited in terms of oral production tasks when using a foreign language. Likewise for teachers, the machinima design, production and implementation process can be creative and experimental, which in turn leads to ownership of the learning resources and materials and potentially provide a positive environment for collaborative and project-based learning approaches to be developed. Designing 3D resources in virtual and immersive worlds can produce activities that appeal across a wide range of content-based areas, from the sciences to the arts and humanities, as well as to different types of learners. For example, learners with special educational needs or who experience higher levels of anxiety in collaborative language-learning environments may benefit from the anonymity of in-world computer-mediated communication or the use of blended learning.

Inevitably, the use of new technologies also presents challenges to teachers and learners alike. Machinima production can be a time-consuming process, particularly during the initial stages of learning new techniques. Moreover, for learners, it can present a higher cognitive load which may risk focusing learners' attention on the technologies rather than the content of the instruction. Indeed, not all learners may benefit from or enjoy the emphasis on screen activities integrated consistently across the curriculum. Technical challenges may inhibit teachers and schools from using these technologies depending on the availability of equipment and the required internet bandwidth and storage requirements (Tüzün and Özdinç 2016).

Methods

North School is a bilingual secondary school in the Netherlands in which CLIL is used consistently across the curriculum to teach subjects through the medium of English. The European and International Orientation is integrated in the programme alongside the International Baccalaureate for English. In this case study, video-based machinima were designed by the classroom mathematics teacher to explore the potential of the technology to aid student engagement and understanding of difficult-to-learn concepts. Typically, the class used paper-based materials in mathematics teaching as key threshold concepts could appear abstract and challenging to visualize in 2D. The in-class-developed experiment utilized 3D objects in *Second Life* followed by producing a digital video recording (machinima) to explain Pythagoras' theorem and the calculation of a space diagonal to students.

The CLIL instructor had been teaching mathematics at the secondary school in the Netherlands to learners aged 13 with beginner-level English proficiency for nine years. During the first eight weeks of each semester the instructor routinely spoke English and Dutch with the students. Following this opening transitional phase, only English was used as the medium of instruction. The instructor had experience of developing a techno-CLIL approach in which he used several interactive web-based applications (e.g. Socrative) to enable students to organize and project manage their work in mathematics. The instructor used his tablet to keep track of students' activities during each class session and to encourage students to use their own tablets and smartphones. The teacher's own digital skills also included the use of 3D animation, and while he had no previous experience with using 3D immersive worlds or machinima video productions, he understood the potential advantages of using these environments to enable communication between students and teachers about the content of each class. The teacher nonetheless remained conscious of the significant added effort required in terms of time, continuing professional development, and expertise required of instructors and students to develop video-based teaching resources of this type.

In order to prepare the machinima-based lessons, the class teacher created a worksheet which enabled the students to take notes and provide scaffolding for the activities, acting at once both as an opportunity to provide structure for their thinking. Students first read the instructions on the worksheet to check if they understood the English vocabulary items (see Appendix). The students proceeded to complete a worksheet in English which asked them questions about Pythagoras' theorem, including the steps used to calculate it, and were exposed to relevant vocabulary to enable them to answer the questions effectively. This was followed by a brainstorming exercise in which the students were asked to compile a list of relevant vocabulary for the mathematics concepts they were about to learn about in the video. The vocabulary items were then discussed by the whole class to make sure the students could understand the machinima about the space diagonal. The students and teachers then watched the video which showed a 3D model about the space diagonal (see Figures 11.1 and 11.2). Finally, the students completed a post-task exercise which addressed their understanding of the key concepts and vocabulary mentioned in the machinima video. To further assess the extent of the students' understanding, they were asked to complete a questionnaire about their experience while the teacher was interviewed separately.

The questionnaire was used to collect data about the students' experience of using the CLIL-based machinima approach. In total sixteen students responded

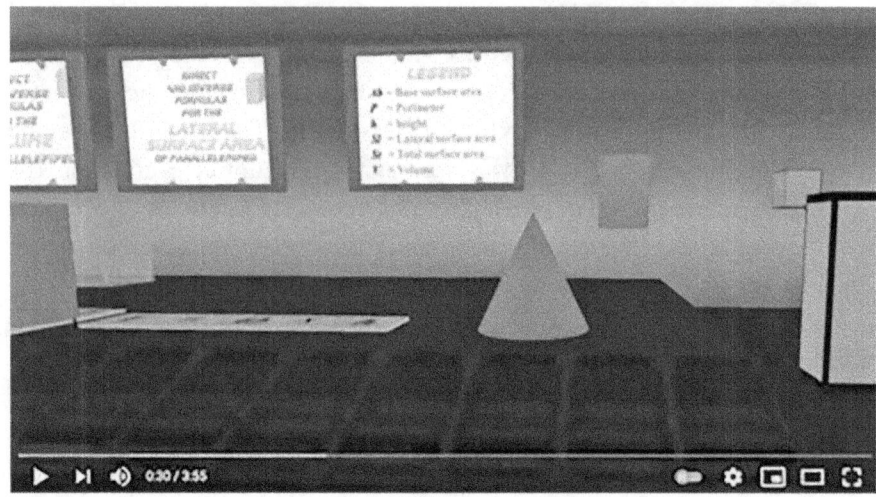

Figure 11.1 Space diagonal instructions in 3D world. Source: CamelotProject.eu (Dir. Occioni, de Boer, Koeraad and Schneider, 2016).

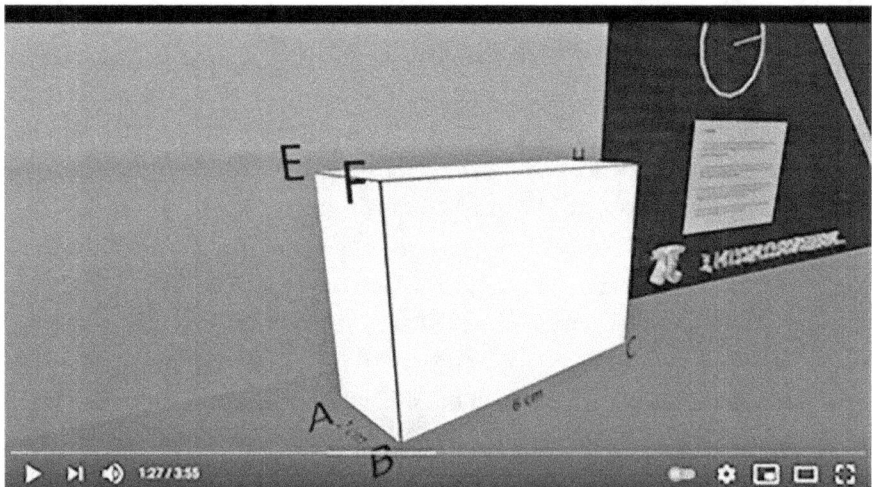

Figure 11.2 Space diagonal formula. Source: CamelotProject.eu (Dir. Occioni, de Boer, Koeraad and Schneider, 2016).

(f=9; m=7) and all of the learners were aged 13. While none of the participants had created machinima, fifteen of the participants were familiar with multiplayer computer games such as *World of Warcraft* or *Minecraft*. The questionnaire used a 5-point Likert scale ranging from 'strongly agree' to 'strongly disagree' to respond to the fifteen-item questionnaire.

The interview with the teacher of the CLIL class consisted of three sections and twenty-nine question items covering his background and experience as a language teacher, the technical challenges he faced during the machinima lessons, and the pedagogical implications of his use of machinima in the mathematics class.

The data from the student questionnaire on the CLIL-based machinima approach were analysed through the use of descriptive statistics and the interviews were audio recorded and transcribed following Braun and Clarke's (2006) iterative open coding approach. Several themes emerged from the two-stage process involving the qualitative data, and Guba and Lincoln's (1994) framework on credibility, transferability, dependability and confirmability guided the cycles of analysis.

Findings

Several positive results stand out from the questionnaire data (see Table 11.3). There is clear evidence for the impact on students' motivation to engage in mathematics as a result of the machinima.

Students overwhelmingly 'agreed' and 'strongly agreed' that they 'enjoyed watching machinima in the lesson' (91.67 per cent), 'learned and understood the subject better with machinima' (70 per cent) and 'learnt a lot with machinima' (58.33 per cent). This positive outlook remained present in responses to questions about how they felt as a result of their use of machinima during the lesson, with students engaged enough to feel motivated (60 per cent), comfortable with this new mode of learning quite quickly (30 per cent) and more curious about the subject matter (20 per cent) than was the case with more traditional approaches.

Qualitative comments from students indicated that they were engaged by the machinima lessons because the video productions and contents were 'clear' and 'simple' as well as 'more professional' and 'explained the problem' more effectively than the traditional approaches. Students also provided specific responses on the machinima content, with positive feedback on 'Is machinima as good as normal video in the lesson?', with 80 per cent in agreement or strong agreement.

Discussion

The use of machinima had several benefits in the CLIL-based secondary mathematics classroom with this group of Dutch secondary-school learners of English. Primarily, it presented opportunities to produce 3D objects which could

Table 11.3 Students' responses to statements on machinima

Statement	No	Strongly agree	Agree	Undecided	Disagree	Strongly disagree
1. I enjoy watching machinima in my lessons.	12	25.00%	66.67%	8.33%	0%	0%
2. I enjoy making machinima in my lessons.	11	0%	27.27%	54.55%	18.18%	0%
3. Short machinima are better to help me learn.	12	8.33%	75%	8.33%	8.33%	0%
4. I learn a lot with machinima.	12	8.33%	50.00%	25.00%	16.67%	0%
5. Machinima help me to learn new words.	12	0%	33.33%	33.33%	33.33%	0%
6. Machinima help me to understand new grammar.	12	0%	50.00%	8.33%	41.67%	0%
7. Machinima help me to improve my listening.	12	0%	50.00%	25.00%	25.00%	0%
8. Machinima help me to improve my speaking.	12	0%	25.00%	16.67%	58.33%	0%
9. Machinima help me to improve my writing.	12	8.33%	8.33%	8.33%	66.67%	8.33%
10. Watching machinima is fun, but I am not learning anything.	12	8.33%	8.33%	8.33%	58.33%	16.67%
11. The avatars don't look natural.	11	18.18%	18.18%	36.36%	27.27%	0%
12. I find it difficult to learn a language if the avatars do not show what they feel.	11	9.09%	27.27%	36.36%	9.09%	18.18%
13. I learn and understand the subject better with machinima.	10	0%	70.00%	20.00%	10.00%	0%
14. I will continue learning with machinima in the future.	11	9.09%	54.55%	18.18%	9.09%	9.09%
15. Machinima help me to learn on my own.	11	18.18%	54.55%	18.18%	0%	9.09%

be used to visualize 'difficult to understand' or 'threshold' mathematics concepts such as Pythagoras' theorem and the space diagonal (Alrehaili and Al Osman 2019). By creating several 3D images, the instructor was able to visualize how to calculate the length of space diagonals (Morozov 2008). Unlike a traditional 2D blackboard image, the use of 3D machinima objects enabled the teacher to animate aspects of the instructional materials so that the students could see changes in perspective, the layering of abstract information, and use a repeatable video format which the students could replay as they wished to recap on important aspects of the instructional content in the target language (De Jong Derrington 2013).

Students' self-reported data allied with the teacher's perspective suggest that the learning was more effective and they felt more motivated and engaged in the technology-mediated CLIL classroom, at least in the short term (Warburton 2009). Students reported an overall sense of increased enjoyment, the potential to learn more input, increased vocabulary and grammar acquisition, improvements in listening, and learner independence (Middleton and Mather 2008). The Pythagoras machinima was a well-conceived production created with input from the teacher. Research suggests that performance and motivational gains are possible when the students participate fully in the design and production phases of machinima video and that the creation process is more valuable than the quality of the final production (Warburton 2009).

Conclusion

This chapter enables comparison between two case studies of techno-CLIL involving video-based learning in secondary schools in Italy and the Netherlands. The first case study in Italy is part of an ongoing, more extensive study on the use of multimodal input in CLIL science and the development of subject-specific language. The findings reported here are, in a sense, limited. In particular, in order to measure learners' vocabulary gains and retention, it would have been beneficial to analyse data also at the delayed post-test phase, but this was not possible. Future research should address questions related to the use of captioned video to teach subject-specific vocabulary in CLIL classrooms, such as:

1. Do elementary learners acquire more subject-specific vocabulary when exposed to L1 subtitles instead of L2 bimodal captions?
2. Does the use of multimodal input contribute to larger EFL vocabulary improvement?

3. Can learners be trained in the effective use of captions, particularly for subject-specific vocabulary learning?

The increasing popularity of multimodal input and language tasks to engage EFL teenage learners has inspired researchers and practitioners to look at its potential and the challenges it raises.

The second case study explored a techno-CLIL approach in the mathematics classroom in the Netherlands. There were several limitations in terms of data collection, as it drew mainly on self-reported data. It will be important in future to undertake more longitudinal studies of students' actual language performance in the machinima-based class, as well as ethnographic studies of the collaborative styles of learning CLIL appears to enable (Boellstorff 2008), from both learner and teacher perspectives. Future research will need to examine more closely the following suggested research questions:

1. To what extent can techno-CLIL using machinima enhance language performance?
2. How can techno-CLIL using machinima develop learners' collaborative literacies?
3. How can techno-CLIL using machinima sustain learners' motivation over time?

The case studies outlined in this chapter have investigated the pedagogical implications of two techno-CLIL approaches that appear to have potential in the language classroom. It is hoped that this comparative format will help teachers and practitioners to continue to bridge the gap between research and classroom practice in language education and to explore how they can research innovative practice in ways that directly impact continuing professional development and learner performance and engagement.

References

Alrehaili, E. A., and H. Al Osman (2019), 'A Virtual Reality Role-Playing Serious Game for Experiential Learning', *Interactive Learning Environments*, 30 (5): 1–14.

Ball, P., K. Kelly and J. Clegg (2015), *Putting CLIL into Practice*, Oxford: Oxford University Press.

Boellstorff, T. (2008), *Coming of Age in Second Life: An Anthropologist Explores the Virtually Human*, Princeton: Princeton University Press.

Braun, V., and V. Clarke (2006), 'Using Thematic Analysis in Psychology', *Qualitative Research in Psychology*, 3 (2): 77–101.
Chapelle, C. A. (2003), *English Language Learning and Technology: Lectures on Applied Linguistics in the Age of Information and Communication Technology*, Amsterdam: John Benjamins.
Chatterjee, B., and K. Kuddus (2015), 'Mass Media Approach to Second Language Acquisition', *Journal of English Studies*, 10 (1): 10–16.
Dalgarno, B., and M. J. W. Lee (2010), 'What Are the Learning Affordances of 3-D Virtual Environments?', *British Journal of Educational Technology*, 41 (1): 10–32.
Dalton-Puffer, C. (2011), 'Content-and-Language Integrated Learning: From Practice to Principles?', *Annual Review of Applied Linguistics*, 31: 182–204.
Dalton-Puffer, C., T. Nikula and U. Smit, eds (2010), *Language Use and Language Learning in CLIL Classrooms*, Amsterdam: John Benjamins.
Dash, A., and K. Kuddus (2020), 'Leveraging the Benefits of ICT Usage in Teaching of English Language and Literature', in S. Satapathy, V. Bhateja, J. Mohanty and S. Udgata (eds), *Smart Intelligent Computing and Applications: Smart Innovation, Systems and Technologies*, 225–32, Singapore: Springer.
De Jong Derrington, M. (2013), 'Second Language Acquisition by Immersive and Collaborative Task-Based Learning in a Virtual World', in M. Childs and A. Peachey (eds), *Understanding Learning in Virtual Worlds*, 135–63, London: Springer.
Dieterle, E., and J. Clarke (2007), 'Multi-user Virtual Environments for Teaching and Learning', in M. Pagani (ed.), *Encyclopedia of Multimedia Technology and Networking*, 1033–40, Hershey: Idea Group, Inc.
Gablasova, D. (2014), 'Learning and Retaining Specialized Vocabulary from Textbook Reading: Comparison of Learning Outcomes through L1 and L2', *The Modern Language Journal*, 98 (4): 976–91.
Goris, J., E. Denessen and L. Verhoeven (2019), 'The Contribution of CLIL to Learners' International Orientation and EFL Confidence', *The Language Learning Journal*, 47 (2): 246–56.
Guba, E., and Y. Lincoln (1994), *Sage Handbook of Qualitative Research*, Thousand Oaks, CA: Sage.
Hall, C. J. (2002), 'The Automatic Cognate Form Assumption: Evidence for the Parasitic Model of Vocabulary Development', *International Review of Applied Linguistics in Language Teaching*, 40 (2): 69–87.
Herrington, J., and R. Oliver (2000), 'An Instructional Design Framework for Authentic Environments', *Educational Technology Research and Development* 48 (3): 23–48.
Herrington, J., R. Oliver and T. Reeves (2002), 'Patterns of Engagement in Authentic Online Learning Environments', *Australasian Journal of Educational Technology*, 19 (1): 59–71.
Kuddus, K. (2018), 'Emerging Technologies and the Evolving Roles of Language Teachers: An Overview', *Language in India*, 18 (6): 81–6.

Lansiquot, R., and C. Rosalia (2008), 'Second Languages, Virtual Worlds: Living Second Lives', in J. Luca and E. Weippl (eds), *Proceedings of ED-MEDIA 2008: World Conference on Educational Multimedia, Hypermedia and Telecommunications*, 2660–4, Vienna: Association for the Advancement of Computing in Education (AACE).

Mahan, K. R. (2022), 'The Comprehending Teacher: Scaffolding in Content and Language Integrated Learning (CLIL)', *The Language Learning Journal*, 50 (1): 74–88.

Makoe, M., and T. Shandu (2018), 'Developing a Mobile App for Learning English Vocabulary in an Open Distance Learning Context', *The International Review of Research in Open and Distributed Learning*, 19 (4): 208–21.

Marsh, D. (1994), *Bilingual Education A Content and language Integrated Learning: Language Teaching in the Member States of the European Union (Lingua)*, Paris: University of Sorbonne: International Association for Cross-cultural Communication.

Marsh, D., ed. (2002), *CLIL/EMILE – The European Dimension: Actions, Trends and Foresight Potential Public Services*, Brussels: European Commission.

Marsh, D., ed. (2005), *The CLIL Quality Matrix. Central Workshop Report*, Gratz: Council of Europe.

Mayo, M. P. G., and A. Lázaro Ibarrola (2015), 'Do Children Negotiate for Meaning in Task-Based Interaction? Evidence from CLIL and EFL Settings', *System*, 54: 40–54.

McDougald, J., and D. Pissarello (2020), 'Content and Language Integrated Learning: In-Service Teachers' Knowledge and Perceptions before and after a Professional Development Program', *Íkala Revista de Lenguaje y Cultura*, 25 (2): 353–272.

Middleton, A. J., and R. Mather (2008), 'Machinima Interventions: Innovative Approaches to Immersive Virtual World Curriculum Integration', *ALT-J, Research in Learning Technology*, 16 (3): 207–20.

Montero-Perez, M., W. Van Den Noortgate and P. Desmet (2013), 'Captioned Video for L2 Listening and Vocabulary Learning: A Meta-analysis', *System*, 41 (3): 720–39.

Morozov, A. (2008), 'Machinima Learning: Prospects for Teaching and Learning Digital Literacy Skills Through Virtual Filmmaking', in J. Luca and E. Weippl (eds), *Proceedings of World Conference on Educational Multimedia, Hypermedia and Telecommunications* 2008, 5898–590, Chesapeake, VA: AACE.

Navés, T. (2009), 'Effective Content and Language Integrated Learning (CLIL) Programmes', in Y. Ruiz de Zarobe and R. M. Jimenez Catalan (eds), *Content and Language Integrated Learning: Evidence from Research in Europe*, 22–40. Bristol: Multilingual Matters.

Nikula, T. (2015), 'Hands-on Tasks in CLIL Science Classrooms as Sites for Subject-Specific Language Use and Learning', *System*, 54: 14–27.

Occioni, M., P. de Boer, T. Koenraad, and C. Schneider (Camelot Project EU), *Space Diagonal*, Youtube. Available online: https://www.youtube.com/watch?v=P7kk8gQmZJE.

Ortega, L. (2015), 'Researching CLIL and TBLT Interfaces', *System*, 54: 103–9.

Pavesi, M., and E. Ghia (2020), *Informal Contact with English*, Pisa: Edizioni ETS.

Pérez-Vidal, C., and H. Roquet (2015), 'The Linguistic Impact of A CLIL Science Programme: An Analysis Measuring Relative Gains', *System*, 54: 80–90.

Peterson, M., M. Thomas and K. Yamazaki, eds (2021), *Digital Games and Language Learning: Theory, Development and Implementation*, London and New York: Bloomsbury.

Pinner, R. S. (2013), 'Authenticity and CLIL: Examining Authenticity from an International CLIL perspective', *International CLIL Research Journal*, 2: 44–54.

Pinner, R. S. (2019), *Authenticity and Teacher–student Motivational Synergy: A Narrative of Language Teaching*, London and New York: Routledge.

Price, K. (1983), 'Closed-captioned TV: An Untapped Resource', *MATSOL Newsletter*, 12 (2): 1–8.

Pujadas, G., and C. Muñoz (2019), 'Extensive Viewing of Captioned and Subtitled TV Series: A Study of L2 Vocabulary Learning by Adolescents', *The Language Learning Journal*, 47 (4): 479–96.

Rieder-Bünemann, A., J. Hüttner and U. Smit (2019), 'Capturing Technical Terms in Spoken CLIL', *Journal of Immersion and Content-Based Language Education*, 7 (1): 4–29.

Taylor, G. (2005), 'Perceived Processing Strategies of Students Watching Captioned Video', *Foreign Language Annals*, 38 (3): 422–7.

Thomas, M., and C. Schneider (2020). *Language Teaching with Video-based Technologies: Creativity and CALL Teacher Education*, London and New York: Routledge.

Tüzün, H., and F. Özdinç (2016), 'The Effects of 3D Multi-User Virtual Environments on Freshmen University Students' Conceptual and Spatial Learning and Presence in Departmental Orientation', *Computers and Education*, 94: 228–40.

Vanderplank, R. (1990), 'Paying Attention to the Words: Practical and Theoretical Problems in Watching Television Programmes with Uni-lingual (CEEFAX) Sub-titles', *System*, 18 (2): 221–34.

Vanderplank, R. (2010), 'Déjà vu? A Decade of Research on Language Laboratories, Television and Video in Language Learning', *Language Teaching*, 43 (1): 1–37.

Warburton, S. (2009), 'Second Life on Higher Education: Assessing Potential for and the Barriers to Deploying Virtual Worlds in Learning and Teaching', *British Journal of Educational Technology*, 40 (3): 414–26.

Winke, P., S. Gass and T. Sydorenko (2010), 'The Effects of Captioning Videos Used for Foreign Language Listening Activities', *Language Learning and Technology*, 14 (1): 65–86.

Appendix

Worksheet Pythagoras 3-D

Name:

Class:

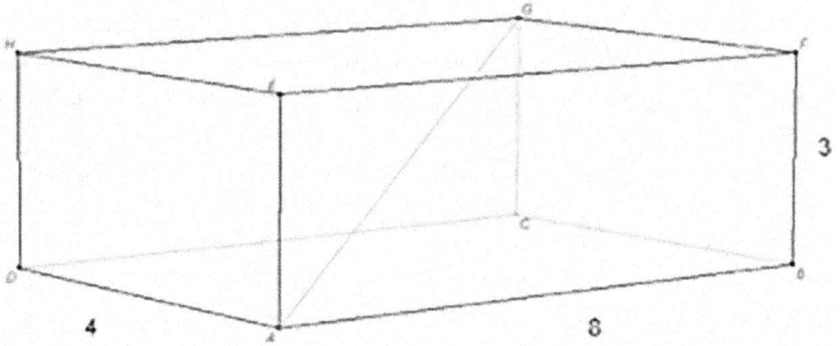

[Figure: 3D rectangular box with vertices labeled, showing dimensions 4, 8, and 3, with diagonal line AG drawn]

Look at the figure above

Q1: What is the name of line AG?

....

Q2: What lines have the same length as line AG?

....

Q3: What line do we need to calculate *before* we can calculate AG?

....

Q4: Write down the steps to calculate a line with Pythagoras' Theorem

Step 1: ....
Step 2: ....
Step 3: ....
Step 4: ....

Q5: Calculate the line of Q3.

....

Q6: Calculate AG.

Figure 11.3 Appendix. Worksheet for teaching Pythagoras in 3D. Source: Author.

12

Participatory Video in Practice: Filming with Women from the Sudanese Community in Bradford

Simona Manni

Introduction

Participatory filmmaking is a form of production which uses video 'as a social and community-based tool for individual and group development' (Shaw and Robertson 1997: 11). In participatory film, professional filmmakers act as, or work with, facilitators to transfer technical skills to participants without imposing their views, which enables the participants to become the authors of the films produced. As Yang (2012: 103) explains, 'as participants blur the boundaries between filmmakers and film subjects or combine the roles, they can construct their experiences uniquely from their perspectives, thereby providing authentic data about themselves'. As such, participatory filmmaking can transform the passive subjects of traditional documentary into active agents who are empowered to shape their own media messages and own the production process. Other forms of art, such as drama and music, have traditionally been more popular in community development work. However, the increasing accessibility and affordability of digital filmmaking tools have made it easier to use participatory video in communities.

Participatory filmmaking is grounded on community-centred values and aspirations that, when translated into reality, can have a dramatic impact on the communities involved. However, achieving this is often difficult in practice. Due to this gap between intentions and realization, many criticisms have been levelled at participatory filmmaking (Shaw 2012; Milne 2016; Walsh 2016). As a participatory filmmaker, I have often witnessed the empowering effects of the process and experienced its many inherent challenges and negotiations. I believe that these challenges can be fruitfully overcome, as long as the needs of the community are kept at the heart of the project. In this chapter, I present a case study of film production in a community setting in Bradford in order to illustrate the opportunities and challenges of participatory filmmaking. I review my approach to this form of practice, which sits at the intersection of media education and community development. In doing so, I pay particular attention to the aspects of the project that fulfilled the original aspirations of participatory video and to the strategies deployed to overcome the challenges faced in the process.

Participatory video

Participatory filmmaking emerged in the context of participatory communication and participatory rural appraisal, families of practices and methodologies which aim at empowering local communities to analyse, articulate and share information on their life conditions (Chambers 1994: Thomas and Mefalopulos 2009). It is based on the assumption that 'through video anyone can express ideas, articulate their viewpoint or voice opinions of importance with no barrier of status or consequence' (White 2003: 64). It enables people to see how they relate to their community and to become conscious of their own needs as well as those of their community (White 2003). Participatory filmmaking is aimed at disenfranchised groups, who feel ignored by society due to inequalities such as unemployment or homelessness (Shaw and Robertson 1997). As stated by Plush (2012: 68), 'with its visual nature and ability to capture the voices of people from marginalized groups, participatory video holds the potential to educate, persuade, and advocate in ways that can bring about positive change'. Being involved in participatory filmmaking can present opportunities to participants, such as developing information and communications technology skills, interpersonal competence, the ability to identify self-development goals, and being able to communicate these to a variety of audiences (White 2003).

From its beginnings, this practice was grounded on Freire's (1970) pedagogy of the oppressed, which focused on transformational and relational education as a process of 'conscientizing' the individual. Roberts and Lunch (2015: 1–2) explained that 'Freire's praxis of reflection upon action can be seen as a means to decode the world, to better grasp the mechanisms of oppression and dehumanization, and better enable the oppressed to interpret and change their reality'. Participatory video aspires to be a tool in this process, by enabling participants to use media-making to reflect and articulate their experiences and circumstances with a view to raising awareness and shaping action. The educational value of participatory video is that it gives the participants the opportunity to become active consumers and producers of media messages, as articulated by Shaw and Robertson (1997).

Central to the practice of participatory filmmaking is the concept of using voice and dialogue to bring about a real change. The dialogic nature of participatory filmmaking works by using communication to modify and correct perceptions and promote in-depth exchanges between individuals (White 2003). Overall, participatory video aims to create a space for community members to define themselves, represent their identities, have a dialogue with other communities, identify ways in which they can control and change their circumstances, and affect change on a larger scale (Shaw and Robertson 1997). According to White (2003: 84), '*self-disclosure* is the act of sharing either verbally or nonverbally those aspects of yourself that would not be readily recognized or understood if you did not dialogue about those aspects'. In essence, the value of participatory filmmaking is that it allows those conversations to happen in a safe space, to be worked through in a narrative form, and to be communicated to others through storytelling.

The practice of participatory filmmaking is varied and diverse (High et al. 2012; Roberts and Lunch 2015), so the modalities of production are more fluid than those of traditional filmmaking. Each practitioner tends to adapt the strategies and tools to the individual community that they are targeting. Since 2015, I have been using participatory filmmaking with community groups attended by people who are recovering from substance addiction and mental health problems, facing homelessness, recovering from abuse or experiencing challenges as migrants. Since 2016, I have also been running film courses for people who are recovering from mental illnesses at Converge, a provider of Educational courses for mental health service users at York St John University. This practice has created experiential knowledge on working with groups by using film to discuss aspects of their experiences. I have witnessed the empowering effects of engaging in visual storytelling that results in films produced collectively by people who are facing similar issues and problems. Taking part in participatory film sessions provides the following benefits: the opportunity to get absorbed in a creative activity; the establishment of a supportive community, which can overcome the sense of isolation experienced by many people in challenging circumstances; an increased sense of agency, which results from expressing one's views on particular circumstances as an artist as opposed to a patient, a service user or a foreigner; and the acquisition of technical and creative skills. Participatory filmmaking opens up the space for much-needed conversations, both among the participants and with the outside world, through screenings and online sharing.

Entering a community: building rapport and trust

One of the most challenging aspects of a participatory video project is the initial phase of entering a community as an external facilitator and establishing a constructive relationship of trust with the participants. A criticism of participatory video is that, in spite of the intention to keep ownership in the hands of the participants, the agenda is often set by funders and commissioners, who are indeed external to that community (Milne 2012; Shaw 2012). This was partly the case for the project discussed in this chapter: the initiative for proposing a participatory video experience came from Bradford UNESCO City of Film, which had already established a connection with the participating community group – the Sudanese Community in Bradford, a registered charity which provides educational, social and recreational activities to Sudanese adults and children in Bradford.

The project was commissioned by Bradford UNESCO City of Film in 2017 as part of its Neighbourhood Film Project, an effort to connect the diverse communities in Bradford through film and creativity. I was contacted about working with the Sudanese Community in Bradford, specifically the women's group, which gathers at the centre every Saturday. I worked with the women for several weeks over two main chunks of sessions from June 2017 to March 2018, which resulted in the production of a short film, *Unity and Community*. In this film, the women discuss the challenges of life in Bradford and how they support each other through their community.

The Neighbourhood Film Project focuses mainly on community film screenings rather than film production. This meant that, for this project, the agenda was kept open and fluid. My main duties were to establish a relationship with the women's group, to watch films together and to discuss the possibility of producing a short film; nevertheless, had the group jointly decided to stick to screenings only, the outcomes of the project would still have been met. This openness meant that there was no pressure to produce specific formats or discuss pre-established themes, which left us in the privileged situation of being able to explore ideas freely.

The first project sessions, in line with many other participatory filmmaking experiences (Shaw and Robertson 1997; Shaw 2012), were dedicated to creating a rapport between myself and the women. I was invited to join the weekly women's group, which took place on Saturdays. The afternoon meetings were for women only and consisted of coffee and catch-ups. The women were then usually joined by the men for a community evening meal. During my first encounter with the women, I was introduced by David Wilson, director of Bradford UNESCO City of Film and executive producer for this project, who talked about the Neighbourhood Film Project and my role in it. I had a general chat with the group, with the support of women who acted as interpreters for others who had recently arrived and were still learning English. The women expressed interest in the project, but they said that they would prefer it if I joined them every other week rather than weekly. The weekly meetings were the only occasion on which the women could meet, catch up with each other's lives and discuss personal matters: although they were interested in the project, they wanted to keep some space for their community time. The commissioners and I agreed that it was essential to respect their wish to act in the least invasive way. This is in line with general practice in participatory video, which aims to keep the community's needs at the centre of the project. I was fortunate to be granted the flexibility to do so.

I quickly realized that organizing structured film technique sessions would not have been appropriate for this community: the women met in groups of around thirty at a relatively small venue, mainly to socialize. Organizing technical tutorials would have meant imposing silence on the women and their children (who were also present at the venue during the meetings) and disrupting their gatherings. They would also have had to wait for a long time to use the camera in turns. This might have been different if the women had been joining me at dedicated film sessions on a different occasion; however, it was agreed that due to financial, professional and family pressures, it would be difficult for all of them to add another commitment to their schedule. As a facilitator, it was my duty to design sessions that could incorporate the film activities into the women's existing social scenario, leaving their time together as undisrupted as possible. Adapting the activities to the community's needs is in line with the foundational principles of participatory filmmaking: the facilitators do not intervene to impose a curriculum; rather, they propose activities that may encourage dialogue and cohesion. Participatory video is centred on the needs of the participants; it aims 'to develop their confidence and self-esteem, to encourage them to express themselves creatively, to develop critical awareness and to provide a means for them to communicate with others' (Shaw and Robertson 1997: 11). Therefore, as filmmakers, we need to let go of what we think a film production process should look like when this would detract from, rather than enhance, the participants' experience.

Traditionally, participatory video sessions begin with camera techniques (Waite and Conn 2012; Shaw and Robertson 1997). However, I often find it more useful to begin by trying to understand what matters most to a community. This makes it possible to centre the activities and exercises around the interests and concerns of the participants, who may not yet be intrigued by the technological side of the work. Introducing camerawork too early may also lead the participants to worry about mastering the technology before solid community work has been done to create lasting engagement in the process. Consequently, we started with discussions about what it meant to be a foreigner in the UK, and in Bradford in particular. Following this conversation, I organized the screening of a few videos that the women could watch while they were having coffee. These would be followed by conversations in English and Arabic. The choice of materials to show was linked to the previous discussion and consisted of archival footage of 1950s and 1960s Bradford and videos of modern Sudan. This stimulated discussion on the women's perceptions of Bradford in comparison with their home countries and the pros and cons of each, in their experience.

During the third session, I introduced visual storytelling by proposing an art exercise that involved using colour to paint over black-and-white images of Bradford. The purpose of this exercise was to translate the discussions from the previous session (where we had watched black-and-white images of Bradford alongside current footage of Sudan) into a visual form. The women used colour to translate their subjective impressions and their cultural heritage onto the images of the city. This activity gave the women the freedom to chat and have fun together while reflecting on the themes that were starting to emerge in the group. While the women were busy with the art, some of the children expressed an interest in my camera, which I had brought along to document the session. With the women's permission, I decided to give them the chance to film their mothers at work: an activity which proved successful, thanks to the familiarity of the young people with current digital technology.

During our final session for this first chunk of work, I simply joined the women for a final chat while showing an edited version of the footage that their children had made. This represented a key stage in the process, as it was the first time the women had watched images of their own community onscreen. The video was light-hearted and fun, not yet addressing the deeper themes that were taking form in the group. The reaction from the group was positive, and the women's motivation to produce a film of their own increased dramatically from this moment onwards. This positive reaction seems to be in line with what is indicated in the literature as an empowering effect of participatory video: by seeing themselves onscreen, the participants exercise reflexivity. According to Yang (2012: 103), 'the reflexive approach to filmmaking – in the sense that film subjects create their own films – is intertwined with the reflexive way of looking: film subjects seeing themselves'. Watching themselves on the recorded material encouraged the participants to reflect and, in doing so, to 'develop a sense of self' (Shaw and Robertson 1997: 21). Some practitioners consider that this 'mirror' aspect is essential for participatory filmmaking, but I usually prefer to leave the community to choose how they would like to represent themselves. Film directors can use a range of expressive tools and metaphors for self-expression without necessarily filming themselves; therefore, if the participants are to be treated as creators, they should have the freedom to decide whether to use autobiographical, symbolic, narrative or documentary expressive devices, and what combinations to use. In this project, however, seeing themselves onscreen acted as a catalyst for the women to consider the opportunities of participatory video, and their level of engagement increased after they watched the clips that their children had filmed.

At this point in the project, the sessions stopped for a few months to allow the Sudanese Community of Bradford to move to a new venue. Meanwhile, I kept in touch with Hafsa Kheri, who acted as the project manager for the sessions and was an intermediary between me and the rest of the women.

Filmmaking: themes and techniques

When I reconnected with the women in January 2018 to resume our sessions, I found that their engagement in the project had not subsided. During the break, the women had watched the video filmed by their children repeatedly and had talked among themselves and decided that they wanted to go ahead with the film production in order to discuss key aspects of their community. At this stage, Hafsa Kheri suggested that we create a subgroup of women who spoke English and could act as intermediaries for the rest of the group during the design of the film. The smaller group would meet before the coffee gatherings and take a more focused approach, and the main group would continue to run afterwards.

Two sessions were dedicated to an in-depth discussion of the themes that would be dealt with in the film. I proposed a brainstorming approach to explore all the aspects that the women felt were important in their experiences of life in Bradford. These conversations were then translated into a list of spoken content paired with a list of visuals to collect. The women compiled the lists with a strong focus on portraying the importance of the Sudanese Community in Bradford in their lives and how its presence had enabled newcomers to settle much more quickly and comfortably in their new city than those who had arrived earlier. However, the women also wanted to discuss the challenges of running a community group with no external support, and their personal struggles as women who were living without the close network of extended families that they had been used to in Sudan. The list included the following themes: settling in a new country; isolation brought about by lack of contacts and poor English-language skills; the resources needed to be able to feel confident as citizens; the role of the weekly coffee gatherings as a way to reconnect with their culture; how women who are more settled support newcomers; how lacking a sense of community affects their lives; the importance of the Arabic school for children that was being run at the Sudanese Community; their educational and professional aspirations and skills; and the challenges faced by the community due to the lack of funding. They also wanted to portray some aspects of their culture: Sudanese coffee-making; the henna and hairstyling skills that many of the women practised on each other; and the strong sense of a common bond. The women were also very specific in defining the visuals they wanted to include: making coffee; practising henna and hairstyles; the new venue; the Arabic school for children; the women's meetings, showing their sense of friendship and mutual support; and some images of the weekly dinner with the men. They also wanted to include some of the children's footage of their artwork. The women were able to articulate their viewpoints clearly, and they spoke with honesty and openness about their experiences. They also discussed aspects of their journey that they explicitly preferred to be kept out of the video, but which they still wanted to articulate to an outsider. Overall, the women felt the need to express themselves and their viewpoints in a society in which they felt neither explicitly discriminated against nor fully integrated. The audience for the film was thought to consist of external communities and wider society as a whole. This would allow the women to represent their community in ways that they felt were not possible in daily life because of a lack of opportunity to establish lasting conversations with those communities.

A discussion also took place around the technicalities of filming. In an ideal situation, the participants would have taken charge of the technical side of filming by learning filmmaking techniques and tools. There is debate in the literature on whether this should be considered a prerequisite for a participatory video project

(Shaw and Robertson 1997; Yang 2012). According to Shaw and Robertson (1997: 36), the participants in such a project must operate the equipment because 'a fundamental aim of the work is to hand over skills to the group so that they are in control of their own communications'. However, most participatory video projects operate on a spectrum of involvement that ranges from ideation only to full technical delivery of the film. It has been observed that too much stress on technical capabilities can be detrimental to certain projects (Yang 2012). As such, 'various degrees of collaborations between participants, researchers, and professional filmmakers need to be considered' so that the participants' reflexivity is not hampered by technical barriers (Yang 2012: 10). In the case of the Bradford project, after careful discussion it was decided that most of the filming should be carried out by me. This was partly because the technical tutorials would have disrupted the normal flow of the weekly gatherings. The women were mostly interested in having an authorial say. Given that a film director normally leads a technical crew, I acted as a cameraperson, following the women's list of visuals and their directions rather than imposing my ideas on what should be filmed. In an ideal scenario, there would have been enough resources to train the women over a long period and equip them with cameras that they could keep, so that they could build their own sustainable filmmaking practice. However, these are rarely the circumstances when working in participatory video, and on this occasion the women were interested in making a powerful film that could express their views as accurately as possible to other communities and the wider society. Having a product that looked professional in its technical execution was more important to them than learning the camera techniques. Overwhelming them with technical responsibilities while reducing their social time would have been, in my view, a detrimental approach and would have undermined the agenda that the women had set up spontaneously. This solution seemed to be successful, and the women were granted editorial control at the end of the filming.

The filming itself was carried out over a number of sessions, starting with a long interview in Arabic led by Hafsa Kheri. This footage was not used in the final cut, due to a lack of funding for the subtitling process; but it was used as a reference for the women who were leading the filming. It helped to give focus to the conversation, and it enabled those women who did not speak English to have a direct say about what content should be present in the film. After this interview, I visited the community to film several gatherings and events, covering all the aspects that the women had requested in their list of visuals. Although it had been agreed that technical involvement was not a requirement, the women helped to record the sound during the interviews while I was filming and occasionally tried out filming on my camera. At the end of this process, Hafsa Kheri and Sohair Norman, a participant in the project, recorded a voice-over track that tried to take into account all the aspects that had been discussed beforehand in a succinct and focused manner. The purpose of the voice-over was to complement the visuals that had been recorded.

At the end of the filming process, I stepped out of the group to edit the film. Editing is a delicate phase of participatory film projects (Mak 2012), because the process can greatly influence the tone and shape of the film's messages. It is still one of the least accessible aspects of this practice, due to the technical requirements it entails. It is at this stage that facilitators and filmmakers can, with varying degrees of consciousness, take over in shaping the overall communicative potential of the film. I have only rarely managed to involve participants in this step. Due to a lack of equipment, I usually work with one laptop, but video-editing tutorials need to be delivered one to one and for several weeks to build participants' proficiency. To avoid the pitfalls of re-establishing power hierarchies at the editing stage, over time I have developed techniques that allow participants to guide the editing without having to operate the video-editing programmes. For example, I have created detailed paper edits, where shots and sounds are represented on paper and are arranged by participants in their preferred order. I also include several rounds of feedback on rough cuts of the film so the participants can correct the direction of the work if necessary. In this case, the paper edit work was minimal: the women had structured the themes and visual elements very carefully from the beginning and expressed clear directions about music and tone, which made my editing job straightforward. Nevertheless, the rough edit was shown to the women in person, and a final cut was circulated online by private link. The women provided feedback in person and in writing, asking me to eliminate a few of the images. The final cut was also sent to the commissioners; they required only minor changes, such as adding logos and an establishing shot of Bradford. Overall, the editing process proved to be unproblematic and satisfying for everyone, thanks to the flexibility allowed by the commissioners and the trusting relationship that had been established with the women.

Showing: final product and screenings

The sessions culminated in *Unity and Community*, a short film of about 10 minutes, in which the two narrators – Hafsa Kheri and Sohair Norman – talk about how the Sudanese Community in Bradford was born and the impact that it has had on their lives, given their struggle to settle in a new country. Hafsa and Sohair speak about the challenges of living abroad without the support of their extended family network and discuss how isolation affects their emotional well-being and their aspirations for the future. The recounting of these experiences is intertwined with a description of the coffee gatherings and a demonstration of how to prepare the traditional spiced Sudanese coffee that they consume. The final part of the film illustrates the women's aspirations for the future of their community, such as their plans to expand their activities to include English and professional courses. According to the women, having a strong community of their own makes them feel more grounded. This allows them to reach out to British society and fulfil their aspirations of studying and getting into employment with increased confidence.

Historically, participatory filmmaking has been more engaged with the process of production and the beneficial effects that this can have on participants, rather than with the final product (Gumucio Dragon 2001; Rodriguez 2001; Benest 2011). However, films that have been produced through participatory filmmaking have been used extensively to spread messages in local communities. The rise of the internet has created new opportunities for individuals and communities to reach wider audiences (White 2003). The process of participatory filmmaking benefits the participants, and the act of articulating their viewpoints and experiences in narrative form can have empowering and even therapeutic effects (Johnson and Alderson 2008). However, neglecting the potential of the final product means that opportunities are left unexplored. As a format, video makes it possible to share knowledge widely with many different audiences, including the participants themselves (Mitchell, Milne and de Lang 2012). The products derived from participatory filmmaking result from a dialogical and inter-relational process; therefore, it would seem sensible to use them as tools for dialogue with external communities. An excessive focus on process at the expense of the final product would mean relinquishing many of the opportunities offered by this practice.

In the case of this project, the women responded to such opportunities; indeed, one of their initial motivations for getting involved in the filmmaking was that they wanted to show their film to external audiences. Therefore, this project had the twofold purpose of self-representing and using a film as a tool to gather support for their community in the form of volunteering or funding. The women were more cautious about using the film online, though. The prospects of hate crime and online abuse, and the difficulty in controlling online responses, led the women to limit online screening to the Neighbourhood Film Project website by embedding the film using Vimeo. They avoided Facebook and YouTube, which they felt were unsafe and more difficult to monitor.

However, before any form of external sharing, the film was screened at the Sudanese Community centre for the launch of the new venue. This internal screening was aimed mostly at Sudanese men and women, with the exception of a few external guests. It is usually good practice to screen participatory films internally to give the participants a chance to gauge the views and reactions of their community of belonging and, at times, to provide a final round of feedback before external publication. It was also important to review the film with the people who appeared in it but were not directly involved in making it, so that they could play a part in determining their representations (Yang 2012). The internal screening was an occasion on which to do so, and women who were not directly involved in the project and men from the community were able to watch the film for the first time. The feedback was overwhelmingly positive, and the group decided not to make any other changes to the body of the film.

Equipped with the confidence that the community liked and took ownership of the film, the commissioners made a considerable effort to locate opportunities for external screenings. These took place in a variety of settings, including public and community screenings in Bradford, an international film festival in the United States, a symposium on education, an academic conference, and a multilingual film festival in Manchester (Beyond Babel). The variety of audiences reached proved that there was a general interest in the subject and validated the women's storytelling. However, as often happens in participatory video, the work was disseminated after the project had formally concluded. This meant that the dissemination was mostly performed by the filmmakers and commissioners in their free time, often in an unstructured manner. In this situation, it is not uncommon for the films produced to be stored and left unseen for long periods. As Miller and Smith (2012: 331) ask, 'the generative possibilities of collaborative creation cannot be underestimated, but must the participatory process end when the work is complete? Is just *making* media enough?' Here, Miller and Smith consider outreach and advocacy, with the direct involvement of the participants as a key and empowering aspect of the project – and rightly so. On the other hand, Kindon, Hume-Cook and Woods (2012) warn about the possible risks and ethical challenges of sharing video work created by community groups. The authors present cases in which the audience response was hostile and had a detrimental effect on the participants. In my experience, those screenings in which the women were directly involved generated fruitful conversations.

However, sharing and dissemination are challenging areas of participatory video work. This calls for a more structured approach that incorporates this part of the work into the body of the project and gives it the same ethical and organizational attention as the ideation and production phase.

The work presented in this chapter may resonate with 'participatory approaches' to language education inspired by Freire (1970), particularly in the field of ESOL: 'As an integral part of language and literacy development, participatory approaches involve reflection on the material conditions of learners' lives and experiences and, where appropriate, involve students in action to effect change' (Cooke, Winstanley and Bryers 2015: 214). The example of participatory filmmaking discussed in this chapter has many common connections with 'participatory ESOL', such as the importance of 'active listening' (Auerbach 1992: 49) and the significance of identifying topics with learners by 'making meaning', 'going deeper' and 'broadening out' (Cooke, Winstanley and Bryers 2015: 218–20). The project provides a valuable model to explore future applications of participatory pedagogy in ESOL practice in mainstream settings and voluntary sectors (see Bryers 2015, and the project Heart and Parcel 2015). It offers significative evidence of the potential of this pedagogic approach that allows ESOL learners to develop a project locally to foster connections with the host community, give visibility to their values and customs, and strengthen the ties within their own group (Goodey 2021).

Conclusion

Overall, *Unity and Community* is a successful example of participatory filmmaking in practice. The women demonstrated an excellent level of engagement with the process, and there was a positive response from audiences when the film was publicly screened. The project avoided many of the initial pitfalls of other commissioned participatory video experiences. Thanks to the flexibility of the Neighbourhood Film Project, I was able to adapt to the community context by setting a more relaxed pace for the sessions and I could invest enough time in establishing a relationship of mutual trust with the women. With no strict agenda for the content, the women could shape the message of the film according to their genuine interests and concerns rather than having to keep to the requirements of an external organization.

The first phase of the project was decidedly freer and more unstructured than the second; this allowed me to build a foundation of dialogue and trust, so that the second phase could become more structured at the women's request, rather than as an imposition from commissioners and the facilitator. These dynamics led to a more successful project, where the women maintained their ownership and agency over the materials produced, in spite of not carrying out the filming themselves. While this lack of involvement in technical training may seem to contradict the foundation of participatory video, imposing a stricter training programme would have damaged the collaborative relationship with the women and detracted from some of the enjoyment they took from meeting together. The women still had the opportunity to learn about producing media messages by shaping the content and message of the film and directing me as a camera operator and editor. Allowing this process to happen spontaneously increased the women's engagement: they proposed investing more of their time in the subgroup work from the second phase onwards.

In addition, gradually introducing visual storytelling by using art exercises that embedded the topics discussed by the women fostered their engagement with the filmmaking while keeping their interests and concerns at the heart of the process. The unplanned short video filmed by the children during the first part of the project was invaluable in engaging the women in the filmmaking process: it gave them a tangible sense of the power of images in representing the complexity and beauty of their community. This shows that engagement must be built gradually and that facilitators must stay open to unexpected opportunities that may arise for the community.

The most challenging part of the project was the use of the film for dissemination and outreach. While the film created interest and the commissioners made considerable efforts to share the film, the women could only be involved partially in this process and it was not always possible for them to attend the screenings. As with most participatory video projects, this is the stage at which the bond that has been created with the participants – and their sense of ownership – may start to weaken. Although this project was relatively successful in using the film for external engagement, it still underlines the fundamental lack of structured approaches to using participatory film for focused outreach that involves the participants. This could be a side effect of the traditional tendency in participatory video practice to value the production process over the final product, and it calls for new solutions for efficiently embedding this final stage into the overall process. The caution that the women exercised about sharing their film online also emphasizes the possible risks and ethical challenges of using the internet to disseminate messages when it comes to marginalized or vulnerable communities, who are painfully aware of the harm that can be done by online hate crime. Online use can widen the reach of these films in fruitful ways, but an ethical framework needs to be developed for doing so safely.

Considering the process of making *Unity and Community* as a whole, tailoring the approach so that the participants' interests, concerns, habits and culture were embedded in the very structure of the project made it possible to negotiate between the ideals of participatory filmmaking and the reality of the practical limitations, without sacrificing the women's ownership of the project.

As I have suggested, this type of project can stimulate debates about integration, education and skills. ESOL practitioners and language teachers in general can use some approaches and techniques from this model of participatory filmmaking in their teaching. Working collaboratively in local areas can contribute to changing the ways in which migrants and refugees are portrayed and open new avenues for projects in which learning is informal and implicit, but highly relevant.

References

Auerbach, E. R. (1992), *Making Meaning Making Change: Participatory Curriculum Development for Adult ESL Literacy*, London: Center for Applied Linguistics/ERIC.

Benest, G. (2011), *A Rights-based Approach to Participatory Video: Toolkit*, London: InsightShare.

Bryers, D. (2015), 'Participatory ESOL', *Language Issues: The ESOL Journal*, 26 (2): 55–7.

Chambers, R. (1994), 'The Origins and Practice of Participatory Rural Appraisal', *World Development*, 22 (7): 953–69.

Cooke, M., B. Winstanley and D. Bryers (2015), 'Whose Integration? A Participatory ESOL Project in the UK', in J. Simpson and A. Whiteside (eds), *Adult Language Education and Migration: Challenging Agendas in Policy and Practice*, 214–24, London: Routledge.

Freire, P. (1970), *Pedagogy of the Oppressed*, New York: Seabury Press.

Goodey, C. (2021). 'Collaboration and Learning in Community Integration: Shifting the Focus', *NYS TESOL Journal*, 8 (2): 29–38.

Gumucio Dragon, A. (2001), *Making Waves: Stories of Participatory Communication for Social Change*, New York: Rockefeller Foundation.

Heart and Parcel (2015), 'About Heart & Parcel', *Heart and Parcel*. Available online: https://heartandparcel.org/about/.

High, C., N. Singh, L. Petheram and G. Nemes (2012), 'Defining Participatory Video from Practice', in E.-J. Milne, C. Mitchell and N. de Lange (eds), *Handbook of Participatory Video*, 35–48, Plymouth: AltaMira Press.

Johnson, J. L., and K. G. Alderson (2008), 'Therapeutic Filmmaking: An Exploratory Pilot Study', *The Arts in Psychotherapy*, 35 (1): 11–19.

Kindon, S., G. Hume-Cook and K. Woods (2012), 'Troubling the Politics of Reception in Participatory Video Discourse', in E.-J. Milne, C. Mitchell and N. de Lange (eds), *Handbook of Participatory Video*, 349–64, Plymouth: AltaMira Press.

Mak, M. (2012), 'Visual Postproduction in Participatory Video-Making Processes', in E.-J. Milne, C. Mitchell and N. de Lange (eds), *Handbook of Participatory Video*, 194–207, Plymouth: AltaMira Press.

Miller, E., and M. Smith (2012), 'Dissemination and Ownership of Knowledge.' in E.-J. Milne, C. Mitchell and N. de Lange (eds), *Handbook of Participatory Video*, 331–48, Plymouth: AltaMira Press.

Milne, E.-J. (2012), 'Saying "No" to Participatory Video: Unravelling the Complexities of (Non)Participation', in E.-J. Milne, C. Mitchell and N. de Lange (eds), *Handbook of Participatory Video*, 257–68, Plymouth: AltaMira Press.

Milne, E.-J. (2016), 'Critiquing Participatory Video: Experiences from Around the World', *Area*, 48 (4): 401–4.

Mitchell, C., E.-J. Milne and N. de Lange (2012), 'Introduction', in E.-J. Milne, C. Mitchell and N. de Lange (eds), *Handbook of Participatory Video*, 1–18, Plymouth: AltaMira Press.

Neighbourhood Film Project (2017), 'The Neighbourhood Film Project', *Bradford UNESCO City of Film*. Available online: https://www.bradford-city-of-film.com/enjoy/neighbourhood/.

Plush, T. (2012), 'Fostering Social Change through Participatory Video: A Conceptual Framework', in E.-J. Milne, C. Mitchell and N. de Lange (eds), *Handbook of Participatory Video*, 67–84, Plymouth: AltaMira Press.

Roberts, T., and C. Lunch (2015), 'Participatory Video', in R. Mansell and P. Hwa Ang (eds), *The International Encyclopedia of Digital Communication and Society*, 1–6, London: John Wiley & Sons.

Rodriguez, C. (2001), *Fissures in Mediascape: An International Study of Citizens' Media*. Cresskill, NJ: Hampton Press.

Shaw, J. (2012), 'Interrogating the Gap Between the Ideals and Practice Reality of Participatory Video', in E.-J. Milne, C. Mitchell and N. de Lange (eds), *Handbook of Participatory Video*, 225–41, Plymouth: AltaMira Press.

Shaw, J., and C. Robertson (1997), *Participatory Video: A Practical Guide to Using Video Creatively in Group Development Work*. London: Routledge.

Thomas, T., and P. Mefalopulos (2009), *Participatory Communication: A Practical Guide*, Washington, DC: The World Bank Publications.

Unity and Community (2018), 'Sudanese Centre in Bradford and Bradford UNESCO City of Film'. Available online: https://vimeo.com/294435741.

Waite, L., and C. P. Conn (2012), 'Participatory Video: A Feminist Way of Seeing?', in E.-J. Milne, C. Mitchell and N. de Lange (eds), *Handbook of Participatory Video*, 85–99, Plymouth: AltaMira Press.

Walsh, S. (2016), 'Critiquing the Politics of Participatory Video and the Dangerous Romance of Liberalism', *Area*, 48 (4): 405–11.

White, A. S. (2003), 'Participatory Video: A Process that Transforms the Self and the Other', in A. S. White (ed.), *Participatory Video: Images that Transform and Empower*, 63–101, New Delhi: Sage.

Yang, K. (2012), 'Reflexivity, Participation and Video', in E.-J. Milne, C. Mitchell and N. de Lange (eds), *Handbook of Participatory Video*, 100–14, Plymouth: AltaMira Press.

Glossary

AHRC – Arts and Humanities Research Council. British Research Council that funds and supports research and postgraduate study in Arts and Humanities subjects.

A-Level – Advanced Level qualifications are subject-based qualification for students aged 16 and above in the UK. They are usually studied over two years, leading to qualifications recognized for entrance to higher education institutions in the UK and many others worldwide.

ALL – Association for Language Learning. One of the major associations in the UK for those involved in the teaching of foreign languages.

AMA – Acronym for 'Ask Me Anything'. It usually refers to a genre of videos, blogs and posts that are created in response to comments or questions from users, members of the audience, participants, etc.

APPG – All-Party Parliamentary Groups (UK). Informal groups with shared interests formed by members of all political parties. They work together to discuss and campaign for certain issues.

AQA – Assessment and Qualifications Alliance. Awarding body in England and Wales.

AR/VR – Augmented Reality/Virtual Reality.

AS Level – Advanced Subsidiary Level qualification. It usually covers the first components of an Advanced Level qualification. It is usually studied over a year, instead of A-Levels, which are studied over two.

ASCL – Association of School and College Leaders (UK).

ASD – Autism Spectrum Disorder.

BFI – British Film Institute.

CALL – Computer-Assisted Language Learning.

CEDEFOP – European Centre for the Development of Vocational Training.

CEFR/CEFRL – Common European Framework of Reference (for Languages).

CILT – National Centre for Languages (UK). It merged the Centre of Information on Language Teaching and Research, and the Languages National Training Organisation.

CLIL – Content and Language Integrated Learning.

CMC – Computer-Mediated Communication.

CPD – Continuing Professional Development.

CSE – Certificate of Secondary Education. It was a predecessor to the current GCSE.

DfE – Department for Education (England).

DiAL-e – The Digital Artefacts for Learner Engagement Framework is an open-access resource designed to support educators in the effective use of digital resources.

EBacc – The EBacc (English Baccalaureate) is a set of subjects at GCSE that are intended to keep students' options open for further study and future careers, focusing on a mixed selection of subjects. To qualify for the EBacc, students must take English language, English literature, maths, science, either geography or history, and a modern foreign language.

Edexcel – Private British examination body owned by Pearson plc.

EFL – English as a Foreign Language.

EHEA – European Higher Education Area.

ESOL – English for Speakers of Other Languages.

ESP – English for Specific Purposes.

FEAC – Further Education Advisory Council.

FILTA – Film in Language Teaching Association.

FLAME – Film, Language and Media in Education. Research group at Manchester Metropolitan University.

GCE – General Certificate of Education in some parts of the UK and Commonwealth. It is composed of three different levels, according to difficulty: the O-Level (ordinary level), the AS-Level (Advanced Subsidiary Level) and the A-Level (Advanced Level).

GCSE – General Certificate of Secondary Education. UK-based qualifications, usually taken as a two-year programme in Years 10 and 11 when students are 14–16. Most students do nine or ten subjects, which must include English, maths and science.

HE – Higher Education.

HEI – Higher Education Institution.

ICT – Information and Communication Technology.

INSET – In-Service Training days. These are training days in educational settings in the UK. There are usually five in a year, when schools interrupt the normal class schedules to provide training for teaching staff.

KS (KS1–KS5) – Key Stage. The national curriculum in England is organized into blocks of years called 'key stages' (KS): KS1, aged 5–7; KS2, aged 7–11; KS3, aged 11–14; KS4, aged 14–16. Post-16 (16–18) education is often referred to as KS5.

L1 – First Language.

L2 – Second and Modern Foreign Language.

MFL – Modern Foreign Language.

MI theory – Multiple Intelligences Theory.

MIE – Moving Image Education.

Ofcom – Office of Communication (UK). The regulatory and awards body for broadcasting, telecommunications and postal industries.

Ofqual – Office of Qualification and Examinations Regulation. Government department that regulates qualifications, exams and tests in England.

Ofsted – Office for Standards in Education, Children's Services ad Skills. Government department responsible for inspecting educational settings. Their publicly available reports and scores are often used as a measure of quality.

OU – Open University. UK university that offers distance-learning degrees.

OWRI – Open World Research Initiative. Investment and Support Initiative under the AHRC that ran between 2016 and 2020. It had four main research programmes to demonstrate the value of modern languages in a globalized environment.

PACTE Group – Process in the Acquisition of Translation Competence and Evaluation Group. Research group founded in 1997 at the Universitat Autónoma de Barcelona.

PBL – Project-based learning.

SBC – School Broadcasting Council.

SLA – Second Language Acquisition.

SpLD – Specific Learning Disabilities.

SVOD – Streaming Video On-Demand.

TC – Translation Competence.

TESOL – Teaching English as a Second or Other Language.

UX – User Experience.

VAK – Visual, auditory and kinaesthetic.

Index

The letter *f* following an entry indicates a page with a figure.
The letter *t* following an entry indicates a page with a table.

A-Level curriculum 55, 71, 72–3, 74, 82
　entry numbers 90
adult education 117, 122, 125–6
Alcober, J. Ruiz, S. and Valero, M. 144
Alles Klar TV series 125
Alm, A. 21
Almodóvar, Pedro 73, 81
Alonso-Pérez, R. 33
Altman, Rick 55
analysing (knowledge process) 49
Anderson-Hanley, C., Tureck, K. and Schneiderman, R. L. 206, 208, 213
apartheid 160, 173
applied linguistics 124
applying (knowledge process) 49
Appuntamento in Italia TV series 125
AQA 71
archives 30
ASD (Autism Spectrum Disorder) 213
assessment template 36*t*–7*t*
audiotape recording 119
audiovisual comprehension 92
audiovisual literacy 91
audiovisual materials
　benefits 92
　Spanish in HE Gen Z classrooms study 93–107, 112–13
audiovisual translation techniques 25, 29–30
auditory learning 204
authentic resources 81
Autism Spectrum Disorder (ASD) 213

Baddock, B. 81
Bateman, J. 50
BBC 5, 30, 116, 130–2
　Bitesize 127, 128
　Covid-19 pandemic 128–9, 130
　Digital Curriculum 127–8
　educational broadcasting 115, 116–17, 120–2, 126–8
　foreign-language education 123–6, 132
　iPlayer 128
BBC Further Education 117, 125–6
BBC Live Lessons TV series 129
Beyond Babel Multilingual Film Festival 27
BFI (British Film Institute)
　Framework for Film Education in Europe 91
　National Archive 30
　Screening Literacy in Europe: Film education in Europe 91
Bitesize Daily TV series 129, 130
Bogost, I. 200, 211
boredom 70, 82
Borrasca, Jarauta 140
Botanicula video game 60
Box of Broadcast 30
Bradford UNESCO City of Film 250
　Neighbourhood Film Project 250
Breakout video game 202
Brevik, L. M. 22
British Film Institute (BFI). *See* BFI
Broadcasting Act (1990) 115, 127
Brooks, R., Cooper, A. and Penke, L. 91–2
Bruffee, K. 141
Burden, K. and Atkinson, S.
　Digital Artefacts for Learner Engagement (DiAL-e) framework 201
Burke, S., Snyder, S. and Rager, R.C. 19–20

Café des Rêves, Le TV series 125
Calhourne, D.
　'Invictus 2010. Review' 160, 164–5, 174
Cambridge Analytica data scandal 179

captions 25, 30, 225–6
   multimodal input in a CLIL science project in Italy study 224–32, 241–2
Carlin, John
   Playing the Enemy: Nelson Mandela and the Game that Made a Nation 164
Carreres, Á., Noriega-Sánchez, M. and Calduch, C. 160, 169*t*–71*t*
   Mundos en Palabras. Learning Advanced Spanish Through Translation 166, 167
casa de papel, La (*Money Heist*) TV series 94, 98, 100–1
CEFR (Common European Framework of Reference) 80, 93, 96
CEFR Companion Volume with New Descriptors (Council of Europe) 168
Celebrity Supply Teacher TV series 129
Chasse au Trésor, La TV series 123–4
chicas del cable, Las (*Cable Girls*) TV series 98, 99–100
China 213
Chou, Y. 201
Chuchel video game 60
CLIL (Content and Language Integrated Learning) 223–4, 226, 231, 233–4
   challenges 234
   multimodal input in a science project in Italy study 224–32, 241–2
   teaching mathematics with machinima in the Netherlands study 232–41, 242, 246
ClipFlair 29–30
CMC (computer-mediated communication) 234
cognitive development theories 206–7
collaborative work 140, 141–3*t* *see also* participatory filmmaking
Common European Framework of Reference for Languages: Learning, Teaching and Assessment (Council of Europe) 23–4, 92
communicative language competences 23–4
community development 247–9 *see also* Sudanese Community in Bradford

Companion Volume to the Common European Framework of Reference for Languages (Council of Europe) 92
competencies 2, 26, 27–8, 32*t*–3*t*
   communicative language 23–4
   twenty-first-century skills 28, 50
computer-mediated communication (CMC) 234
conceptualizing (knowledge process) 49
confidence 73
Connecta Project 33–4
Content and Language Integrated Learning (CLIL). *See* CLIL
conversational language 25
cooperative work 140, 141, 143*t*, 172
copyright 29
Corrigan, Timothy
   Short Guide to Writing about Film, A 160–1
course management systems 182
COVID-19 pandemic 7, 10, 128–9, 130
Crayons, Les (Barcelo, Didier) 59
Creative Europe Programme 91
creative literacy 74
Crimson Room video game 60
critical essays 161
critical framing 49
critical literacy 59, 74, 75
critical thinking 26
'Culturema' project 34
cultural activities 27
cultural knowledge 26, 55
   film 73
   intercultural appreciation 79–82
   learning/teaching 79–80
   Spanish 73
cultural literacy 74
cultural mediation 168
curriculum, the 48–9, 54–5
   A-Level 55, 71, 72–3, 74, 82
   BBC Digital Curriculum 127–8
   criticism 72
   film in 70–6
   GCSE 55, 71–3, 74–5
   LTC 173
   statutory 119, 126–7

Dance Dance Revolution video game 208
dance education
 high-stakes learning environments
  213
 parallels with language education
  207–8
dementia 213
Dès le Début TV series 125
Descubra España TV series 125
Despacito song 94
Dewey, John 119
DiAL-e framework 209, 210*t*, 211
Dicho y Hecho TV series 125
differentiation 205
difficulty 69, 90, 92
Digital Artefacts for Learner Engagement (DiAL-e) framework (Burden, K. and Atkinson, S.) 201
digital devices 28
digital games 21–2 *see also* video games
 selecting 28
digital literacy 51
digital storytelling
 without dialogues 10–11
distribution technology 121, 127, 128, 130
diversity 173, 250
Dogme approach 211
dual-focused education 233
Durken, K., Boyle, J., Hunter, S. and Conti-Ramsden, G. 213
Dussel, I. and Gutiérrez, D. 50–1

Eastwood, Clint 164–5
 Invictus 160, 164–5, 172, 173
Edexcel 71
Education Act (1944) 119, 121
Education Reform Act (1988) 115, 119
education system 118, 119, 121, 124, 126–7, 129–30
education theory and practice 118, 119–20, 127
educational broadcasting 115, 129–30
 BBC 115, 116–17, 120–2, 126–9, 130–2
 BBC foreign-language education
  123–6, 132
 broadcast series 135
 Covid-19 pandemic 128–9, 130
 dramatized format 123–4, 125

education theory and practice 118, 119–20, 127
 music programmes 122
 national education system 118, 121, 126–7
 statutory environments 118, 119, 121, 127, 130
 strengths 121–2
 technological development 118–19, 121, 125, 127, 128, 130–1
 television 122, 123
Edwards, M. 159–60, 164, 172
EFL (English as a Foreign Language) learners 226, 227
EHEA (European Higher Education Area) 139–40
emotion 35, 50. 51
enactive experience 214
English as a Foreign Language (EFL) learners 226, 227
English for Speakers of Other Languages (ESOL) 259
English for Specific Purposes (ESP). *See* ESP
entertainment 19
Entire Journey, The (Brunners) 59
ESOL (English for Speakers of Other Languages) 259
ESP (English for Specific Purposes) 181
 Facebook 181–91
Europe 139
Europeana 30
exams
 difficulty 69, 90
 grading 69, 90
exergaming 199–200, 201–3
 benefits 212–14
 cognitive development theories
  206–7
 dance 208, 209–11
 high-stakes learning environments 213
 learner engagement 208–12
 learning styles 203*f*–6
 neurodivergent students 213
 non-communicative teaching approaches 213–14
experiencing (knowledge process) 49
exploitationware 200
extra-linguistic sub competence 162, 163

Facebook 179, 180, 182
   Cambridge Analytica data scandal 179
   ESP 181–91
   student attitudes towards 184, 185*t*
   Universidad Politécnica de Madrid study 182–91, 196–8
Fawkes, S. 73
FEAC (Further Education Advisory Council) 117, 122
Ferrés, Joan 51
film 25, 78 *see also* participatory filmmaking; *Teacher Training Project: Film, Languages and Pedagogy*
   copyright 29
   creative approach to 57–8, 74
   critical approach to 57, 59, 74, 75
   cultural knowledge 26
   in the curriculum 70–6
   curriculum integration 47–8
   curriculum requirements 54–5
   definitions 63 n. 2, 108 n. 3
   education framework 56–8*f*
   emotion 51
   foreign film pedagogy 69–70
   intercultural appreciation 79–82
   literacy 91
   motivation enhancement 76–9
   and reality 81
   selecting 28, 56
   Spanish 98, 99, 101–2, 105
   teachers' perspectives 52–4
   thematic content 28
   writing about 160–2
Film English website 34
Film in Language Teaching Association (FILTA) 30, 33, 52–3
Film, Languages and Media in Education (FLAME) 3, 47
film reviews 159–62
   Invictus 160, 164–5, 167, 169*t*–71*t*, 174
   translations 159–60, 162–4, 167, 169*t*–74
filmmaking 161
FILTA (Film in Language Teaching Association) 30, 33, 52–3
FLAME (Film, Languages and Media in Education) 3, 47

For a European Film Education Policy (Lardoux, X.) 91
foreign film pedagogy 69–70
foundational knowledge 141
Fowler, F. J. 183
Framework for Film Education in Europe (BFI) 91
Freire, P. 248, 259
Friends TV series 98, 99
Fuentes, R. 80–1
functional linguistics 124
further education
   BBC Further Education 117, 125–6
   broadcasting 122
Further Education Advisory Council (FEAC) 117, 122

Gablasova, D. 226–7
game-based practice 22
game-enhanced practice 21–2
game-informed practice 22
gameful thinking/gamefulness 201
gamification 9, 201, 211
   exergaming 199–200
   learning engagement 209
   research 199, 200–1
'Gaming and Storytelling in the Modern Foreign Language Classroom' INSET 60–1
Garcia Martin, Jorge 34
Gardner, Howard 203, 205
GCSE curriculum 55, 71–3, 74–5
   entry numbers 90
   marking 75
Gee, J. P. 200
Generation Z (Gen Z) students 93
   audiovisual materials in HE Spanish classrooms study 93–107, 112–13
globalization 10

Halliday, Michael 124
Hanna, J. L. 208
Harry Potter: Wizards Unite smartphone game 200
HE (Higher Education) 90, 91 *see also* Universidad Politécnica de Madrid study; University College London; University of Córdoba project

audiovisual materials in Gen Z Spanish classrooms study 93–107, 112–13
BBC 117
EHEA 139–40
ESP learners 181
Herrero, C. 23, 24f, 27, 92
   assessment template 36t–7t
Herrero, C. and Vanderschelden, I. 91–2
high-stakes learning environments 213
Higher Education (HE). *See* HE
Hjorth, L. and Richardson, I. 202, 206
HolaCandela.com 31
HOME Arts Centre 60
Howard-Jones, P. A. 205
Hoy no estoy (Taretto, Gustavo) 59
Hubbard, Philip 200, 211
Huw Baird College 60

immersive virtual worlds 232–3, 234, 235–6
inclusion 173
informal learning 3–4
Institute Cervantes 30
instrumental/professional sub-competence 162, 163
interaction 168
interactive media 9
intercultural appreciation 79–82
intercultural competence 80
intercultural literacy 80
interculturality 80–1
interlinguistic capabilities, developing 162–4
International Tourism Fair 140
internet
   regulation 131
Into Film 2
Invictus (Eastwood, Clint) 160, 164–5, 172, 173
'Invictus 2010. Review' (Calhourne, D.) 160, 164–5, 174
   pre-translation textual analysis 169t–71t

Just Dance video game 199, 202, 207, 208, 214

Kheri, Hafsa 253, 255, 256–7
kinaesthetic learning 204, 206

Kindon, S., Hume-Cook, G. and Woods, K. 258
Ko, M. H. 21
Kontakte TV and radio series 126
Kress, G.
   Literacy in the New Media Age 50
KS3 70–1
Kukulska-Hulme, A.
   Mobile-Assisted Language Learning framework 201

laberinto del fauno, El (del Toro, Guillermo) 78
language 124
language education, parallels with dance education 207–8
Languages for the Future (British Council) 90
Language Learning Journal, The 55
language-learning-technology 200
language skills deficit 89–90
language sub-competence 162–3
learners *see also* students
   behaviour 9
   engagement 208–12
   preferences 203f–6
learning *see also* participatory learning
   in-person 93
   apps 22–3
Learning by Design project 49
learning styles 203f–6
learning technology 200, 209, 211
   enhancement and augmentation of learning 211–12
LessonStream 34
Liberating the Curriculum (LTC) project 173
linguistic mediation 168
linguistics 124
   linguistic comprehension 27
listening
   comprehension 25
   film 73
literacy 49–51, 73–5
   audiovisual 91
   digital 51
   film 91
   Herrero, C. 92
   intercultural 80

media 26, 74–5, 77
multiliteracy 49–51, 78
visual 75–6
Literacy in the New Media Age (Kress, G.) 50
Liu, M. and Jackson, J. 213–14
LTC (Liberating the Curriculum) project 173
Lumière online library 30

McGonigal, J. 201
Machinarium video game 60
machinima 224, 233, 234–6
    teaching mathematics in the Netherlands study 232–41, 242, 246
Madrid, D. and Pérez Cañado, M. L. 94–5
Maldonado Pérez, M. 141–2
malo, Lo (Ocaña, Aitana) 98, 102
Maman(s) (Doucouré, Maïmouna) 59
Mandela, Nelson 164
Marée et Ses Secrets, La TV series 125
marginalized groups 248, 249
María, llena eres de gracia (Marton, Joshua), 60
Mario and Sonic at the Olympic Games video game 199
Marsh, J. and Bearne, E. 75
maximum contextualization 56
maximum control 56
media consumption patterns 9
media literacy 26, 74–5, 77
Media Literacy Task Force model 73
mediation 93, 168–9, 172, 173–4
metaphors 76
MI (Multiple Intelligences theory 203*f*, 204–5
Miller, E. and Smith, M. 258
Minecraft video game 234, 238
Mobile-Assisted Language Learning framework (Kukulska-Hulme, A.) 201
Money Heist (Antena 3 and Netflix) 10
monolingualism 72
motivation 70, 94–5, 104, 107
    collaborative work 142
    exergaming 208
    using film to enhance 76–9
movie reviews 161
Movieclips.com 30

Multilingual Digital Storytelling project 34
multiliteracy 49–51, 78
    framework 49–50
multimodality 49–50, 59, 207–8, 224–32
Multiple Intelligences (MI) theory 203*f*, 204–5
Mundos en Palabras. Learning Advanced Spanish Through Translation (Carreres, Á., Noriega-Sánchez, M. and Calduch, C.) 166, 167
music programmes 122
music videos 98, 102–3, 105

national identity 82
Navés, T. 233–4
Netflix 10, 20
neurodivergence 206, 213
'New Approaches to Transmedia and Language Pedagogy' conference 3, 61
New Approaches to Transmedia and Language Pedagogy Project 47–8, 61–2, 63
'New Approaches to Transmedia and Language Pedagogy' webinars 62
New London Group 49
new media 11
    taxonomy of 8–9
new textual experiences 8
Newmark, P. 175 n. 1
Newsom Report 122, 125
non-communicative teaching approaches 213–14
non-foundational knowledge 141
Norman, Sohair 256–7
North, B. and Piccardo, E. 168–9
North School, Netherlands 236–41

Oak Academy 129
observational experience 214
Ocaña, Aitana 98
    malo, Lo 98, 102
Ocho apellidos vascos (*Spanish Affair*) (Martinez-Lázaro, Emilio) 98, 101–2
Ofsted Curriculum Research Review 55
One Piece (Toei Animation) 10
online distribution 127, 128, 130, 257–9, 260–1

online learning/teaching 7, 20, 29, 52
   BBC 115, 127–31
'Open Educational Resources for Students by Students' project 34, 61–2
Open University (OU) 117
Open World Research Initiative (OWRI) 'Cross-Language Dynamics: Reshaping Community' 3, 47
OpenSim immersive virtual worlds 232–3, 234
operant conditioning 208
oppression 248
Ortí Teruel, R., García Collado, M. A. and Bendriss, N. 77
OU (Open University) 117
overt instruction 49
OWRI (Open World Research Initiative) 'Cross-Language Dynamics: Reshaping Community' 3, 47

PACTE (Process in the Acquisition of Translation Competence and Evaluation) 160, 162–3
participatory filmmaking 247–61
   benefits 249–50, 257
   editing 256
   ESOL 259
   final product and screenings 256–9
   reflexivity 253
   sharing and dissemination 258–9, 260–1
   technology 252, 255, 256
   themes and techniques 253–6
   trust and rapport 250–3
participatory learning 51 *see also* participatory filmmaking
PBL (project-based learning) 33, 35, 143–5
pedagogic mediation 169
pedagogical approaches 48–52
pedagogy of the gaze 50
Pei-Shei, W. 206
Peng, W. 214
Perdiendo el norte (*Off Course*) (García Velilla, Ignacio) 98, 99, 101
Peripheria (Coquard-Dassault, David) 59
personalization 209
Piaget, Jean 119
Pienso en tu mirá (Rosalía) 98, 102–3

Playing the Enemy: Nelson Mandela and the Game that Made a Nation (Carlin, John) 164
pluricultural competences 80
Pokémon GO smartphone game 200
post-method approach 211
Pratten, Robert 9
Prescott Thomas, John 124
Process in the Acquisition of Translation Competence and Evaluation (PACTE) 160, 162–3
progressivism 119–20, 121
project-based learning (PBL) 33, 35, 143–5
pronunciation 25
prosumers 26, 180, 181
psychophysiological sub-competence 162, 163
public service broadcasting 127, 131

questionnaires 183

radio, educational broadcasting 118
reality perception 81
recording 119, 121
reflexivity 253
Reinhardt, J. 20, 21
Reinhardt, J. and Sykes, J. 21–2
remote learning 7–8, 128–9, 130, 155
resource providers 118, 119, 129
   BBC 118, 121
   unfair competition 127–8
Rieder-Bünemann, A., Hüttner, J. and Smit, U. 227–8
Ring-Fit Adventure video game 199
Rodríguez-Sandoval, E., Vargas-Solano, E. and Luna-Cortés, J. 144
Rosalía 98
   Pienso en tu mirá 98, 102–3
Russian Language and People TV series 126

Samorost video game 60
SBC (School Broadcasting Council) 120–1, 123, 127
school broadcasting. *See* educational broadcasting
School Broadcasting Council (SBC) 120–1, 123, 127

Science 101 videos (National Geographic) 227–8
screen culture 17
screen media 17–37
   activities and learning projects 27–34
   assessment template 36t–7t
   as entertainment 19
   functions and guidelines 23–7
   history of 18–19
   locating 30
   post-viewing activities 31–3
   pre-viewing activities 31–3
   project-based learning 33, 35
   selecting 27–8
   types 30–1
   while-viewing activities 31–3
screen studies 3
Screening Literacy in Europe: Film education in Europe (BFI) 91
screening reports 161
screens 1–2
Second Language Acquisition (SLA) research 211
Second Life immersive virtual worlds 232, 234, 236
self-development 95
self-disclosure 249
self-efficacy 214
self-regulation 209
Sense 8 (Netflix) 10
Shaw, J. and Robinson, C. 255
Short Guide to Writing about Film, A (Corrigan, Timothy) 160–1
simulations 232–3
situated practice 49
Skinner, B. F. 208
SLA (Second Language Acquisition) research 211
smartphone games 199–200
social media/networking 20–21, 180, 181–2 *see also* Facebook; YouTube
social mediation 169
social video 2
socioeconomics 130
sociolinguistics 124
soft skills 168, 202
South Africa 160, 164, 173
Spain 81, 82

Spanish 69–70, 73, 81–2, 91
   Almodóvar, Pedro 81
   audiovisual materials in HE Gen Z classrooms study 93–107, 112–13
   popularity 94
   student numbers 90
Sparc VR video game 202
speaking assessments 75
specific learning disabilities (SpLD) 206
Spires, H. A. and Bartlett, M. E. 51
SpLD (specific learning disabilities) 206
Squid Game (Netflix) 10
state education 118, 119
Stories from World History radio series 123
Stranger Things (Netflix) 10
strategic sub-competence 162, 163
streaming 19, 20
   laws 29
stress reduction 95, 96
student-centred learning 140
students *see also* Generation Z (Gen Z) students
   behaviour 9
   EFL learners 226, 227
   engagement 172, 208–12
   grouping 172
   interlinguistic capabilities, developing 162–4
   neurodivergent 206, 213
   numbers 4, 69, 72–3, 90
   participatory learners 51–2
   PBL 144, 145
   preferences 203f–6
   role of 143–4
   self-regulation 209
   of Spanish 96
study modules 27
subject-specific vocabulary 226–8, 229t–32
subtitles 25, 77–8, 225, 226, 231
success 95
Sudanese Community in Bradford 250, 251, 253
   Unity and Community 250–61
Superhot VR video game 202

TC (translation competence) model 162–3

Teacher Training Project: Film, Languages and Pedagogy 47–63
  key concepts and pedagogical approaches 48–52
  teachers' perspectives, praxis and curriculum requirements 52–5
  workshops, activities and resources 55–62
teachers
  collaborative work 142
  educational broadcasting 120, 121
  PBL 144
  perspectives 52–4
technological development 118–19, 121, 125, 127, 128, 130
technology learning 200, 209, 211
TED talks 20
television
  copyright 29
  cultural knowledge 26
  educational broadcasting 122, 123
  selecting 28
  Spanish 98, 99–101, 105
  thematic content 28
  vocabulary 24–5
Tetris video game 60
Thaler, E. 27
thematic content 28
theoretical essays 161
Thirty Years of Language Teaching (CILT) 72
Thorndike's 'Law of Effect' 208
3D environments 232–3, 234, 235–6, 238f, 239–41
Tinsley, T. and Board, K. 90
Tout Compris TV series 125
transcultural competence 26
transfer sub-competence 162, 163
transferable skills 212
transformed practice 49
translation 93, 165–6
  Carreres, Á., Noriega-Sánchez, M. and Calduch, C. 166, 167t
  extra-linguistic sub competence 162, 163
  film reviews 159–60, 162–4, 167, 169t–74
  instrumental/professional sub-competence 162, 163

  language sub-competence 162–3
  mediation in 168–71, 173–4
  PACTE 160, 162–3
  pre-translation textual analysis 167t, 169t–71t
  psychophysiological sub-competence 162, 163
  strategic sub-competence 162, 163
  transfer sub-competence 162, 163
  translation competence (TC) model 162–3
Transmedia Literacy project 52
transmedia skills 52
transmedia storytelling 10–11
'Transmedia Theory and Practice in Teaching and Learning' symposium 61
Travel Talks radio series 123
Treffpunkt Deutschland TV series 123
trends 7–11
Trim, John 126
twenty-first-century skills 28, 50

Unity and Community (Manni, Simona and Sudanese Community in Bradford) 250–61
Universidad Politécnica de Madrid study 182–91, 196–8
  data analysis 184–9
  discussion 189–91
  method 182–4
University College London 166–7
  LTC project 173
  Modern Languages degree 166
  SPAN0034 Translation into Spanish module 165, 166
  Spanish and Latin American Studies degree 165
University of Córdoba project 140–56
  background 145–7
  collaborative work 140, 141–3t
  cooperative work 140, 141, 143t, 172
  French Culture and Civilization Module 145–53
  methodology 147–51
  PBL 143–5

results and discussion 151–3
theoretical framework 140–5
Translation and Interpreting degree 145–53
user-generated content 10, 33–4
'Using films creatively in the language classroom: Visual literacy and critical thinking' workshops 61
'Using Short films for Critical Analysis in Language Teaching and Learning' INSET 59–60
'Using the short film to develop language skills and intercultural competence in language learning (French/Spanish)' INSET 58–9

VAK (visual, auditory and kinaesthetic) learning styles model 204f–5
video 18–20, 48, 223 *see also* participatory filmmaking
  Altman, Rick 55–6
  captions 25, 30, 225–6
  machinima 224, 233, 234–6
  multimodal input in a science project in Italy study 224–32, 241–2
  music 98, 102–3, 105
  pedagogy 55–6
  recording 119, 125
  social media 20–21
  subtitles 25, 77–8, 225, 226, 231
  teaching mathematics with machinima in the Netherlands study 232–41, 242, 246
  user-generated 10

video games 2, 9–10, 60, 221 *see also* digital games; gamification
  cognitive development theories 206–7
  dance 208, 209–11
  exergaming 199–200, 201–6, 208–14
  learner engagement 208–12
  learning styles 203f–6
  lusory attitude to 202, 206
  non-verbal 60
  physical activity 199–200, 201–3
  smartphone games 199–200
virtual worlds 232–3, 234, 235–6
virtualized experiences 10
visual, auditory and kinaesthetic (VAK) learning styles model 204f–5
visual culture 1–2
visual learning 204
visual literacy 75–6
vocabulary 24–5

Waterhouse, L. 205
Web 2.0 technologies 180
Webb. S. and Rodgers, M. P. H. 24
White, A. S. 249
Wii Fit video game 202
Wilson, David 251
World of Warcraft video game 234, 238

Yang, K. 253
Young, M. R., Klemz, B. R. and Murphy, J. W. 212
YouTube 19–20, 30
  Gen Z students 93
  videos 8–9

www.ingramcontent.com/pod-product-compliance
Lightning Source LLC
Chambersburg PA
CBHW071808300426
44116CB00009B/1240